Kafka's Other Prague

Kafka's Other Prague

Writings from the Czechoslovak Republic

✦

Anne Jamison

NORTHWESTERN UNIVERSITY PRESS
EVANSTON, ILLINOIS

Northwestern University Press
www.nupress.northwestern.edu

Printed in the United States of America

10 9 8 7 6 5 4 3 2 1

Cataloging-in-Publication Data

Names: Jamison, Anne Elizabeth, 1969– author.
Title: Kafka's other Prague : writings from the Czechoslovak Republic / Anne Jamison.
Description: Evanston, Illinois : Northwestern University Press, 2018. | Includes bibliographical references and index.
Identifiers: LCCN 2018004075| ISBN 9780810137202 (pbk. : alk. paper) | ISBN 9780810137219 (cloth : alk. paper) | ISBN 9780810137226 (ebook)
Subjects: LCSH: Kafka, Franz, 1883–1924—Criticism and interpretation. | Kafka, Franz, 1883–1924—Knowledge—Czech language. | Kafka, Franz, 1883–1924—Homes and haunts—Czech Republic—Prague. | Prague (Czech Republic)—Intellectual life—20th century.
Classification: LCC PT2621.A26 Z7468 2018 | DDC 833.912—dc23
LC record available at https://lccn.loc.gov/2018004075

for Mirek

CONTENTS

Acknowledgments *ix*

Introduction *3*

Chapter 1
Kafka and Czech: Away from "Minor Literature" *27*

Chapter 2
Kafka and the Czech Press *43*

Chapter 3
Language Territories *61*

Chapter 4
"Is There a Castle Here?" An Architecture of Disappearing Lines *77*

Chapter 5
Reading Klam(m) *105*

Chapter 6
F:M (The Correspondence with Jesenská) *113*

Chapter 7
"Official Decisions Are as Shy as Young Girls": Gender in *The Castle* *131*

Chapter 8
Of Mice and Music *159*

Conclusion *191*

Notes *195*

Index *217*

ACKNOWLEDGMENTS

Different stages of my research for this book have spanned many years and benefitted from the help of more people than I can acknowledge here. The book owes its single greatest debt to Stanley Corngold for years of careful reading and decades of conversation about Kafka. From this project's earliest stages, I am grateful for the very patient guidance of the late Peter Kussi, the more stringent but no less generous help of the late Karel Brušák, and the insights and experience of the late Eduard Goldstücker and František Kautman. I owe David Short everything I know about vowel shifts, vestiges of the dual, shrikes, and meadow saffron. Robert Pynsent had a unique influence on my understanding of Czech history and literature, not least because of the unusual seminars he convened on Czech literature at the School of Slavonic and East European Studies at the University of London. David Chirico and Tim Beasley-Murray have been at different times generous and exciting interlocutors, as were Jindřich Tomán and members of the Czech Studies Workshop. Peter Steiner taught me a great deal about the Prague School. Marjorie Perloff has been generous with her time and support. I owe ancient and last-minute debts to my *spolužák* for life, Alex Zucker. Kevin Power is in his own category of influence—in a lot of ways, but also in terms of his intellectual and editorial help in shaping my manuscript.

At Princeton University, my work received generous support from the Graduate School, the Department of Comparative Literature, and the Council for European Studies. Earlier drafts of two chapters here benefited from the guidance of Claudia Brodsky and Michael Wood. The University of Utah has supported my work through a Faculty Fellowship, numerous international travel grants, a Faculty Research Award, and a fellowship at the Tanner Humanities Center. My friends and colleagues in the English department have been uniformly generous and supportive of my comparative work, for which I am eternally grateful. In particular on this project, Vincent Cheng and Howard Horowitz have been valuable readers, Scott Black an important interlocutor on the novel, and Barry Weller as always a tireless editor and supportive chair as well as a dear friend. Nancy Roche and Jace Brittain also provided timely assistance, as did Stuart Culver, Andrew Franta, Cynthia Stark, and Elizabeth Swanstrom.

Many of the materials this study has relied upon were provided to me by archivists and other staff: in Prague at the Národní Knihovna, the Ústav pro českou literaturu, the Památník národního písemnictví, the newspaper archive of the Národní Muzeum, and the Společnost Franze Kafky; in Brno at the Moravská zemská knihovna; and in Oxford at the Bodleian Library, where Malgorzata Czepiel gave me crucial assistance with Kafka's manuscripts. Malte Kleinwort has been generous with his time and work on the manuscripts, and Roland Reuß was kind enough to let me see his work on the manuscripts as well.

Portions of this book have been published previously, in considerably different form. Part of chapter 1 appeared in "Kafka and Czech: Away from Minor Literature" in *The Journal of the Kafka Society of America* 27, nos. 1–2 (2003). A portion of chapter 2 appeared in "Kmen: A Faraway Magazine about Which We Know Nothing" in *Comparative Literature Studies* 44, no.2 (2007), and elements of chapters 2, 4, and 5 appeared in "Klamm and the Double Asymmetry of the Castle," chapter in *»Schloss«-Topographien: Lektüren zu Kafkas Romanfragment*, edited by Josef Vogl and Malte Kleinwort (Berlin: Transcript Verlag, 2013). At Northwestern University Press, I would like to thank my first editor Henry Carrigan and my current editor Gianna Mosser; project editor Anne Gendler and the rest of the production team, including the creative director, Marianne Jankowski, and the production manager, Dino Robinson; and in sales and marketing, JD Wilson, Emily Dalton, Greta Bennion, and Parneshia Jones.

My parents, my children Deborah Penham, Juliana Penham, and Miles Dworkin, and my partner Craig Dworkin have been incredibly patient with my Kafka years and their attendant abstraction, travel, basement apartments, and general mess. (My first gift to Craig was a copy of *The Castle* as a guide to understanding a particular institution.) All of my Prague research has been enhanced by my dear friend Zora Hornová; František Matějka was one of my earliest guides to Prague literature, culture, and architecture; Miroslav Ambroz began our friendship by rescuing me from a party and has continued to be the most generous friend and colleague in the decades since—my life and work have been incalculably enriched by his kindness and knowledge, and it is to him that I dedicate this book.

Kafka's Other Prague

INTRODUCTION

> German and Czech so close to each other?
>
> —Kafka, letter to Milena Jesenská, April 1920

Scott Spector begins his book *Prague Territories* with the image of a writing desk. The desk is fitted with spikes that bruise the knee of the seated writer, exciting or agitating him enough to make him tremble; it is a desk that "disciplines," "warns," and "censors in advance." Drawn from a very young Franz Kafka's 1902 letter to his friend Oskar Pollak, the image of this desk lays the groundwork for Spector's discussion of Prague, Kafka, and "the painful confrontation of text and context."[1] The same letter furnishes a phrase now well known enough to appear (in several different languages) on T-shirts sold in tourist stalls throughout Kafka's home city: "Prague doesn't let go. Neither one of us. This little mother has claws" ("Prag läß nicht los. Uns beide nicht. Dieses Mütterchen hat Krallen").[2] This letter proves prophetic for the later Kafka: in late 1921, Kafka writes that he "never made [his] escape from Prague" because he "allowed only absurd [senseless] things to claim my attention, my law studies, or the job at the office."[3] Prague, then, as a metonym for its contingent, quotidian concerns, still weighed on Kafka's mind. But if the worry, the conflict, and the desire for escape remain constant, the city itself had greatly changed in the intervening decades, and never so rapidly as during the period between the end of World War I and Kafka's death in 1924. In focusing on "the Czechoslovak Kafka"—that is, on Kafka's writing life in the wake of the fall of the Habsburg Empire and the formation of the Czechoslovak state—I make a case for the increased importance of Czech language and culture in Kafka's life and work in his final years. Czech came to the fore in Kafka's life on several fronts during this time: political (this change to a nation-state defined and delimited by the Czech and Slovak languages); professional (his attendant increased reliance on Czech at work); personal (he fell in love with the Czech writer Milena Jesenská; his sister married a Czech man); and writerly (Jesenská translated a number of his stories, which appeared in print in Czech-language newspapers and periodicals; she also wrote to him in Czech). This increase in the quality and quantity of Kafka's attention to the Czech language accompanied and even inspired shifts in the way he understood national and ethnic identity, gender and sex, and—paramount for Kafka—writing and language per se. On a broader scale, too, in Prague, questions of language use—which language, when, how often, for what—were highly charged as determiners of identity, civic status, and even property lines and (in theory, at least) borders. In this "city of sharp edges," as the Czech critic Josef Kroutvor has termed it, intellectual, cultural, and physical territory had long been contested along linguistic lines. The state's transformation meant that not only national borders but all manner of boundaries delimiting identity, economics, and property shifted and impinged on one another, emerging intertwined, but in unexpected configurations. As these sweeping political and social changes brought the power and the problem of language to a head across the region, on a more intimate level Czech became, to continue with the metaphor, a more prominent spike in Kafka's Prague writing desk.

A clarification: Franz Kafka was not a Czech writer in any sense in which the word was used in his own historical and cultural context. His father had been raised speaking Czech, his mother German, but German was the couple's common language and the language in which they raised and educated their children. Kafka did speak Czech, however, and well: he grew up speaking it with nannies and servants, and later studied it in secondary school. In a letter to Jesenská, he explains his relationship to the two languages as follows: "I have never lived among the German people, German is my mother tongue and so more natural to me, but Czech seems much warmer"[4] ("Ich habe niemals unter deutschem Volk gelebt, Deutsch ist meine Muttersprache und deshalb mir natürlich, aber das tschechische ist mir viel herzlicher").[5] Some linguistic gallantry is likely at work in this early letter to a woman in whom Kafka had taken a keen interest, especially since shortly thereafter, Kafka claims that Jewish ears experience the Czech sentence "Are you a Jew?" ("Jste žid?") as the blow of a fist. Gallantry notwithstanding, however, the passage clearly stakes out a place for Czech in Kafka's personal linguistic landscape, and it does so in rhetorical terms that were at once politically charged and deeply familiar in Prague. Citing German as his "mother tongue" or native language would identify (on the census forms of the new Czechoslovakia) Kafka as German, but he is quick to disclaim any commonality or even association with "the German people"—a division between ethnic and linguistic identity at odds with nation-state logic that aligns language with cultural and territorial belonging. Furthermore, both passages consign Czech to the realm of affect and, specifically, to the body (the heart, the fist), an association that Kafka develops further: now that Jesenská writes to him in Czech (she had begun their correspondence in German), he claims he sees "the movements of [her] body" and hands. Kafka's bodily experience of even Jesenská's *written* Czech has powerful implications, and is exemplary of the kind of cascading effects this new linguistic attention could have on Kafka's worldview. For Kafka, generally speaking, writing and the body are at odds. While Stanley Corngold and Benno Wagner have argued that in Kafka's personal favorite story "The Judgment" (1912), writing achieved a kind of fusion with carnal life such that "writing, when it went well, was fucking," they also stress that this relation of the written with the sexual was more likely to be governed by an intense sublimation.[6] In fact, Kafka often construes writing and the pleasures of bodily life as nearly incompatible. In his journal earlier the same year, Kafka claims that when he pursued writing with intensity, "everything rushed in that direction and left empty all those abilities which were directed toward the joys of sex, eating, drinking, philosophical reflection, and above all music."[7] Nearly a decade later, Kafka's relationship with Jesenská—pursued with great intensity, in writing—would radically disrupt his sense of how these directions and abilities might relate, his increasing intimacy with Czech *as writing* and with a woman *as a writer* further complicating the equation.

For Kafka, the question of which language he would use, and when, had long been fairly straightforward. Despite or because of Kafka's claims for Czech as a language of emotional and bodily intimacy, with the exception of a handful of letters, Kafka's oeuvre is written in German, the language he spoke with his family, the vast majority of his friends, and in which he conducted most of his professional life. In the logic of the Habsburg Empire in which Kafka lived for his first thirty-five years, this "everyday use" of German would make him a German writer. Yet even at the state level, the questions asked of language—those questions asked as a gauge of identity—were contested and changing in both rhetoric and practical effect. In the census logic of Czechoslovakia, the nation-state formed in 1918 of which Kafka was a citizen until his death in 1924, it is the fact that Kafka wrote in German *first*—that he identifies German as his mother tongue—that would make him a German writer. By citizenship, Kafka could be identified as a "Czechoslovak" writer after 1918, but "Czechoslovak" (or then, Czecho-Slovak) did not name an ethnicity popularly recognized within that nation's own boundaries; it named a state, a passport, a politically expedient conflation of two identities (Czech and Slovak) that were generally felt to be quite separate, and a civic identity on a world stage. Ironically, according to the letter of the 1920 constitution's language law, it also named an official state language that did not exist per se but rather referred to either of two languages, Czech and Slovak.[8] Czecho-Slovakism, growing out of pan-Slavism and fully theorized by the new state's founders, answered more to establishing a territorially viable state independent of imperial rule than it did to expressing an overwhelming feeling of unity on the domestic front between linguistically similar but culturally, economically, and geographically distinct populations. Furthermore, the existence of the extralinguistic ethnicity to which Kafka also belonged—Prague Jews were not Yiddish speakers—tended to highlight the inconsistencies entailed in using language as a proxy for questions of identity.[9] The 1920 Czechoslovak constitution guaranteed protections to linguistic minorities who met a 20 percent population threshold within their civic districts. The census that set out to measure these populations offered "Jewish" as an option for the first time, but in contrast to the Czech and German identities that were determined by native language ("mother tongue"),

Jewish identity had no language question proxy.[10] Neither Habsburg nor Czechoslovak logic, however, nor indeed any logic recognizable to Kafka would have identified him as a *Czech* writer, although he is sometimes called that today. Rather, the sudden closeness of Czech and German, even the possibility of a "faithful" translation of his own German-language writing into Czech, is one of the first surprises his correspondence with Milena Jesenská affords him.

That these Prague tensions around identity and language were never fully resolved is evidenced by the extent to which institutions in Germany, Britain, the Czech Republic, and Israel continue to argue about who can lay claim to the Bohemian-German-Jewish-Czechoslovak writer Kafka's literary legacy. Most recently (June 2016), Israel's Supreme Court ruled that Max Brod's literary estate, including unpublished works by Kafka, should remain in the National Library in Jerusalem. Judith Butler has contended that Kafka was not a German writer, but was "certainly Czech"; Pascale Casanova identifies Kafka as a Yiddish writer, although that was not a language he knew at all well; and David Suchoff further emphasizes Kafka's Jewish languages, arguing persuasively for the interlinguistic play with Hebrew and Yiddish in Kafka's later work.[11] Indeed, the fact that Kafka also turned more seriously to the study of Hebrew in his last years only further attests to his changing relationship to language and languages. Yet Kafka's relationship to Jewish culture, including his interest in Yiddish and Hebrew, has been subject to intensive research and widely influential publication and discussion, while this is far from true of his relationship to Czech, fine work by Czech scholars and Slavicists notwithstanding.[12] In practice, furthermore, Czech was also a language of Prague Jewry—in 1910, 54 percent of Bohemian Jews declared Czech as their language of everyday use.[13] Czech-speaking Jews were prominent in Czech journalistic and print culture precisely in those venues that first published Kafka in translation. Thus my book in its emphasis on Kafka's engagement with Czech language and culture should augment rather than displace existing research on Kafka and Jewish languages. I have no interest in staking yet another claim on Kafka's "true" ethnic identity, nor am I arguing that in his later years Kafka became Czech-identified, that Czech became his primary language, that it eclipsed his interest in Hebrew, or that Czech literature became his greatest influence. I am happy to let others fight over who gets to plant which flags in Franz Kafka and his work. Rather, in contrast to the either-or logic of the nation-state, I contend that in response to a changed political, civic, professional, and personal linguistic landscape, the Czechoslovak Kafka's relationship to languages is best characterized by a heightened awareness of proximity, multiplicity, and shift. These changes also led to a reevaluation of a whole range of issues related to language and identity—not solely or even primarily ethnic or national—and, I argue, destabilized Kafka's sense of himself and his world. Despite what I see as a dramatic shift in these last years, however, it could not be said that Kafka ever occupied a comfortable or stable sense of himself with relation to any language or community whatsoever.

If Kafka has become the patron saint of contested identity, this is only appropriate given his feelings on the subject: "What have I in common with Jews?" he asked in 1914. "I have hardly anything in common with myself."[14] His doubts about belonging go even further, as he would also ask of himself: "What is it that binds you more intimately to these impenetrable, talking, eye-blinking bodies than to any other thing . . . ? Because you belong to the same species? But you don't belong to the same species, that's the very reason why you raised this question."[15] This framing of difference and commonality in terms of *species* also strikes a common chord with the rhetoric around identity throughout the region. This rhetoric—of a difference in kind rather than tongue—sounds a counterpoint to the more liberal-minded linguistic ideology then ascendant, although an organicist, *Volkisch* notion of language and kind was embraced by more extreme nationalists on all sides. The rhetorical and philosophical tension between identity-as-language and identity-as-species finds its way into Kafka's late fiction, where I will argue it plays out in one way in *The Castle*, another way in "Investigations of a Dog" (1922), and comes to a head in the last stories "The Burrow" (1923–24) and "Josefine, the Singer" (1924). In all these works, the perceptions and pronouncements of others—as recognition or the lack thereof—also wield performative power to identify, withhold, and even impose identity and define community. These questions seemed to spur Kafka to write: when in late 1920 he broke a fictive silence of almost three years, one of his first texts was a parable that Max Brod later titled "Gemeinschaft"—translated alternatively as "Community" or "Fellowship." And prior to that, Kafka's correspondence with Milena Jesenská, which I would argue constitutes a major work in its own right, returns often to these issues as well. Thus Kafka may have felt his vantage point on such questions to be external or even alien, but this question of commonality—what could be held in common, who shared it, when, and why—would often occupy him in his final years.

In this preoccupation, Kafka was hardly alone. What had long been a regional obsession was interrogated with all the more urgency in the transition from empire to nation-state. Both the Habsburg Empire and the Czechoslovak Republic needed systems by which to sort their citizens, and both relied on language for the purpose, but the meaning of "which language" and how it would determine identity and life circumstances had changed with the change in government. Before 1918, Kafka's status as a German-speaker aligned him with the culturally, politically, and economically privileged ruling minority, although this dominance had been in decline for decades. After 1918, with the German-identifying minority no longer in power even in name, the German lawyer Franz Kafka retained his post by virtue, suddenly, of his knowledge of Czech and his Czech-sounding name. In short, his ability to function as "František Kafka" with the occasional grammatical help of his Czech brother-in-law meant that Kafka went from being one of only two Jews in a German firm to being the only German in a Czech firm. Kafka's own most involved commentary on the challenges that linguistic affiliation posed to Jews in the post-Habsburg era comes in an April 1920 letter to Max Brod:

> There was a Prague Jew, who until the break-up [of the Habsburg Empire] (this in confidence) was a member of the Deutsche Haus as well as of Měšťanská Beseda, and now, thanks only to his high connections, has obtained his release from the Casino [Deutsche Haus] and promptly had his son transferred to the Czech Realschule and "now he won't know either German or Czech, so let him bark."[16]

This anecdote about a fellow patient (Kafka was convalescing in Meran, Italy) condenses a number of anxieties then plaguing Prague Jewry. While a stranger to the Prague culture wars might see belonging to both Czech and German cultural societies as only rational—getting the best of both worlds, so to speak—Prague natives like Brod and Kafka would immediately recognize it as an admission to be made only "in confidence," since membership in both organizations would constitute a transgression against both sides which if discovered might end in ostracism by each. The two strains of rhetoric around identity (language and species) here share an uncomfortable proximity that reveals an ideological overlap: the barking of the Jew devoid of language painfully aligns the nation-state's insistence on linguistic affiliation *as* identity with the species-centered rhetoric of a common antisemitic slur.

Kafka's fellow patient also introduces a further figurative vocabulary into the mix: if languages are homes, they are not just territories but houses, three-dimensional structures. Later the same year, Kafka returns to this notion in the short fiction "Community" ("Gemeinschaft"): "We are five friends, we once came out of a house one after another" ("Wir sind fünf Freunde, wir sind einmal hintereinander aus einem Haus gekommen").[17] Like this later story, Kafka's April 1920 anecdote fuses language, community, structure, and territory, the last more visible when the locations of the Casino and Beseda are taken into account. The two Prague cultural houses occupied the areas of the city generally associated with their respective linguistic groups: the Deutsche Haus was on the Graben (the German name for the street on the former moat by then officially named Na Příkopě), which was considered the German side of Wenceslas Square, while the Beseda was located just above what had recently become Narodní (the former Ferdinandova/Ferdinandstrasse), which led from Wenceslas Square to the iconic Czech National Theater. This separation of the two languages into cultural territories that are further concretized as buildings—tailored for that very purpose by original design (in the case of the Czech building) or renovation (in the case of the German)—gives visual and physical form to a cultural isolation that was almost a regional article of faith, for all that it was often more theoretical than actual. Arising from the aftermath of the 1848 nationalist uprisings, the societies and eventually the buildings that housed them contributed to the increasing linguistic segregation of cultural activities; the intended function of the buildings was to mark, separate, foster, and enclose distinct identities. The story "Community" adheres to this sense of causality: the five friends emerge one by one from a single house until they all stand together, at which point the public notices them and only *then* associates them with one another, by virtue of their relation to the house: "People took note, they pointed at us and said: Those five just came out of that house. We've been living together ever since" ("Die Leute wurden auf uns aufmerksam, zeigten auf uns und sagten: Die fünf sind jetzt aus diesem Haus gekommen. Seitdem leben wir zusammen").[18] Identity here is purely metonymic. The dual forces of contiguity (with a house and, as a result, with one another) and public recognition render the association binding. It almost immediately emerges that the union of the five would be peaceful enough were it not for the efforts of a sixth, whose outsider status seems to stem wholly from the fact that he did not emerge from the house with the first five but is rather attempting to join them. The parable offers no organic or intrinsic reason to associate the five or exclude the sixth: there is no trace of species separation, but since the "sixth one"came later, he will never, ever be accepted. The arbitrary, inorganic distinction nonetheless presents as so fixed and the five perform their exclusion of the sixth so thoroughly that the difference between them might as well be species—but it isn't. Had the sequencing been a bit different, the story seems to acknowledge, things might just as easily have gone another way.

Similarly, the symbolic, territorial, and architectural isolation of the two cultural houses, the public associations of their members, and the public assumptions made about them were often presented as absolute, an unbridgeable divide: and yet the actual physical distance between the Casino and the Beseda was only half a mile. The apparently segregated territory they occupied was commercially and architecturally hybrid: Czech banks with nationalist friezes by national artists rose up on the Graben;[19] intellectual Czechs frequented German cafés to catch up on their newspapers and journals; German intellectuals—including Kafka and many of his friends—could be found in Czech cafés reading and meeting friends as well as attending the portentously iconic Czech National Theater. Kafka's closest friend Max Brod was a one-man engine for cross-cultural translation and exchange. People had affairs. To imagine that social or physical structures such as the cultural houses were wholly successful in segregating civic or cultural life is to underestimate the overlap and mixing of lives lived in close proximity over a small territory. Czech and German peoples and cultures had coexisted in Prague more or less uncomfortably for centuries. Affiliation with one language or the other was subject to huge shifts in social and political meaning. As Tara Zahra argues, language *as* identity was paramount for nationalists, but for many under Habsburg rule, language was a practical matter and nationality was a matter of "indifference." Residents of the region might identify primarily in other ways: by religion, certainly, but also by region, city, profession, or family.[20] Pertinently for Kafka, I would add, artists often identified around little magazines or aesthetic affiliation. And yet the patient in Meran in 1920 was not wrong in his assessment of what it meant to attend this cultural house or that school, and secretly hedging his linguistic bets was understandable. Prague *was* "a polemical city," as Max Brod wrote. Battles over even street signs *could* become violent, and did. Huge, dominating edifices were erected in the spirit of the Czech National Revival, of which the gold-trimmed Czech National Theater with its giant proportions guarded by allegorical statues in bronze and stone is the most prominent example. Actual interethnic relations were of course more complex and nuanced—less easily mapped—than the Wenceslas Square face-offs or theater boycotts that find their way into cultural narratives suggest, especially at the personal level. These cultural proximities and interactions, however, lacked buildings or territories of their own. They also lacked a single native language. Cultural realities such as bilingualism, intermarriage, and translation had no icons, no theaters, no founding myths; they took place across the city's sharp but shifting boundaries, neither shoring them up nor erasing them. And then, when the entire culture and many of the people that produced it were eradicated or expelled later in the century, these cross-cultural commonalities left less imposing traces than the conflicts did.

Perhaps for this reason, literary and cultural scholars, particularly in the West, long understood Prague's tiny German Jewish minority to exist in a state of near-total intellectual and cultural isolation from the city's Czech majority culture. They presented this state of affairs as absolute, dismissing any individual efforts to bridge the divide as ineffectual and, in essence, statistically unimportant. The divided city took on mythic proportions until for a long time no historical treatment of Prague cultural and civic life of the period seemed complete without the image of the Germans promenading on Na Příkopě, the Czechs promenading on Národní Třída, and the two groups seldom meeting in the center except to exchange insults and blows. This tradition of a starkly divided Prague begins early in discussions of Kafka—in fact, it begins with those who lived through the period. Pavel Eisner, another of Kafka's early Czech translators, presents Prague Germans as self-ghettoized behind "walls" as impermeable as the physical barriers of centuries past: "The Germans in Prague became a small enclave which, both within and without the walls, was cut off from the homogeneous Czech population." Eisner describes a "social Ghetto" that, "owing to the exclusion of everything Czech—an exclusion whose motives were resistance, suspicion, arrogance . . . became also a Ghetto in matters of language and culture. To this Ghetto with invisible walls the German Jew in Prague attached himself."[21] The influential mid-century Kafka scholar Klaus Wagenbach not only emphasized this cultural isolation, but made it central to Kafka's entire oeuvre:

> Fundamental to his range of themes was the insular seclusion of the Germans in Prague. . . . Although Germans held nearly all the socially important positions, they were by then a minority of just 7%. . . . The German writers showed hardly any interest in their surroundings. Few Czech authors were welcomed into the coffeehouse circles where German writers established and reinforced their reputations. Apart from Kafka, hardly any Prague-German writer had a decent command of Czech, with the result that their occasional, tentative approaches remained little more than patronizing and Romantic Czechophile gestures.[22]

These generalizations oversimplified a complex situation, but it was hardly by choice. Mid-century scholars had little access to anything but broad trends and the occasional anecdote. The political division of Europe after World War II and the restrictions imposed by the totalitarian Czechoslovak government long made an unchallenged belief in Kafka's German Jewish isolation all but a critical necessity: the resources and access needed to complicate such a view were simply unavailable to most scholars, including Czechs.

Indeed, no discussion of research in this area can go far without running up against dominant narratives of twentieth-century history—naturally enough, since Prague's own history placed it at the crux of many of Europe's most dramatic upheavals. The city saw (1) the dissolution of its governing empire in World War I and its near-simultaneous establishment as the capital of a new Czechoslovak nation-state (October–November, 1918); (2) its use as a pawn traded to a totalitarian state in a failed attempt to stave off a second World War (Munich Agreement, 1938); (3) its attendant occupation welcomed by a substantial minority of its population, the ethnic "Sudeten" Germans (1938–45); (4) the subsequent incarceration, deportation, and mass murder of a significant minority of its population (Czech and German Jews), including a large number of the city's cultural elite; (5) the expulsion of a large proportion of its citizenry on ethnic grounds after Germany's defeat (the forced migration of over 2.5 million ethnic Germans); (6) the rise of yet another totalitarian regime—this time Communist—in 1948; (7) the 1952 Stalin-inspired Slánský show trials, purges, and executions of Communist party members, most of them Jews; (8) in 1968, the Warsaw Pact invasion to quash the period of liberalization known as the Prague Spring; and finally (9) Soviet Communism's fall in 1990 and the economic uncertainty that ensued. Even when presented in the most condensed, matter-of-fact form, as above, it is a strikingly turbulent history, and such events cannot help but reflect back on what came before. Only one of these major changes happened during Kafka's lifetime, but the overwhelming upheavals that occurred after his death nonetheless color perceptions of his life, his work, and his relationship with his city and its citizens. Then, of course, as a sad footnote to the human cost of this history, came the cost to research archives—many were lost, scattered, or simply long inaccessible. All who are interested in Kafka's overshadowed Prague history owe a tremendous debt to the work of Czech scholars for whom Kafka studies amounted to a political act of resistance in the years leading up to the Prague Spring in the late 1960s, and even more so thereafter. Much of the record was preserved by countless acts of "stealth" conservation. Yet the contributions of such scholars—among them Josef Kroutvor, Kurt Krolop, Eduard Goldstücker, and František Kautman—were long politically and even linguistically segregated from broader international conversations, an exclusion exacerbated by decades of political repression, censorship, lack of access, and, after 1990, chronic underfunding. In many ways, the linguistic, ethnic, political, and even disciplinary boundaries that divided Prague cultural life during Kafka's lifetime were less impermeable than those that have divided its study since.

This state of affairs has long since improved, and studies such as Spector's *Prague Territories* (2001) have made it clear that the invisible walls of Eisner's Prague were frequently breached, whether punched through or less violently permeated. "Paul/Pavel Eisner," as Spector calls him, was himself a German Jew who learned literary Czech and felt the oddity of his doing so, but he was not as alone in this activity as it must sometimes have seemed to him. Eisner's account of Prague's cultural division emphasizes his own importance as a maverick at the expense of conveying a range of complex interethnic, interlinguistic social relations he clearly knew of. We know he knew of such dynamics, furthermore, because they are precisely the focus of another of his early works, the 1930 *Milenky* (*Sweethearts*), a proto-cultural studies examination of the phenomenon of intellectual Jewish men dating intellectual young Czech women—a trend that encompassed Franz Kafka's relationship with Jesenská (another of Kafka's translators) as well as her relationship to her first husband, the writer Ernst Pollak.[23] Jesenská is only one of many Czech women translators who were influential and active during this period. And, as Spector's careful study of German Prague Circle translation activity has documented, Kafka's friends Otto Pick, Rudolf Fuchs, Max Brod, and even Franz Werfel, on occasion, all took an active interest in Czech literature and culture and worked variously to translate and promote it with far more seriousness than the occasional "Romantic Czechophile" gestures that Wagenbach dismisses. The long-accepted accounts of isolation also paid no attention to Prague's Czech-speaking Jews, who especially as editors and writers were central to the literary and cultural life of the emerging Czechoslovakia, and particularly to Kafka's experience of it.

Such details have become plentifully available today, and my own work has immeasurably benefited from many excellent recent studies on Prague intellectual and cultural history, in addition to those more specifically on Kafka. Among the latter, to give just two examples, the linguist and critic Marek Nekula has done most to illuminate the intricacies of Kafka's knowledge of Czech literature and culture, while Michelle Woods's study of Kafka's translators sheds light on Kafka's early Czech reception, including an important treatment of the culture of translation that led Jesenská to approach Kafka.[24] But earlier scholars were also intrigued by Kafka's experience of Czech literature and addressed it imaginatively long before it could be addressed in concrete historical terms. Angelo Ripellino begins his unusual city portrait *Magic Prague* with an imagined scene that features Kafka and the Czech writer Jaroslav Hašek wandering the streets conversing with their respective protagonists, Josef K. and Švejk; for obvious reasons, such a meeting never took place, and it is unknown whether the two authors (sans characters) were even known to each other personally, despite murky reports of Kafka's having attended Hašek's anarchist meetings.[25] Regardless of the truth in such myths or the fictionality of Ripellino's happy dream, by the 1920s Kafka would have seen work by Hašek, who was publishing short pieces in a newspaper Kafka read regularly (*Tribuna*, see chapters 2 and 6), and would probably have read parts of *The Good Soldier Švejk*, then in the process of being released as a multi-volume novel, because his closest friend and literary confidant Max Brod was one of *Švejk*'s early champions. Brod wrote the first critical response to it, in a 1921 review of an early (and unauthorized) theatrical adaptation; two years later, he became the first to translate any part of the novel (see chapter 8 for a more extensive discussion). Would Kafka have managed to miss any trace of Hašek before then? It is possible. Yet it seems unlikely—while Kafka was a quiet man, Hašek emphatically was not, they had acquaintances in common, and Prague was a small city. I consider some implications for Kafka's proximity to Hašek and his antics later, but would now offer a different, documented example of the kind of proximity I mean, of the kind of small-scale but high-impact relationship that was also part and parcel of Prague cultural life but was overlooked or (in this case) known with a knowledge fragmented among different constituencies of scholars, fields, and archives. Two friendships illustrate both the scale of Prague as a metropolitan center and its divided yet bound-together nature. In the time of their obscurity (that is to say, during their lifetimes), Kafka and Hašek—the two men who would become Prague's best-known writers of their era—became friends with two very different brothers: Kafka with the German-identified, eastward-looking, Orthodox Jewish mystic Jiří (Georg) Langer; and Jaroslav Hašek with the Czech-identified future Legionnaire Army doctor and (later) leading playwright and presidential confidant František Langer. These brothers and their friendships are exemplary of contradictions, overlaps, and uneasy proximities that characterized and destabilized the relationships between language and identity in early twentieth-century Prague.

The Langer family were members of a group that was long all but erased from narratives of Prague culture: Czech-nationalist Jews—who exist, for example, only as a single bitter footnote in Frederick Karl's voluminous biography *Franz Kafka: Representative Man*. Czech Jews, however, not only had their own distinctive political organizations and journals, but also edited two of the leading liberal Czech-language daily papers, *Lidové noviny* (first out of Brno, then Prague, and still a paper of record today) and *Tribuna*, in which Jesenská published some of her Kafka translations. The Langer family were secular, assimilated, Czech-identified Jews. František Langer was not only friends with Hašek but later with the first president of Czechoslovakia, Tomáš Masaryk, and his circle. But before his long success as a playwright, rivaled only by that of his friend Karel Čapek (who shared with him close connections to the Czechoslovak political establishment), František Langer was party to many of Jaroslav Hašek's anarchist jokes, including his fraudulent 1911 bid for a seat in the Habsburg Parliament. This campaign for "the Party of Moderate Progress within the Bounds of the Law" consisted mostly of drunken ramblings in pubs and promises to buy beer for new voters. The war changed František Langer, however, and he went on to have a most sober and successful mainstream Czech career, largely eschewing any Jewish topics or representations in most of his work. He and his family were entirely secular, and therefore had been unprepared when his young brother Jiří—Kafka's particular friend, known to him as Georg—became interested in Orthodox Judaism, took off to Galicia, and came back in robes, beard, and curls, unwilling to look a woman in the face or speak in any language but Hebrew.[26] It was shocking to the family. František reflects movingly on these topics in his 1937 essay on his brother (published only in 1956), which is known particularly for its account of Jiří's return to Prague as a Hasidic Jew:

> Father told me with a note of horror in his voice that Jiří had returned. I understood what had filled him with dread as soon as I saw my brother. He stood before me in a frayed, black overcoat, clipped like a caftan, reaching from his chin to the ground. On his head he wore a broad round hat of black velvet, thrust back towards his neck. He stood there in a stooping posture, his whole face and chin were covered with a red beard, and side whiskers in front of his ears hung in ringlets down to his shoulders. All that remained to be seen of his face was some white, unhealthy skin and eyes which at moments appeared tired and at others feverish.
>
> . . .
>
> The attitude of our family to Jiří seemed to us at the time to resemble the situation in Kafka's novel, *Die Verwandlung*, in which an entire family finds its way of life completely upset when the son of the house is suddenly changed into an enormous cockroach, and consequently has to be hidden from the rest of the world.[27]

Here, an established Czech writer borrows a metaphor from a "German" writer to express the family reaction to his brother's transformation *into a Jew*—yet all three writers are Jewish. The transformation experienced as analogous to Gregor Samsa's was from "Jew" to "Jew," *within the same family*, a response that undermines any sense of "Prague Jewry" as a single identity. Again, all three writers are Jewish, but the commonalities shift among the three depending on the kind of identity in question: František and Jiří are aligned by blood; Jiří and Kafka are aligned by German (the language of their friendship) and Hebrew (Kafka knew little when he was most intimate with Jiří Langer, but would go on to study it, while Langer was the first Prague author to publish in Hebrew); František and Kafka are aligned by assimilation and secularism.

Each of the three represents different versions of Prague Jewry, only two of which—Czech-identified and German-identified Jews—were common in Prague. Eastern European Jewry hardly existed in Prague; they were exotics, and some in Kafka's circle both essentialized and idealized this culture as authentic and earthy—including Kafka himself. However, according to his friend Max Brod, Kafka viewed the Hasids he met through his friend Jiří as akin to "African savages," living on "pure superstition," though he studied Hebrew and copied some of Jiří's Hasidic tales into his diary. He also copied some memories:

> With Max and Georg [Jiří] Langer at the wonder-rabbi's on Saturday. . . . All rabbis look like savages, Langer said. This one was in a silk caftan, trousers visible under it. Hair on the bridge of his nose. Furred cap which he kept tugging back and forth. Dirty and pure, a characteristic of people who think intensely. Scratched in his beard, blew his nose through his fingers, reached into the food with his fingers; but when his hand rested on the table for a moment you saw the whiteness of his skin, a whiteness such as you remembered having seen before only in your childhood imaginings—when one's parents too were pure.[28]

The figure of the Hasid, then, is both animal and "pure" and "white"—essentialized, alien, transcendent. "Dirty" and "pure"—apparent binary opposites uncomfortably sharing a single identity. Interethnic relations, then, were not so simple as Czech against German against Jew. Here, Czech- and German-identified Jewish writers alike frame the unassimilated Jew in animal terms: it is not the language, but rather the clothes, the hair, the skin that divides them. Eastern Jews are described physically, taxonomically, in recognizable patterns employed by German writers to describe Czechs and by Czech writers to describe Germans (and by everyone to describe women: a passage from Kafka's 1917 diary reads: "The wisdom of the children. The primacy of the animals. The women. Cows moving across the square in the most matter-of-fact way").[29] In a land where language will be established as the primary determiner of identity, and therefore nationality and even territory, the common rhetorics of these "animal-others" cross language boundaries and are employed *within* languages—that is, they define territories and identities not necessarily equivalent to the linguistic boundaries on which the logic of the nation-state relies.

This logic of "species" at once underlies and undermines the notion of a people defined by language that in turn demarcates territory. The complex familial and cultural history of the Langer family illustrates the untidiness of these relationships, and yet a whole range of Prague cultural orthodoxies needed such relationships to be clearly and cleanly delimited. Logic and identity politics yearn for binaries: P or Not P; Czech or German. Language wants them, too: voiced or unvoiced, singular or plural. Prague may furnish such binaries, but it also overlaps them in ways that threaten the logic of the nation-state: Czech Jewry, bilingual families, non-native speakers. Jiří/Georg/Mordechai Langer bridged and undermined all such binaries; he published in three languages and multiple genres; he never chose definitively among his languages; he transgressed more than one boundary simultaneously, writing, for example, the first Hebrew collection of openly homosexual poetry, and theorizing a specifically Jewish homosexual identity.

If Kafka's friend Langer could convene so many different, contradictory, even (by some accounts) mutually exclusive identities in a single person, it can't be so difficult for them to come together in other circumstances. The family and its friendships also serve as a reminder that on a small scale, locally, in a small city, different kinds of people might simply meet one another, no matter how polemical the surrounding streets (or street signs). Newspapers and coffeehouses or shared friends and tastes might bring them together. As the editor of the very interesting and more than usually cosmopolitan Czech art publication *Umělecký měsíčník* (*Art Monthly*), for example, František Langer wrote to Franz Kafka about obtaining short stories to appear in translation. By Langer's account, that is when he received *The Metamorphosis* and also when he read "The Stoker," the first text Jesenská would later translate. He sent Kafka some of his own work in exchange—but the translations never happened, the war began, the magazine like many others went under, and František Langer joined the volunteer Czechoslovak Legion. The Legionnaires fought alongside the Russians against the Austrian interests largely supported by Prague's German Jews, and so in large-scale political terms, Langer and Kafka became fellow countrymen who supported different sides in a devastating world war. But before the war, Langer often went to the Café Arco where Kafka and his friends used to meet. While this "Prague Circle" spoke and wrote in German, František Langer's German, unlike his brother's, was not very strong—if he chatted with Kafka, they spoke in Czech. After the war, František Langer's work was translated by Kafka's friend Otto Pick.[30] Many such individual meetings and exchanges long went unrecorded or at least unattended. They lack historical impact on the scale of empires falling or being founded or entire populations facing extermination or mass expulsion. Cultural life is nonetheless shaped by such "minor" interactions: points of contact and exchange that, while small in scale, are significant in impact in intellectual and writerly life. And for Kafka, the man who recorded the outbreak of World War I with the same urgency and affect with which he reported swimming that afternoon, this impact might have been of the greater importance.

Prague language politics—national, local, and personal—and the issues around identity they both demarcate and destabilize indeed wielded an important influence on Kafka during this period. However, I would not argue that such issues constituted his *primary* interest in language. The identity that mattered most to Kafka was his identity as a writer, and whatever else changed for him during these last years, this primacy did not. Much of this book will seem distant from broader cultural and political topics as well as from the intricacies of café friendships or family dynamics, as it progresses through structure, rhetoric, word and, eventually, letter—but the presence or absence of a single letter could signify a name's (and hence a person's) linguistic and national identity in this world. Such uncomfortably close proximities between spheres and modes once relied upon to be disparate (including, at the most basic level, "writing" and "the world") constituted major preoccupations for Kafka throughout this period. The Czech context most pertinent theoretically and interpretively to this literary, writerly language ironically shares a name with the unrelated group of writers with which Kafka was associated: there were two Prague Circles, one each for two writers whose work would go on to be studied in fields and disciplines divided by boundaries more impermeable than those of the "small nation" in which they both lived. The Russian linguist Roman Jakobson and Franz Kafka were first published in Czech translation in the same year and in the same journal, *Kmen*. Jakobson would go on to help found the Prague Linguistic Circle two years after Kafka's death; Kafka was interested in linguistics to the extent of subscribing to the leading Czech philological journal *Naše řeč* (*Our Language*). The loose-knit group of German Jewish writers was not concentric, nor did it much overlap, with the linguists and literary critics known by the same name. Yet throughout this book, I have found it productive and illuminating to consider Kafka's twin interest in language and social structure in connection with Prague School structuralism: the shared name in the shared city is more telling than mere coincidence. In recognizing the circle as a demarcation of territory, "a charting of inclusion and of exclusion" that attempts also to define periphery versus centrality, Spector reads the German Prague Circle's efforts at self-definition in terms of the culturally pervasive desire to define identities in terms of place, language, and national affiliation.[31] The figure of a circle describing Prague linguists also draws such a line, and both Prague Circles sought to mark linguistic and literary territory for themselves—to create and hold a common ground.

Much early Prague School activity involved inventing, designing, and policing a common terminology, built on shared theoretical positions—and those members who deviated would be expelled from the group. With more direct pertinence to Kafka, the policing of language was also a main preoccupation of the journal of a very different group of Slavic linguists. The "gentlemen from *Naše řeč*," as Kafka called the editors of this journal, studiously sought to distinguish authentically Czech constructions and vocabulary from corrupting German influences.[32] Prague structuralism departed markedly from this more traditional philology (though future members were represented on its pages), but it shared this interest in identifying and maintaining clear linguistic boundaries. Thus even the Prague School with its scientific ambitions and rhetoric reflected its home city's environment: language excludes as well as includes; language determines, explicitly in Prague then as in few other places, where you belong and even what belongs to you. But as Spector argues, the German Jewish "circle," at least, "opened their eyes to see themselves precariously suspended between territories, with no firm ground beneath their feet."[33] The relationship between fluctuating language politics and territory, which should theoretically imply some ground to stand on, produced this sense of precarious suspension: this vertiginous experience of territory from which there can be a precipitous fall. An awareness of this experience leads Kafka to reconfigure the relationship of territory and language as a multidirectional and multiply unstable structure—most thoroughly explored in *The Castle*—in ways that simultaneously anticipate and critique the dynamic structures of the Prague School.

Even in a theoretical system so heavily reliant on a community of native speakers, however, a core theoretical text acknowledges the potential for the slippage that even native speakers must contend with. The Saussure student and Prague School member Sergei Karcevskij would define such a problem in 1929 as "the dual asymmetry of the linguistic sign": to paraphrase, not only are we cursed with synonymy (morphologically different words can have similar or identical meanings), but with homonymy as well (the same word, or similar or identical words, can have different meanings). Even in a native language, spontaneous comprehensibility is hardly a given. Internal divisions and distinctions render a "standard language" less clear and stable than a system of communication based on norms and differences probably needs to be. Despite such acknowledged problems, a community of native speakers who spontaneously comprehend norms is the foundational basis for Prague School theory, just as it is for the nation-state. The language politics of this shared city, however, complicate the central Prague School tenet wherein texts that focus attention on language (or "foreground," by means of violating of a norm) over what it communicates are poetic. By this definition, the Prague of Kafka's day is exploding with poetry, because language there is *always* foregrounded—disrupting communication and more: language disrupted the streets, gave way to riots among linguistic factions.

Historical overlaps and geographical proximities perhaps make it less remarkable that Kafka takes up in his late work, as I argue, very similar concerns to those of Prague School theory: in particular, a vision of language as internally fissured, in a state of tension, violation, and assault within itself, a state in which language at once violates boundaries and produces literature. Yet while the Prague School posits a "common language" as central to its theory and practice, Kafka imagines the ramifications of such a model in the absence of a common language or, as the logic of the times insisted was synonymous, a common ground. When the Prague School would theorize that "poetic language radically violates the norm," they assumed the norm would be known, understood, recognizable. When Kafka writes that "this whole literature is an assault against boundaries," the nature of the boundaries in question—and even whether the sentence refers to boundaries as concept or to a certain set of them—is undefined and, in context, indeterminable.[34] Kafka wrote this sentence in his journal shortly before beginning work on his last novel, *The Castle*. *The Castle* centers around a strangely shifting, oddly linguistic structure—as will the Prague version of structuralism, in which literary structures are not fixed but dynamic, shifting with time and usage but often violently, internally at war in a struggle for dominance. While I suggest a significant parallel between the work of two of the best-known and influential cultural exports from a single city, arrived at within the space of a few years, I also argue that while they shared a common territory—and even elements of a common model of how language might work, and work to produce literature—they did not share a vision of what that model meant.

These aspects of Kafka's world, while not yet widely understood, are slowly but steadily being examined, and I refer to many recent studies devoted to different aspects of Prague history and culture throughout this volume. By way of introduction to Czech-informed Kafka scholarship and the new insights it can provide, I want to consider in more detail two recent readings of a story that further interrogates—from a highly skeptical perspective—the link between language, politics, and buildings that the two Kafka texts from 1920 discussed above (the patient's anecdote and "Community") suggest more obliquely. These readings did not lead me to the conclusions reached in my own chapters—the bulk of my research had been done before I came across either—but rather dovetail with my thinking in some ways while in others pointing to different paths of interpretation and connection, confirming my long-held sense that sustained and varied study of Kafka from the perspective of Czech language and culture will yield insights heretofore unavailable to even the most astute of his many excellent critics.

Kafka's short story "The City Coat of Arms" ("Das Stadtwappen") dates from the same period of productivity as "Community," a time when Prague's own divisions had been frequently breached rather than bridged in bouts of extreme polemical and physical violence. The story offers a compressed account of a century of nationalist architectural conquest, abstracted enough to be recognizably Kafkan but equally recognizable as Prague, its current scene, recent past, and longer history at once towering and collapsing together (as happened in literal enough ways on Prague streets). References to Prague politics recur throughout Kafka's late fiction, but never again so explicitly:

> Every nationality wanted the finest quarter for itself, and this gave rise to disputes, which developed into bloody conflicts. These conflicts never came to an end; to the leaders they were a new proof that, in the absence of the necessary unity, the building of the tower must be done very slowly, or indeed preferably postponed until universal peace was declared. But the time was spent not only in conflict; the town was embellished in the intervals, and this unfortunately enough evoked fresh envy and fresh conflict.[35]

In Nekula's view, Kafka rejected the "monolingualism" that dominated public discourse around language and instead took an active interest in "a confusion of tongues," a phrase drawn from a 1911 entry in his travel notebook that poses such confusion as a potential answer to nationalism. Nekula's own work seeks to critique and counter "Czech/Slavic-German polarization and the monolingual interpretation of the world" and sees Kafka as engaged in a similar project, although "The City Coat of Arms" arguably takes a darker perspective on such multiplicity. Nekula's sense of Kafka's critical stance toward monolingualism, however, led me to draw a straight line from this story to the elements in *The Castle* that first gave me the idea for this book many years ago. "The City Coat of Arms" anticipates a dynamic I see in the later novel between vestiges of a nineteenth-century novella's precise linguistico-architectural primer and Kafka's own unchartable (unsurveyable) architectonic landscape. *The Castle* parses single-minded architectural clarity—a material analogue of monolingualism—with the protagonist K.'s nostalgia for a remembered tower, one he compares unfavorably with a haphazard collection of buildings that seem to confuse tower with everyday dwelling. I connect this kind of nostalgia for clarity with various nationalist projects such as the Czech National Revival's desire to resurrect literary Czech from centuries past rather than from what (common) people were currently speaking, attempts to purge Germanisms from the modern language, and the need to discover and perform national customs in music and myth even where such discovery amounted to invention. The "City Coat of Arms" tower at first seems to have a clarity of direction akin to K.'s remembered tower—both in the sense of a single direction or goal (skyward) and a clarity of direction "on the ground" complete with signs and interpreters. But this early sense of priority is quickly lost, and attention turns from tower to dwellings for workers. Nationalities fight over who would get the best quarter, and the tower's building is delayed. Only in the "pauses" between these struggles is the city built, an entire city arising as the afterthought of national conflict. It is an origin story that in 1920 the Czechoslovak nation-state might well seem to share. I will not detail here the myriad ways in which

The Castle takes up concerns raised in this earlier story (they become clear in the chapters), but I would like to highlight a particular difference, also relating to origin and history: in “The City Coat of Arms,” as Nekula points out, Babel was the governing structure of language from the outset, “confused and divided before the Tower of Babel was built.”[36] Whereas *The Castle*’s K. *may* remember an actual tower, no such tower in “The City Coat of Arms” was ever built. The notion is clearly a holdover from the misconceived plans of the people’s forebears, although this awareness seems to do little to stop the ongoing process of failing to implement them: “To this must be added that the second or third generation had already recognized the senselessness of building a heaven-reaching tower; but by that time everybody was too deeply involved to leave the city.”[37] The last clause resonates bitterly with Kafka’s own sense of his life as well as a pessimism about national projects and their ill-begotten if ancient origins. Perhaps this is why “all the legends and songs that came to birth in that city are filled with longing for a prophesied day when the city would be destroyed by five successive blows from a gigantic fist.”

Of course, “The City Coat of Arms” is not all Prague. Like so much in Kafka’s work, it fuses contemporary local, even personal referents with national and transnational mythologies; here Babel itself provides a global perspective on misconceived linguistic building projects, but the story implicates particularly regional antecedents as well. In keeping with his titular theme of *Prague Palimpsests*, Alfred Thomas sees “City Coat of Arms” as evoking not only biblical Babel but also its distinctive role in the medieval Czech *Chronicle of Dalimil*, which employs the image “as a metaphor for [Czechs’] own defensive position vis-à-vis their German neighbors” in order to address local anxieties about immigrants and language.[38] In Kafka’s story, leaders are ineffectual against such conflict, seeing it only as proof that “in the absence of the necessary unity” the tower must be built slowly or “preferably postponed until universal peace was declared.” Bringing his reading back to contemporary Prague, Thomas extends the scope of this critique of incrementalism to the new Czechoslovakia and its president Tomáš Masaryk’s emphasis on slow progress through gradual “good work” rather than revolution.[39] Even more particularly and locally, Thomas relates the projected fate of the tower to a very recent event in Kafka’s own Prague, the toppling of the Marian column on the city’s Old Town Square. Inspired by a very different political impulse from Masaryk’s incrementalism, the fall of the column was major political news even in the early days of a new republic.[40] For Kafka, it also transformed the space in which he’d lived almost his entire life. Kafka was born on Old Town Square; his first and last homes, his Gymnasium and later his father’s shop (in the same building, the Kinsky Palace) all opened onto it. He would have passed this Marian column almost every day of his life—until it was pulled down by a mob of anticlerical nationalists within a week of his new country’s establishment. Not that he would have witnessed the actual event, as Kafka was then dangerously ill with Spanish flu and double pneumonia and spent the final days of the Habsburg Empire and the first of the new Czechoslovak state bedridden in his parents' apartment (so while he could have seen the column fall from his window, he was likely too sick to do so). But when he did recover, the absent column outside his window would have provided his first glimpse of the material manifestation of his now-transformed world.

There is no indication that Kafka paid close attention to this political upheaval during his near-fatal illness, and he kept no journal that year. Later letters to Max Brod reveal that he *did* pay close attention to monuments, but everyone paid attention to the Marian column—even before its downfall. It's a perfect example of the way in which architectural styles and structures, language, and national identity bind together in densely overdetermined signs whose value is as variable as it is political and polemical. The Baroque column had been erected in 1650 in honor of the Habsburg defeat of the Swedes and their subsequent withdrawal from Prague, a monument to the city's successful resistance against a foreign invader: Bohemia against the world. By the nineteenth century, however, its cultural meaning had shifted. Most Czechs had come to believe the column instead celebrated their 1620 defeat at the Battle of White Mountain, which the National Revival movement saw as the beginning of Czech cultural and linguistic erasure by German hegemony. Without any change to its actual structure or to any of the historical events at issue, the column's meaning for Czechs changed from commemorating the city's independent stance against foreign invasion to memorializing its cultural, political, and linguistic subjugation. Its very architectural style had fallen out of favor, as Czech nationalists came to reject the city's many Baroque buildings as further reminders of Austrian rule. Prague politics had its own dramatic metamorphoses, but instead of individuals awakening as vermin, monuments of independence "awoke" (National Revival activists were known as *buditelé*, literally, "awakeners") to find they had been transformed into symbols of oppression; subjects of an empire awoke as citizens of a nation-state; German lawyers awoke as nominally Czech—but unlike poor Gregor Samsa, who had grown extra legs and a pair of mandibles, none of these changes effected an immediate physical transformation of daily life—or in the case of the Marian column, at least not until a mob arrived.

The structural mode of representation I see throughout Kafka's late fiction reflects his own difficulty of negotiating boundaries between inner and outer realms, both of the writer and the text. It is less representation than a kind of transposition, a deformation that recognizable forms and structures are subjected to when subsumed by the novel and its world. Walter Benjamin wrote that Kafka "divests the human gesture of its traditional supports and then has a subject for reflection without end."[41] In these late texts, in place of the gesture we have whole social structures, each dimension as unstable as the gesture and just as resonant. Much of the resonance Benjamin describes, however, derives from what has been cut away: he speaks of "traditional supports"—which might be historical or literary referents, religious, social, or philosophical context, or the traditional trappings of the novel: plot advancement, character development, and actions. This volume shows how the "traditional supports" provided by Kafka's "other Prague" and his experience of its Czech literary and political culture shaped his late work and contributed to its resonance in ways that are only beginning to be recognized. Did Kafka live "between languages" in some way, never feeling at home in either, as he would sometimes claim? And, if so, does this make his experience in the context of modernity peculiar, rather than exemplary as is often felt? And if the latter, if the problem of living between languages looks like one we all face, what does that say about language as structure, as codifiable, comprehensible entity founded on perceivable, identifiable differences? How are the tensions between two languages qualitatively different from tensions that arise within our experience of language generally? And if we implicitly rely on language to distinguish and codify the differences that render our identities, how can we know that we are relying on the same language to do so? These are the broader questions I see raised in and by Kafka's late fiction, a body of work I find closely tied to the world in which he lived but resonant far beyond its perimeters.

In my first chapter, "Kafka and Czech: Away from 'Minor Literature,'" I take issue with Deleuze and Guattari's influential essay *Kafka: Toward a Minor Literature* as responsible for a number of misunderstandings about Kafka and language. I correct several misconceptions it has created and clarify the matter of Kafka's knowledge of Czech language, literature, and culture, which this well-known essay has tended to obscure by seeming to present it as a known quantity—when in fact it has been understood very little. My second chapter, "Kafka and the Czech Press," takes up the question of Kafka's specific knowledge of Czech print culture of the 1920s, the years when he was most actively engaged with contemporary Czech culture and began publishing in translation. I identify and gloss several Czech magazines and newspapers Kafka read, published in, or which were edited by his friends, reserving the most extensive examination for *Kmen*, the first periodical to publish Kafka in translation. *Kmen* provides a window on the small but active and influential world of leftist Prague, in which nationalism, cosmopolitanism, and radical politics came together in surprising, even counterintuitive ways.

In chapter 3, "Language Territories," I consider the question of territory so prominently raised by Deleuze and Guattari and explored with so much more precision by Scott Spector. I explain how, as Spector argues, the relationship between language and territory in the Czech lands had long been extremely concrete, a fact that the disputes around borders and language in the new nation-state could only accentuate. In a nod to this state of affairs, Kafka's protagonist in his last novel is a Land Surveyor. This chapter considers what such surveying would actually mean in literal, material terms, how it was implicated in the new country's recent history, how languages figured into the question of borders and property, and how these languages themselves were surveyed or measured. Yet *The Castle* itself represents neither land nor map, instead chronicling the travails of a Land Surveyor stymied by an incomprehensibly shifting architectural and political landscape. It cannot be mapped—at least not by K.

Following on from the apparent exhaustion of the territorial figure, in my fourth chapter, "Is There a Castle Here?," I argue that Kafka's heightened awareness of language's power to configure and confuse required a figural system with more dimensions than the flat space implied by the territory evoked by a Land Surveyor protagonist. Despite K.'s (purported) profession, the novel's dominant figure and governing system are more architectural than territorial, and the instability of rhetorical, social, and spatial relations in the novel has its analogues in Prague politics, in which language directly shaped not only the city's social and civic structures but even its actual material architecture. I read Kafka's novel in conjunction with Czech texts that are also concerned with the relationship of language, architecture, and social space. The nineteenth-century novelist Božena Němcová and the twentieth-century theorist Jan Mukařovský both posit a common language as the key to navigating both physical and social architectures. By contrast, I argue that *The Castle* presents the problems of approaching such structures as a non-native speaker, likely to miss nuances in meaning that the natives take for granted and incapable of reliably distinguishing individual error from systemic flaw.

The conceptual tension suggested by the difference between "language" and "languages"—the question, rather, of difference within language or between languages—proves central to *The Castle* by virtue of a complex pun on a single word. My fifth chapter, "Reading Klam(m)," briefly but intensely illustrates how the macro structures I detail at length in the preceding chapter are replicated on the micro level, including the level of the letter as seen in the Castle notebook manuscripts. Questions of multilingualism and the travails of the non-native speaker manifest in the novel at the lexical and sublexical level through interlinguistic puns. Words operate along the same shifting, unpredictable structures as the central edifice itself, with the problems always entailed in homonymy cubed in the face of homonymy across language boundaries. Small-scale as they are, these dynamics—materially manifest on the pages of the manuscript—wield considerable interpretive power regarding K.'s political, social, and sexual relationships.

My sixth chapter, "F:M (The Correspondence with Jesenská)," argues that Milena Jesenská and all she represented had a profound and disruptive effect on Kafka. With their relationship, the Czech language became central in Kafka's emotional life and daily reading, gaining new importance for him as a written language, and this reading also constituted the most attention he had ever paid to a woman as a writer (that is, a writer who identified as such professionally and personally). Until their correspondence, Kafka had written of no woman writer, nor indeed of any Czech writer, in very positive terms; this now changed. I situate Jesenská in terms of the prominence of women in Czech myth and literary history, the political investments and expectations projected onto women's education in Kafka's day, and the lengths to which Jesenská went to disrupt such aims. Jesenská's frank depiction of her sexual, social, and economic situation in Vienna excited Kafka's sympathy and jealousy—of her texts, which not only he but anyone could read. Jesenská's feuilleton "Kavárna" ("The Coffeehouse") particularly claimed his attention, and the piece's portrayal of social architecture places her in conversation with both Němcová and Kafka's future novel *The Castle*. My seventh chapter, "Official Decisions Are as Shy as Young Girls," shows how the influence of Jesenská as a destabilizing force reverberates throughout *The Castle*. I argue that *The Castle* invokes Jesenská's "Kavárna" feuilleton and, furthermore, draws on it in depicting female characters and the Castle world's complex system of gender and power relations. Jesenská confuses binaries by which Kafka had previously constructed his identity as a man and writer, and we see an analogous confusion play out in gender and sexual relations (which do not align as one might expect) throughout the novel—again, at the level of structure, grammar, and word.

Finally, my eighth chapter, "Of Mice and Music," reclaims Czech contexts for Kafka's late animal stories, many of which engage with the prevailing need to sort humans and their activities into kinds different enough to be analogous to species. Hašek's early animal writings reveal and revel in the fraudulent use to which this need can be put, while *The Good Soldier Švejk* further defies categorizing convention by confusing the linguistic binary that divided Czech into a "literary" written language and a spoken colloquial one. Kafka's late animal stories also invoke the categories of sound, noise, or music, specifically considering how they might (or might not) be distinguished. That Czechs were natural musicians was a common period stereotype, and this Czech identification with music acts as a counterpoint to Kafka's lifelong *dis*-identification with music. In Jesenská's writing, however, he hears a "music of language." Having been guided by the belief that certain pleasures—including both music and carnal and domestic life with a woman—were incompatible with his writing life, Kafka confronts the possibility that he had denied himself on the basis of category errors—not in the sense that he had sorted these elements into the *wrong* categories, but rather that they did not belong to such different categories after all. The creatures of his late stories hear the same sounds differently—as music, as noise, as threat—depending on their own experience, knowledge, and situation. In this final chapter, I argue that these late stories with their concerns about perception, community, and musicality represent Kafka's aesthetic mediation between and among modes of being and expression that he had long assumed were different in kind.

Chapter 1

✦

Kafka and Czech

Away from "Minor Literature"

A wide-ranging discussion of Kafka, Prague, and languages began with Deleuze and Guattari's *Kafka: Toward a Minor Literature* (1975). In large part as a result of this essay, a great deal has been said with regard to mapping linguistic territory in Kafka's Prague and charting Kafka's place within it—as well as outside it, on the broader world stage. *Minor Literature* argued that Kafka's "Prague German" constituted an upstart, rebellious "minor literature" within the master discourse of German, but the reach of the essay is far, far broader. Deleuze and Guattari placed Kafka, in name at least, at the heart of essays on Chinese, Palestinian, Puerto Rican—indeed, on any number of literatures which can claim to be, or to harbor within themselves, a potentially "minor" literature, a "gypsy nomad" literature written of necessity in "the language of the masters" but out to deform or disrupt it from within.[1] This flowering of interest attests to the paradigm's relevance to an array of voices and literatures eager to lay claim to common ground in a global conversation, and it has proven fruitful for a broad range of political conversations about power, state recognition, and minority status. *Minor Literature* has seemed relevant to nearly everyone—with the occasional exception of those most concerned with its purported inspiration. That is, the essay has been treated with more skepticism by some Kafka scholars—Stanley Corngold the most vocal and prominent among them—on the grounds that it distorts considerably Kafka's relationship to the German language and literary tradition (the essay's "major literature" or "language of the masters") on the one hand, and that it is based on largely unresearched and unverifiable claims about Prague German, a now extinct linguistic form the essay uses to define its particular sense of "minor," on the other.[2] The essay's relevance for Kafka studies, of course, has never been the main source of scholarly interest: it is "minor literature's" transposability as a paradigm for other apparently analogous cultural situations that is responsible for its enduring influence—in the past several years alone inspiring essays on topics ranging from television and gaming to Nubian and Haitian literature to disability studies. Its efficacy or applicability *outside* of Prague is not my concern here, but rather the fact that the essay's purported object of analysis, Kafka and his relationship to Prague language culture, has remained a reference point in this broader discourse without actually being actively engaged or even known. In fact, such is the power and reach of the essay's claims that Deleuze and Guattari's "minor literature" has obscured important elements of Kafka's *own theory* of minor literature. Lowell Edmunds has effectively carried this point by drawing attention to what we might understand as the "minor literature" remainder, those less insurgent attributes Deleuze left by the wayside: Kafka's sense that minor literature benefits from a pool of mediocre talent, that it is characterized by a certain "liveliness," and, most ironically given its afterlife, that minor literature's connection with politics renders it not liberatory or revolutionary but rather "harmless" and even conformist.[3]

Similarly, Deleuze and Guattari's account of "minor literature" has placed Prague culture—with Kafka as its ambassador to the world—in a regrettable double position of exemplarity and obscurity. Although on the strength of this essay, Prague has been offered as a model of political and linguistic relations that provides a basis for global comparison, this very ubiquity has granted an aura of settled fact to Deleuze and Guattari's reading of Kafka and his milieu. This ubiquity as well as the framing of the essay itself gives the impression not only that Prague language politics are widely felt to be relevant to a global discourse on literature, language, and power, but also that they are widely understood—well enough to be referred to as a model. At the time Deleuze and Guattari were writing, however, no such research had been conducted—or at least, it was not available to them. Since the essay was written, a number of more historically informed studies have shed light on these relations. Spector's *Prague Territories* focuses needed attention on the complexities of German linguistic and ethnic politics in the city, while Nekula's work brings a linguist's methodologies and meticulous research to the question of exactly what languages Kafka knew, when he used them, and what it meant when he did.[4] Outside the more narrow confines of Kafka studies, such research is even more plentiful, as cultural and political historians, linguists, and Jewish studies scholars have turned their attention to Prague cultural and language politics.[5] Yet none of these efforts has attained the broad currency of Deleuzean "minor literature" in literary critical discourse.

Deleuze and Guattari, of course, never claimed to be writing a historicist account of Prague culture. They base their general understanding of German-Czech-Jewish triangulation on Kafka's fiction, several letters and diary entries, and occasional citations from Max Brod's biography and Gustav Janouch's much-disputed *Conversations with Kafka*—little else would have been available to them even had they been more interested in painstaking historical research. Furthermore, the "minor literature" they seek to define is "that which a minority constructs within a major language": not Czech, but a literature that would be particular to Kafka's Jewish Prague German.[6] To this end, they make the theoretically expedient but historically and linguistically outlandish move of substituting Kafka's views on Czech and Yiddish for his views on his own relationship to German literature. This chain of substitutions has substantially undermined any broadly held understanding of Kafka's relationship to Czech, which has always been the most marginalized, least researched aspect of Kafka's thoroughly researched life. Although *Toward a Minor Literature* has little to do with Czech except as a vague ethnic heritage, it nonetheless takes as its occasion Kafka's 1911 journal entry about Czech and Yiddish as "minor" literatures and transposes these remarks to reflect on Kafka's writing in German. In addition to errors the essay makes about Kafka's German (that he wrote in a variety of dialect), this linguistic transposition rests on an equally troubling misunderstanding of Kafka's knowledge of and relationship to Czech. While Deleuze and Guattari present the possibility of writing in Czech as an equally viable option open to Kafka, one he simply doesn't choose, Kafka's command of Czech, particularly written Czech, never equaled his command of German—which was the language in which he conducted the overwhelming majority of his personal, professional, and literary life. It is clear he was highly conversant in Czech, but the gap between informal spoken and written "literary" Czech is broad.[7] Any choice by Kafka to write literary Czech would not only have meant a strong and highly charged rejection of the German literary and cultural tradition, but would also have required a rigorous program of linguistic and literary study on his part.

Throughout most of his life, however—until the period with which this book is concerned—Kafka makes scarcely any mention of Czech language or literature. The journal entry on which so much of *Minor Literature* is based is an anomaly. Similarly taking issue with Deleuze and Guattari's linguistic and cultural assumptions, Charles Sabatos resituates this December 25, 1911, diary entry in the context of Kafka's disappointment with a Czech play he'd recently attended, Jaroslav Vrchlický's *Hippodamie*. In one of the few references to Czech literature dating from this era of his life, Kafka calls it a "bad play," somewhat randomly derivative of Greek sources; he finds even the good production of it "nothing but an imitation of Reinhardt" and concludes that "all this must be sad for a Czech who knows even a little of the world."[8] Even in as established and dominant a figure as Vrchlický, then, for Kafka, Czechs are imitative and parochial; their estimation of their own accomplishments would surely be diminished by a more international, cosmopolitan perspective. Such opinions about Czech literature were not unusual among German intellectuals and are in keeping with comments Kafka makes elsewhere. But in terms of Deleuze's "minor literature" paradigm, Kafka's characterization of Czech here hardly seems "deterritorialized." As Sabatos argues, for Kafka, "Vrchlický's work is a force of innovation within the Czech context [but] seems to reflect the limitations of a small literature without the benefit of 'liveliness.' "[9] Kafka's journals display far more positive associations with Yiddish theater than with Vrchlický's play, but in fact he knew very little of Yiddish or its theatrical traditions beyond the performances of the theater troupe he'd recently been taken with. And furthermore, Kafka's analysis of the "national struggle" of Yiddish writers takes as its point of reference Bedřich Smetana's *Prodaná nevěsta* (*The Bartered Bride*, 1870), which consciously drew on Czech folk sources in order to create a "national opera." Ironically, for Kafka, the operatic referent is more likely to magnify rather than diminish his perceived distance from the Yiddish theater, given his lifelong belief that he had no sense for music. In the same journal entry, in fact, he claims to "hate" Franz Werfel because he is everything Kafka is not: "gifted with a sense of music, he has done good work early and easily, he has the happiest life behind him and before him, I work with weights I cannot get rid of, and I am entirely shut off from music."[10] Music, while almost incalculably central to Czech national culture, is if anything *more* foreign to Kafka than these languages in which he does not write. Certainly none of this framing suggests a particular affinity between any of these contexts and Kafka's own writing.

The clearly marginal status that Czech long occupied in Kafka's writings might suggest that little is at stake if *Kafka: Toward a Minor Literature* has gotten this linguistic relationship wrong. Such a dismissal might be justified had Prague's language politics and Kafka's relationship to them remained constant over time—but this presumption of constancy is one more flawed impression that *Minor Literature* creates. In the "minor literature" paradigm, Kafka's relationship to and knowledge of Czech is taken as a stable given, established in a 1911 journal entry, against which his relationship to German can be understood—but it was no such thing. Not only, then, does the essay read this early journal entry about Czech and Yiddish as a means of understanding Kafka's relationship to German, but it takes these thoughts as being equally applicable to a late text like *The Castle*—as if nothing might have happened in the intervening decade to alter Kafka's relationship to questions of language, literature, and politics. Yet political history, Kafka's employment and personal relationships, his correspondence and, as I suggest throughout this volume, his fiction, all make clear that Czech was more prominently on his mind during this time, and in a new way. It is only natural that this change would leave its mark in his writing. Bound up with this new awareness of his other language, we find Kafka's changing views on questions of spoken and written language, literary value, ethnic and gender identity, and sexuality: all of them are subject to reflection and change in his last years.

During the last six years of his life, several factors profoundly altered the nature of Kafka's relationship to Czech, particularly with regard to writing. First: the balance of linguistic and political power shifted when post-Habsburg Prague became the capital of the new Czech nation-state, greatly emphasizing the importance of Czech for Kafka's working life. Kafka was able to retain his post, unlike many German speakers, by virtue of his knowledge of Czech and his Czech-sounding last name: "Franz" could become "František" Kafka. With these political changes, the "minor" literature became, if not the "major literature" Kafka saw in Goethe's German, then at least the "major literature" of national bureaucracy, and Kafka had more need for written Czech. He took concrete steps to become better acquainted with the written language, subscribing to the philological journal *Naše řeč* and reading more Czech literature. As early as the fall of 1917, for example, he praised the then newly released letters of Božena Němcová, and, early the following year, he referred to Jaroslav Vrchlický's correspondence with the writer Sofie Podlipská, also published in 1917. He apparently took a personal interest in young Czech writers such as Gustav Janouch and Michal Mareš, and often consulted his Czech brother-in-law for help in writing business letters.[11]

It is also far from insignificant that Franz Kafka had a Czech brother-in-law to consult, his beloved sister Ottla having married: a striking change for a man not given to taking familial relations lightly. Furthermore, Ottla was not the only Kafka sibling to become involved with a Czech gentile. When in the spring of 1920, Kafka entered into the bilingual correspondence with Jesenská, suddenly all the most urgently anticipated and deeply felt documents of his reading life—Jesenská's letters and journalism—were written in Czech. And last but not least, since this relationship began with Jesenská translating Kafka's own writing into Czech, his writing appears in print in Czech alongside new Czech writing as well as other German writers also translated into Czech. His surprise at what he deems the success of these translations seems genuine and profound, as if the possibility of his own fiction appearing in Czech—the majority language of his home country—had never occurred to him. Czech was thus newly "foregrounded" for Kafka, as the Prague School would put it. That does not mean he did not know it before, only that following his Gymnasium study of Czech literature, it passed rather to the background—a minor literature and not a major concern.

Kafka's Czech

> "Brief lesson in Czech"
>
> —Kafka's note over the Czech letterhead of the Workers' Accident Insurance of the Kingdom of Bohemia in Prague, letter to Felice Bauer, 1914

> I understand your Czech very well, I also hear your laughter but I keep digging into your letters, burrowing between your words and your laughter—until I then hear one single word, one word which is, moreover, my very essence: fear.
>
> —Kafka, letter to Milena Jesenská, June 12, 1920

The extent of the change in Kafka's relationship to Czech in the last years of his life emerges in sharp relief when we consider, by way of example, how

Czech figured in his earlier correspondence with his German fiancée Felice Bauer. These references are neither especially numerous nor revealing, but together do cumulatively reveal Kafka's sense of Czech as it pertains to various kinds of writing. In a letter of January 29, 1913, Kafka alludes to Max Brod writing his novel *A Czech Maidservant* (*Das Tschechische Dienstmädchen*); his imprecise mention of the work's title (he calls it "Die Tschechin," or "The Czech Girl") is the full extent of this reference, which instead focuses on his own apathy and incapacitation while listening to Brod write as they shared a room.[12] Here, Czechness is specifically gendered female; the novel values but eroticizes the maid's Czech identity while is itself of course written in German. Another reference dates from a letter of March 20, 1913—as Kafka discusses a possible Easter visit to Berlin, he remembers that Easter usually brings

> meetings of all kinds of societies to discuss accident insurance, where representatives of the Institute speak on some subject or other . . . and in fact today two such invitations arrived. The federation of Czech Milling Associations holds its convention in Prague on Monday, and the Czech builders from the Sudetenland have theirs in Brünn on Tuesday. Luckily, the meetings are in Czech, and my Czech is at best deplorable . . . but in accordance with the distribution of work within the Institute, it would undoubtedly be my concern.[13]

In a further letter, the Czech millers' convention "is still threatening." So Czech appears as both bureaucratic obstacle and threat—but threat by virtue of its status as obstacle, an obstacle from which Kafka's lack of knowledge of Czech may deliver him. It is, in any case, a distraction from matters of greater importance. In another instance (May 28, 1914), Kafka writes on Czech company letterhead, adding the title: "Brief Lesson in Czech" above the heading.[14] These few references clearly establish Czech as a part of his work world, but as an extraneous detail, a professional annoyance interfering in urgent personal matters—here, a misunderstanding with Felice: "At the office. There is a lot to do. I wasn't cross. I was furious, sad. . . ." The Czech language could hardly be more marginal, appearing, as it does, in a letterhead.

In a different vein, Kafka alludes to Czech in a more literary context—of a sort—writing of a Czech neighbor that he is "a teacher and author of erotic novels . . . on the title page there is a picture of a lady juggling with burning hearts . . . I don't know why I always picture this man, without concerning myself with him in any way, as a little black creep."[15] Kafka mentions that he "heard a Czech novelist" (not that he read him, but rather heard an account he gave) dismiss the work of this neighbor with the remark that "erotic novels written by a dried-up little teacher with no experience of the world and from his little hole in the ground are bound to be somewhat ridiculous." When Kafka finally meets his neighbor in the elevator, he declares him a "magnificent, enviable man!"—by virtue, apparently, of his pretending to be French, explaining: "The Czechs, you know, are very much inclined to emulate the French. . . ."[16] As represented in this correspondence, then, Czech writing is either bureaucratic—concerned with workmen, their machines and finances—or pornographic and derivative. In either case, in context the Czech language amounts to a kind of background noise; it is what goes on in the corridors where one lives and works, what threatens to disrupt the occasional holiday plan or appears by default on stationery. Czech, like the background noise of the Burrow Creature's home, is usually relegated to the background; it can come to the fore as an annoyance, but it does not threaten. Insofar as the minor literature paradigm applies at all to these sparse references, Czech's minor disruptions are opposed to, not aligned with, Kafka's own efforts.

Written a decade after these letters, Kafka's story "The Burrow" ("Der Bau," 1923) offers an excruciating account of the changing effects of an aural phenomenon as the result of a listener's increasing attention. The kind of background annoyance typical of Czech's position in the Felice Bauer letters resonates with the early stages of the Burrow Creature's experience of annoying yet potentially threatening "whistling" or "hissing" ("Zischen"). The creature first associates the noise with the "small fry" ("Kleinzeug") and their interfering tunnels; he thinks initially he didn't hear the sound at all, and then that it is "comparatively innocent"; he subsequently maintains he must always have heard it and only now has noticed it—that he needed to feel at home with it, that it was "audible only to the ear of the householder."[17] Although he calls his investigation of the sound "most urgent," his central concern—much like Kafka's expressed worry that Czech millers may disrupt his holiday plans—is that the noise is wasting his time: "these little creatures take up much, far too much, time that could be better employed"[18] ("Viel Zeit, viel Zeit, die besser verwendet werden könnte kostet mich das kleine Volk").[19] Over the course of the story, however, the nature of the noise—or the nature of the creature's relationship to the noise—changes. The more he pays attention, the more he distinguishes qualities of sound, insisting that his ear is getting trained: "I hear it now more and more distinctly, for my ear has grown keener through practice."[20]

The relationship of ear and mouth to Czech resurfaces often in Kafka's letters to Jesenská and, as I argue at greater length in my chapter "Of Mice and Music," in his animal stories of this late period, because Czech was primarily a spoken as opposed to a written language for Kafka—a particularly keen difference in Czech. We see Kafka's own sense of the discrepancy between his command of ordinary spoken Czech (*obecná čeština*) and formal written Czech (*spisovná čeština*) on display in his 1922 correspondence with his employers and with his Czech brother-in-law. Since after 1918, much more of Kafka's working life was carried out in Czech—in particular, his requests for health-related leave—he consistently passed drafts of this official correspondence to his brother-in-law, a kind of anxiety he never displayed with regard to his German writing. During the same period, however, he happily and fluidly wrote less formal Czech letters and cards to the same brother-in-law, and these letters display no signs of hesitation and very few errors: he knew Czech very well, but writing it correctly in formal situations gave him pause.

And yet, according to Marek Nekula, Kafka's education in eighteenth- and nineteenth-century Czech literature and history was comparable to that of a student attending Czech secondary schools.[21] As early in his career as 1908, in a letter to the Workman's Accident Insurance Institute sent in both Czech and German versions, Kafka describes himself as having strong spoken and written Czech, signing the Czech version of the letter "František Kafka."[22] Nekula dismantles myths about Kafka's Czech at both extremes—that he was wholly bilingual in spoken and written Czech and German, or that he grew up with Czech as his native, primary language, on the one hand, and, on the other, that his Czech was so rudimentary that he could not write a basic, communicative letter. Kafka's written Czech is always clear and comprehensible, but displays a range of minor mistakes: missing accents often (some of these are mistakes a literate but not highly educated Czech might make), a German-inflected word order, or even mistakes of aspect—a characteristic of verbs in Slavic languages that native speakers almost never misuse, but which proves difficult for even highly adept non-Slavic-native speakers.[23] These texts and their errors demonstrate that Kafka *could* write Czech, and well, but also that it did not come as easily to him as German. This analysis only confirms Kafka's own accounts of his Czech—depending somewhat on his mood and audience—but given the continuing confusion about Kafka's languages, it is of great value.

The Czech literature and public art that would have dominated Kafka's early exposure was certainly engaged in the attempt at constructing, maintaining, and policing a stable linguistically based national identity. Several strains of Czech modernism approached the question differently or resisted it altogether, and some of these would have found their way to Kafka's reading list as well. Then, too, Kafka's knowledge of Czech enabled him to read Russian works in translation in a language closer to the original, as Jürgen Born's catalog of Kafka's personal library suggests that he did, and his readings in the Czech press broadened his knowledge of other literatures as well, fueled by a vibrant Czech culture of translation. Nekula argues that Czech should also be viewed as a "medium" language for Kafka, a means by which he gained access to other literatures and cultures as well as one in which he conducted an increasing amount of his professional lawyerly life. (It did not hurt, of course, that Milena Jesenská was one of Tolstoy's translators into Czech.[24] Kafka also advised her on her Czech translations.) So Kafka's reading in Czech is not always a matter of reading Czech literature, and is not necessarily operating in the national-linguistic binary that governed so much of Prague's discourse on language.

Kafka's Knowledge of Czech Culture

Thus Kafka spoke Czech, could write it but without native fluency (due in part to the marked split between spoken and written Czech), and had a solid foundation in Czech letters at the secondary-school level. Furthermore, as Nekula also details, nationalist civic art in Prague meant that the streets themselves memorialized the Czech cultural pantheon and national mythology. Simply walking the city would have reinforced Kafka's formal schooling in Czech literary and cultural history because building facades and public sculptures—or their destruction, as in the case of the Marian column on his native Old Town Square—formed the background of his daily life. Maiden and Hussite wars, national martyrs, and even—Prague language politics being what they were—lexicographers and linguists were everywhere immortalized in monuments and paintings. From 1915 onward, the square outside Kafka's parents' home and his father's shop centered on a monument to the national hero Jan Hus by the sculptor Ladislav Šaloun (Kafka did not think much of it). Moreover, the Czech National Theater and many buildings throughout the country were decorated by "national artists" such as the sculptor Josef Václav Myslbek, whose work included the statue of Saint Wenceslas on Wenceslas Square and decorative work for the National Theater, and by the painter Mikuláš Aleš (the mural in the National Theater and countless facades throughout the country, including a prominent bank near the German cultural center or Casino in the heart of the German-dominated Graben). Czech myths and legends had thus become part of the scenery, but they were also central to the most prominent and celebrated works of Czech culture. The national mythology begins with Praotec Čech (Forefather Czech) finding and naming the land, but soon gives a prominent place to female figures such as Libuše, the founding matriarch who married a plowman and foretold a city named "threshold" (Prah). Her story, for example, is told in a novel by Franz Grillparzer (a German writer much beloved by Kafka), an opera by Bedřich Smetana, and a sculpture by Myslbek then on the Palacký Bridge. Another legend of female power, the Maidens' War, is the basis for the "Šárka" part of Smetana's symphonic poem collection *Má vlast* (of "Vltava" or "Die Moldau" fame). In this legend, the warrior maiden Vlasta rebels against Libuše's widower, the Přemysl patriarch, and Šárka then entraps his army by tying herself to a tree, pretending to be the helpless victim of other maidens, getting her rescuers drunk on mead, and putting them to sleep in order to slaughter them more easily (she loses eventually). The prominence of the matriarch Libuše, the maiden warriors, their colony Děvín, and their fight against patriarchy put a dramatic and surprisingly long-standing feminist stamp on Czech culture as Kafka would first have encountered it; the association between strong, rebellious women and Czech nationhood was well established.

These legends were central not only to nineteenth- and twentieth-century public art and music, but also to the broader sweep of Czech literature from its origins in the early fourteenth-century Czech document *The Chronicle of Dalimil.*[25] *Dalimil* was proudly touted as a testament to the longevity of the Czech literary heritage, and the *Chronicle* itself stresses the importance of the Czech language and of using it to resist German cultural hegemony. Had nineteenth-century nationalists commissioned an early work, they could hardly have done better. That didn't stop someone from trying, however. With even more prominence if less authenticity, Czech national mythology was further embellished and popularized in a pair of forged medieval manuscripts "discovered" in 1817, manuscripts that would figure variously and importantly in political discourse for at least the next hundred years. Championed by nationalist historians and artists throughout the nineteenth century as establishing Czech as a literary language with a longer history than German, the 1817 forged manuscripts were definitively exposed in 1886 by none other than Tomáš Masaryk, the future first president of Czechoslovakia. The manuscripts' fraudulent origins were then cited by German chauvinists as evidence of Czech literature's inherent derivativeness and false premises, while the sober demystification that surrounded the fraud's exposure became a touchstone of Masaryk's "realist" political movement, bolstering his own legend as a fair-dealing, iconoclastic, rationalist leader of a nation whose authenticity had no need of such falsehoods. These myths and figures, their literary and artistic legacy and their political valences, would simply have been part of Kafka's consciousness since childhood, since which time the Czech cultural marking of Prague's streets and buildings had only increased. Such monuments were not *only* background made invisible by habituation, however, but were often suddenly (and sometimes violently) "foregrounded," to literalize the Prague School term. The Jan Hus memorial erected on Old Town Square in 1915, for example, dramatically altered Kafka's personal Prague landscape by placing an enormous monument to Czech martyrdom in front of his old German high school. The 1912 unveiling of Myslbek's statue of Saint Wenceslas on the city's main square and the artistic conflicts between traditional Realist and more modern (Art Nouveau, Expressionist, and even Cubist) designs for the city's Žižka and Palacký monuments all gave form, substance, and a heightened sense of currency to Czech literary and cultural nationalism, inserting not just the legendary subjects but the artists and their aesthetic programs into public discourse and front-page news. And while Czech national mythology was an ever-increasing part of the city's landscape throughout Kafka's lifetime, the founding of a nation-state in part based on this mythology surely "foregrounded" this cultural legacy.

In addition to going about his business against a background more and more crowded with Czech myths in bronze and stone, Kafka began to more actively seek out Czech literature, apparently for the first time since secondary school. For instance, he would have read primary works by the nineteenth-century authors Božena Němcová and Jaroslav Vrchlický—the Czech cultural equivalents of a George Sand or Victor Hugo—in school, but he hardly mentions them for many years. During his time in Zürau (Siřem) in 1917–18, however—months before the official founding of Czechoslovakia—Kafka read the recently released volumes of correspondence by each writer, suggesting less a passive curiosity than a particular interest, especially given the importance Kafka seems to ascribe to his own letter-writing.[26] During the same period, he asked Max Brod to send more Czech literature and claimed to be restricting himself to works in Czech and French. He left no detailed record of this reading other than these names, but his future correspondence and fiction offer evidence of a sustained and thoughtful engagement with Němcová's work especially.

Even had Kafka never mentioned such reading, his formal schooling and daily life as a Prague citizen guarantee his basic familiarity with established—and establishment—Czech culture, particularly nationalist culture. But of its modernist strains, of the Decadent, Symbolist, or other avant-garde Czech literary movements—the more cosmopolitan, less intensely nationalist elements of Czech culture—less is clear. Kafka himself displays little awareness or interest in these elements of Czech culture until this later "Czechoslovak" period. This does not mean he did not have *any* interest, of course, especially given his enthusiasm for the visual arts which were so central to Czech culture at this time. During Kafka's lifetime, there were *many* "Prague Circles" in addition to the two groups which are known by that name; that is, much of Prague culture revolved around groups of artists and writers—often associated with a particular little magazine—who exhibited and published together. For the generation prior to Kafka (or rather, during Kafka's youth), the extraordinary fin-de-siècle *Moderní revue* was the standard-bearer of the Czech literary (and to some extent visual) avant-garde. Taking its cues from Oscar Wilde, Aubrey Beardsley, and French Symbolism, it was dedicated to an aestheticist and cosmopolitan ethos and in its early days published in multiple languages. Kafka doesn't mention it, although Nekula makes a convincing case that he may have traveled in the same social circles as *Moderní revue* artists, but other proximities exist as well: divided as it was, the Prague art scene was small enough that no game of "six degrees of Franz Kafka" is likely to get beyond degree 2. Otokar Březina, for example, the great Czech Symbolist poet, was strongly associated with *Moderní revue* (both rose to prominence in tandem) as was František Bílek, an artist and sculptor Kafka very much admired (as I discuss more fully below) who illustrated Březina's work. Kafka's friend Franz Werfel translated Březina, thus Kafka had a copy of the poet in translation, while Milena Jesenská wrote Březina heartfelt fan letters as a teenager (and later translated both Werfel and Kafka). Jesenská's aunt Růžena Jesenská was also associated with *Moderní revue*, and Kafka seems familiar with her work in his letters to her niece, although he never mentions any such interest before that. In short, it is difficult to imagine anyone in Prague even vaguely curious about art and literature not being aware of the visual artists and writers around this publication.

Somewhat later but still before World War I, the Cubist-oriented groups Osma and Skupina (reformed as Tvrdošíjní [The Obstinate Ones] after the war) became dominant. (In keeping with the city's divisive nature, Czech Cubists also split into two groups along not only aesthetic but national lines, with some adhering to the more purist French style and theory and the others wishing to seek a more local, or national, inflection.) Although these Cubist groups were more visually focused and formally declared than the loose and expanding associations that formed around little magazines, it was a central, defining feature of Prague culture at this time that visual artists, designers, critics, architects, and writers all moved in these circles to various extents. František Langer, the Czech-identified brother of Kafka's friend Georg/Jiří Langer, edited an arts magazine in which he had wanted to publish Kafka, but the magazine folded with the onset of World War I.[27] The war naturally had a dampening effect on culture (perhaps particularly on Czech-German overtures), but with its end, and with the promise and energy of a new state, Prague saw an explosion of little magazines and collaborations—some of these supported by the government, which had strong ties to the arts. Not that all avant-gardes, naturally, were in lockstep with Czechoslovakia's nascent liberal capitalist democracy. The most internationally influential of these groups, Devětsil, was first formed in 1920 in reaction against the by-then establishment Cubo-Expressionists like Karel and Josef Čapek and their progressivist connections to Masaryk and his government. The more hard-nosed, ideological, polemical, and leftist Devětsil was unquestionably the most significant avant-garde group from the interwar period, and included the writer Vladislav Vančura, whom Kafka mentions with admiration and who had known Jesenská at university, and Jaromír Krejcar, the architect whom she married after Kafka's death. Although the group's greatest reputation and influence also came after his death, during Kafka's lifetime Devětsil writers and artists published often in the Czech leftist magazines in which Kafka himself appeared; Kafka received his own issue of *Kmen*, discussed in detail in the next chapter, while Devětsil had a dedicated issue of *Červen*, *Kmen*'s sister publication that published art and graphics as well as political and literary writing. (See figure 1.)

As with the Prague Linguistic Circle, Kafka and Devětsil were fellow travelers for a brief time. As he was coming to the end of his life, these major interwar groups were only nascent, but some of these forward- and outward-looking Czechs sought him out (although he was hardly well known), and he seems to have responded with his own interest. A number of Kafka's friends, of course, were much more directly involved in the Czech art scene than he; Max Brod would give the first favorable review of the Osma Cubism exhibition in 1908, and Kafka's school friend Oskar Pollak also went on to be a prominent art critic. But Kafka's knowledge and interest did not rely on such personal connections. His interest in the visual arts and graphic design (Brod

ČERVEN

PROLETKULT — KOMUNISM — LITERATURA — NOVÉ UMĚNÍ

ROK IV. ČÍSLO 12 VEDE STANISLAV K. NEUMANN 22. ČERVNA 1921

U.S. DEVĚTSIL * * * !

zvláštní číslo

Artuš Černík: Smutný den

Tichá hodina jakoby nebyla z tohoto města,
neboť ani pták v kleci nad svým osudem nejásá:
zamyslili se lidé nad svým životem,
rozsypala rosu šedá nebesa?
Boží den a v ruce vztažené,
děvče svírá žlutý růženec,
děvče, které v letních dnech
hledělo do studánky.
Má v tvářích bledých nemocné rysy,
umírá touhou a volá zpátky
veselé srdce a horské ptáky.

Bystřiny, pádící mechem,
kameny na rozcestích,
nejste-li led a sníh,
nejste-li neděle truchlivých zadumání?

Ztratily barvy hřejivé tváře,
pozbyly domy vlídnost,
již vítají člověka cizího, člověka věřícího,
tržiště nekonečné, bída dláždění
zajaly do zrádných sítí ženu.

A v tento den,
byť v kostelích byl zpěvem posvěcen,
a ženy, jimž rudá krev byla dána,
aby z ní zástupům vyrostla slávobrána,
byť zpěvem políbily nejzazší skaliny a chaty,
je smutná sousedka nad podzim tesklivější
a ještě modliteb než leta zapomněla,
a růžencem žlutým v rukou
nad světem se modlí u okna:

— Vy oblaka, jichž ruka nespoutala,
vy stromy, kterým ústa dána nebyla,
vy vzdechy, které světem plujete,
vy smutní mrtví, kterých neskryla
však mramorová deska třpytivá,
má mrtvá sestřičko, již láska zavraždila,
vy ptáčci, keře, oči zamyšlené,
pastviny skutečné i louky sněné,
bude mi umříti
za takového dne,
v mlhavém polibku sluneční pochodně.

— Den snese se na lehkých perutích,
odpusťte bledé holčičce tíživý hřích.

— Uprostřed zahrad a zpěvu ženců
a kytek na mezích
kdys z neznámého večera
jsem v život vkročila
jak vlnka jezera,
jak pěnkava . . .

— Leč domy cizí, města, města, okna,
jednou mne nesl vlak
do vašich objetí,
ni zahradám, ni vsím jsem s bohem nedala
ni hnízdům ptáčat v lesním údolí.
A hřešit nechtějíc, jsem těžce zhřešila,
svůj život krášlic perlami.
Člun na jezeře v bouřích ulomil
a lípu v květu milují milenci.
Mé oči za večerů v městě vybledly
a nikdo nevrátí mi dětské duše.

Figure 1. *Červen* (sister publication of *Kmen*), June 1921. Cover of issue devoted to the avant-garde group Devětsil. *Červen: tendenční čtrnáctidenník*. Prague: Fr. Borový, June, 1921. Vol 4, no. 12. Moravská zemská knihovna v Brně / The Moravian Library in Brno.

had planned to publish a selection of his drawings) guarantees he would have been aware of the major trends in Czech art, which during his lifetime had intense and distinctive Decadent, Expressionist, Cubist, Dada, Nativist, and Futurist movements (and various combinations of them all). He shared common interests with the Czech art scene—Gauguin, for example: his paintings at the 1907 Prague exhibition of French Impressionist and Post-Impressionist painters took the city by storm, wielding a huge influence on artists from Josef Čapek to Josef Váchal, while Kafka read his artist writings. As a matter of fact, the French influence on Czech culture that Kafka explained somewhat disparagingly with relation to his Czech neighbor (see above) was, in fact, extremely strong in both letters and the visual arts—the 1919 *Červen* issue devoted entirely to Apollinaire's *Zone* (translated by Karel Čapek,

Rok I. Číslo 21. a 22. ČERVEN 6. února 1919

Guillaume Apollinaire: Pásmo

Přeložil Karel Čapek

Obrazy ryl do linolea Josef Čapek

291

Figure 2. Cover for the issue of *Červen* devoted to Apollinaire's *Zone*. Translation by Karel Čapek; cover art (linocut) by Josef Čapek. *Červen: tendenční čtrnáctidenník*. Prague Fr. Borový, 1921. roč.1, č. 21-22 (February 6, 1919), 290. Moravská zemská knihovna v Brně / The Moravian Library in Brno.

illustrated by Josef Čapek) was another such French-inspired watershed in Prague culture. (See figure 2.)

Of these Czech movements, the connection to Kafka is most evident in the Expressionist and Cubist strains, which combined in the Czech lands in distinctive ways. Cubism was particularly strong in the Czech lands, where it extended into furniture and design and even—also uniquely—into architecture: "Kafka's Prague," as Josef Kroutvor has explained, "that city of sharp and wounding edges, was also the city of Czech Cubism." In 1911 the first Cubist building in Prague, the House of the Black Madonna, went up just around the corner from Old Town Square, the center of Kafka's own Prague. Several commentators—including Kroutvor—have noted Cubist qualities in some of Kafka's representational strategies; Kroutvor cites the cramped stairwells and passageways in *The Trial* as examples of the "descriptions and feelings" that approach Cubism in Kafka's work, remarking that in the end, even Kafka's gravestone is Cubist. Kroutvor appears to tie this tendency back to Prague politics by virtue of what he calls the city's "sharp edges": "both forms, literary and visual, have wounding edges, because both are at the intersection of two worlds: the conflict of human inwardness and personal perspective against supra-personal geometry and its laws."[28] This formulation is a potent reminder of the aesthetic and representational issues, the kinds of artistic identity, that mattered most to Kafka.

Nonetheless, however comprehensive Kafka's knowledge of any of these movements in Czech art or literature *may* have been, it must be acknowledged that in his adult life, active, sustained interest in them seems to have been scant until his later years, if we judge by his writings. In his voluminous letters to Felice Bauer, these Czech cultural movements appear only in the passing reference to Kafka's "creeping" Czech novelist neighbor. As Kafka followed Jesenská's and Brod's writings and translations in the 1920s, this would certainly change, and comments in his late letters suggest that his curiosity did not limit itself to his friends' careers. To return, for a moment, to the topic of monuments: Kafka's correspondence with Brod shows that Kafka *had* been considering the topic of monuments closely, and had formed definite opinions about them, opinions that indicate an increased awareness of and sensitivity to the more modern strains in Czech culture. Šaloun's Hus monument on Old Town Square apparently displeased him enough that he had researched alternative versions. Kafka championed designs by a very different sculptor, František Bílek.[29] Of the two, Bílek's style is more Decadent, fin de siècle-inflected, but both artists had ties with Mánes, the prominent, internationally engaged society of modernist Czech artists. Around the time that Kafka was writing to Brod about monuments, the Czech-language daily *Tribuna* that Kafka often read had recently touched on the subject. That article may have prompted his commentary, but Kafka had clearly already thought extensively about the topic. He displays a thorough knowledge of what he considers Bílek's superior sketches for monuments that had not been cast and advocates that Brod take up Bílek's cause, suggesting that a "government organ" ("Regierungsblatt," meaning the new *Prager Presse*) would be the appropriate venue.[30] These letters emphasize Kafka's awareness that the cultural interpretation of Czech history was far from monolithic and that Czech nationalism and cosmopolitanism were not necessarily opposed. This sense of such differences and nuances could not have been gained passively. It is one thing to have an opinion on the enormous statue that shows up outside your house but quite another to become intimately familiar with alternative designs that never came to fruition.

I dwell on this brief exchange because I find it exemplary of the qualitative shift in attention that often characterizes Kafka's "Czechoslovak" period.

In one way, the exchange about the monument plans is very simple—Kafka had been reading a Czech-language newspaper, something caught his fancy or interest, and he followed through on it after some reflection. No similar instance figures in his earlier writings, however, while his letters and journals from this later period display a familiarity with various Czech publications and often with the individuals involved. The context in which Kafka made these remarks—he had been reading *Tribuna*, he suggests material for the *Prager Presse*—attests to his immersion in left-leaning Czech newspapers and periodicals (the *Presse*, while published in German, like *Tribuna* was dedicated to featuring both Czech and German writers). In part, Kafka's newfound interest was personal, but this personal interest reflected political change: in the new Czechoslovakia, the Czech press published and employed his friends, colleagues, and lover—and even incredibly (to Kafka) translated and published Kafka himself. Kafka by no means engaged in these journalistic and collaborative activities to the same extent as his friends, and furthermore, his failing health often took him outside of Prague during his time as a Czechoslovak citizen. Yet his friends were deeply involved, and friends and family sent him papers and clippings while he was away. If Czech print media would not otherwise make its way to foreign locales like Meran and Berlin, he could certainly find it in the domestic spas and villages he also spent time in.

Thus the contemporary Czech works *in print* (excluding private letters) that we have the greatest reason to believe Kafka read carefully during his last years appeared in these newspapers and journals, to which I devote the next chapter. As I will explain in detail, the postwar Prague press challenges in its complexity the notion of stable identities constituted by language that the very same papers often promote and try to maintain. The paradigm of "minor literature" is inadequate to the intricacy and conflict these publications display, as well as to the concerned ambivalence with which Kafka himself approached these issues. A more richly informed understanding of "minor literature's" Prague context shows at once how apt was Deleuze and Guattari's focus on Prague's language politics and how limited their historical and even theoretical understanding of the relations they examine. Their post-World War II suspicion of unity as hegemony and their embrace of instability and rupture as inherently liberating is anachronistically applied, distorting Kafka's complex and changing engagement with questions of language, identity, territory, and the instability and permeability of their relations. Rather than substitute an alternative paradigm, my own work sees the anxious variety with which these issues play out in Kafka's work as being resistant to such a project: though patterns do emerge and repeat, they also contradict. As more recent work fills in the gaps left by Deleuze and Guattari's argument, a new understanding is developing not only of Prague cultural history but also of its theoretical implications—for Kafka's work and beyond.

Chapter 2

✦

Kafka and the Czech Press

Gustav Janouch's *Conversations with Kafka* portrays Kafka as "a passionate reader of newspapers and magazines" who, although cynical about the press, kept contemporary issues of Czech, German, and French reviews on hand in his office and "referred to their contents in conversation."[1] Janouch's reliability is contested and inconsistent, and his accounts are best believed when his claims can be corroborated by other sources, as this claim certainly can be. When, for example, Janouch mentions that Kafka had two bound volumes of the philological journal *Naše řeč* and had been studying them, wishing for earlier issues, there is little reason to doubt him because Kafka mentions the publication elsewhere.[2] And when Janouch's Kafka remarks that "the greatest difficulty of the Czech language is to demarcate it properly from other languages," it indeed sounds like the reflection of someone well steeped in this philology journal.[3] Kafka had been paying attention to both popular journalistic and more specialized discourses about Czech, a fact not established but rather confirmed by the *Conversations*. Czech periodical and newspaper culture was indeed central to Kafka's experience of Czech letters.

First, Kafka's interest these publications is explicable solely on personal grounds. Leaving aside for a moment the question of Jesenská's influence (to which I devote a great deal more space in later chapters), Max Brod's engagement with Czech culture, always strong, only intensified during this period. In 1921, this interest extended to taking a position as critic in the new Czech government-sponsored *Prager Presse*, a German-language newspaper whose cultural pages presented Czech culture to German audiences. Otto Pick, a longtime friend of both Kafka and Brod, was editor-in chief, and his newspaper went on to publish stories by Kafka. While Kafka was recuperating at Matliary in Slovakia (December 1920-August 1921), Brod wrote of two different possibilities for employment at the new paper, and Kafka responded knowledgeably. Kafka advised Brod against taking a job as editor-in-chief, which struck Kafka as "impossible," and he further worried that the newspaper in question would be like the *Gazette des Ardennes*, a notorious German propaganda organ published in French in German-occupied France and Belgium (1915–18) and distributed to prisoners in camps. It is hardly a flattering comparison, and Kafka finds the thing "unworthy" of his friend. As to acting as critic for the *Prager Presse*, however, Kafka finds that unobjectionable: "Why should that not be possible? For which the government would pay? The government is so totally improvised, so precarious, that it is bound to do some first-rate things now and then."[4] While Kafka's interest may first have been inspired by his friends' involvement, these are the remarks of someone who has spent some serious time and effort thinking about the fate of newspapers not only in the new Czechoslovakia, but elsewhere during the war and postwar periods. "Besides," reasons Kafka, "things of this kind are not only happening in Czechoslovakia; they are the happy accidents of press arrangements improvised during wartime."[5]

Dedicated in part to presenting the Czech government's side of any given story to German readers whose own newspapers, it was felt, could not be relied upon in this regard, the "happy accident" of the *Presse* employed serious journalists and was embraced by many of the Prague Circle writers of Kafka's acquaintance, including Brod and Pick. Pick, a tireless translator and promoter of Czech literature who was responsible for the introduction of Karel Čapek to European audiences, was the paper's literary editor. Importantly, the *Presse* provided a venue for Prague German writers, publishing them alongside more broadly known German writers and thinkers such as Albert Einstein and Herman Hesse, and this patronage generated goodwill. More unusually, however, the *Presse* published full-broadsheet, photographically illustrated introductions to Czech architecture, literature, and painting, one of the only German-language publications to do so. It also published German translations of both leading and emerging Czech writers—many of them translated by Pavel Eisner, Kafka's translator after Milena Jesenská. The *Presse* presented a broadly cosmopolitan image of Prague—an image that was both more true than would appear from the nationalist newspapers of the time, but also *less* broadly true than the paper's own hopeful project made it seem. The *Presse* exemplified the hopes the Czechoslovak government held out for Prague as a cultural "Center of Europe": they envisioned the city as a cultural crossroads, which must naturally include cultural contact and contiguity between its Czech and German citizens. While the *Prager Presse* was not a Czech-language paper, its role in presenting Czech and German writers on the same pages, in German, was representative of other new efforts to increase cultural collaboration, although the paper's semiofficial state status also set it apart.

Prague newspapers must be understood not only as providing political and historical contexts for literature but as literary spaces themselves, as popular venues for publishing short prose pieces, following from the nineteenth-century rise of the feuilleton in France. The bottom section of most Bohemian (that is to say, Czech and German) newspapers at this time was devoted to belletristic literary and cultural material. All the major writers of the day published in this feuilleton (in Czech, *fejeton*) space: essays, excerpted novels, short stories, poems, reviews, and the like by writers from

Jaroslav Seifert and Karel Čapek to Franz Werfel and Gustav Meyrink and everyone in between—including, thanks to Brod and Jesenská, Franz Kafka. Above the line (the feuilleton section was blocked off by a boldface margin), the papers dealt with nationalist conflict, the end of the war and its aftermath, the founding of the new nation-state, and so on. Most newspapers were closely politically and financially aligned with political parties; some were neutral or "independent" in that they were not financially dependent on political affiliation (although that doesn't mean they steered clear of politics). However, it was not uncommon for literary writers to publish feuilletons in a newspaper whose political platform they did not endorse, and so the feuilleton section could be much more cosmopolitan and eclectic than the political positions taken in the reporting "above the bar."

By far the *least* cosmopolitan of the Czech papers Kafka would read was the pro-Czech, anti-German, and often antisemitic *Venkov* (*The Countryside*), the newspaper of the Czech Agrarian Party. While in residence in Matliary in 1921—weakened by his disease and disheartened by the dissolution of his relationship with Milena Jesenská—Kafka mentions this publication in a damning if perversely gleeful (by his own account) manner. He writes to Max Brod of a Czech patient whom he first categorizes as a "disturbance":

> a new table-mate, an elderly spinster, repulsively powdered and perfumed . . . also unhinged by nervousness, talkative in company, as a Czech partially dependent on me, and deaf in the ear on the side away from me. . . . I have one weapon that I hope will be effectual: today she mentioned (not to me) that her favorite paper was Venkov, especially because of its editorials. Delighted, I have been thinking of that all evening.[6]

What this preference for *Venkov* indicated needed no explanation: bias, anti-German and anti-Jew. That Jesenská's ultra-nationalist aunt Růžena Jesenská was often published in its pages likely only fed the understandable bitterness and less understandable (or at least less palatable) misogyny that Kafka displays here. As it happened, he misjudged the woman—though he waited with a strange eagerness for her to embarrass herself with an unforgivable antisemitic comment in front of him, she didn't, and he grew to like her. Yet a preference for *Venkov* would indeed imply all that he initially understood from it. *Venkov*'s nationalist political impulse toward purism, however, did not prevent it from publishing mainstream Czech critics such as Arne Novak and F. X. Šalda alongside writers active in smaller avant-garde magazines at the opposite end of the political spectrum.

Long before this exchange with Max Brod about the *Venkov*-reading patient—in September 1918, in fact, just prior to the establishment of Czechoslovakia—Šalda responds in *Venkov* to Josef Čapek (artist and essayist, brother to Karel) and his call in the magazine *Červen* for a less chauvinistic, more internationally oriented Czech art. Šalda quotes Čapek as complaining that art under the flag of nationalism, racism, Czechness, and so on is reactionary art that ignores the long-permeable boundaries of the Czech lands, and he argues that any call for purity is inimical to art. Šalda responds that German internationalism in the arts is a cover for the Germans' own nationalism, a cover for the hegemony of larger nationalities. When such an exchange is accompanied in the news sections of the paper by the telltale blank spaces of the imperial censor—a frequent feature of *Venkov*'s pages in these last days of the empire—the terms of the debate, like the relationship between politics and publishing, or literature and politics, seem writ very large indeed. (See figure 3.)

Heavy censorship of the news sections notwithstanding, the cultural sections even of so anti-imperial a paper as *Venkov* had freer rein. Sentiments like Šalda's expressed *above* the line marking off the feuilleton space would have been removed. Arguably, this more liberal policy in regard to the political content of cultural works drove more politics into such works, intensifying the inescapable political stakes of cultural life in Prague. This exchange illustrates—as do so many similar ones—the intensity with which questions of art and literature were bound up not only with questions of identity, but with questions of actual state boundaries, which were then specifically at issue in the news sections and implicated in the nationalism-internationalism debate. Furthermore, the visible boundary on the printed page between the cultural and political sections of the newspaper also served as a material link between them, binding them to the "same page" while also delimiting a recognizable "cross-newspaper" (and therefore cross-political and trans-linguistic) literary space.

Tribuna, a Czech-Jewish-headed and -funded daily founded in 1919, was very much at the other end of the Czech political spectrum. *Tribuna* was founded in response to a meeting of the Association of Progressive Czech Jews that called for publication of a left-centrist, largely pro-government daily newspaper in order to provide a balanced account, in Czech, of Czech Jewry and its efforts in the new republic as well as to focus on issues of economic, political, and cultural interest to a broader Czech audience—but all in the context of a venue free from antisemitic remarks.[7] *Tribuna* was edited by Czech Jews—among them Ferdinand Peroutka, who would go on to become one of the most prominent journalists of the interwar period, and Arne Laurin, who would leave to take on the *Prager Presse*. Like the *Presse, Tribuna* dedicated much of its space to publishing new works by Czech writers as well as works by Prague German-Jewish writers—who were often appearing for the first time in Czech translation. It was also international in scope, publishing, for example, an excerpt in translation from a novel by G. K. Chesterton and Jesenská's weekly columns from Vienna. *Tribuna* published several of Kafka's early publications in Czech, translated from the German by Jesenská, who also wrote the paper's fashion section. Overall, this daily newspaper had an impressive track record of finding exciting new work, publishing, for example, the first translation in any language of Robert Musil—"Die Affeninsel"

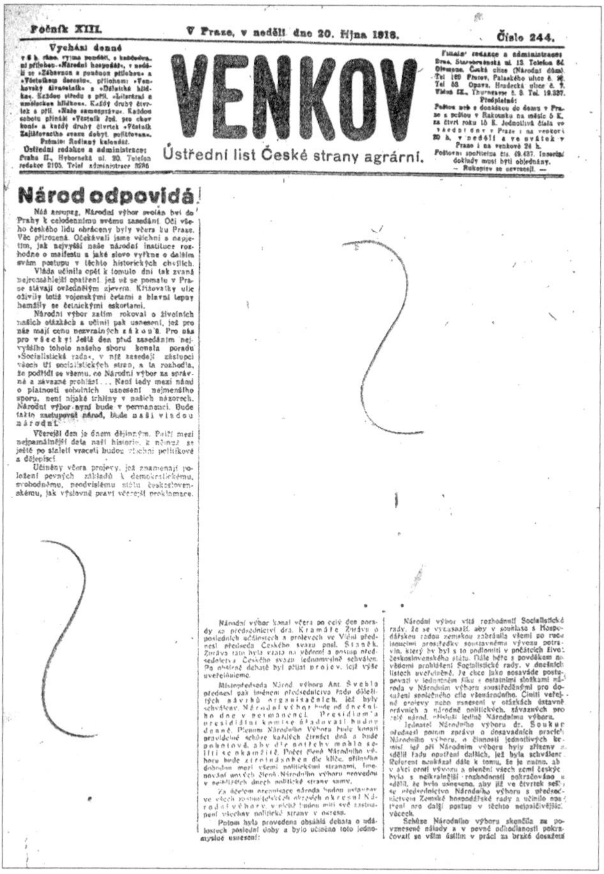

Ročník XIII. V Praze, v neděli dne 20. října 1918. Číslo 244.

VENKOV

Ústřední list České strany agrární.

Národ odpovídá!

Figure 3. Censored front page of *Venkov* two days after the Czechoslovak Declaration of Independence had been signed in Paris. *Venkov: orgán České strany agrární.* Prague: Tiskařské a vydavatelské družstvo rolnické, 1918, vol.13, no. 244 (October 20, 1918). Moravská zemská knihovna v Brně / The Moravian Library in Brno.

("Opici ostrov," "Monkey Island"), and later hiring Musil to write cultural columns.[8] In short succession, it also published Gustav Meyrink (of *Der Golem* fame), Kafka's "Report to an Academy," Jaroslav Hašek of *Švejk* fame, and the strange, Nietzschean philosopher and fiction writer Ladislav Klíma.

In his book largely debunking many claims by Kafka "fabulists" who traded on his name after Kafka's death, Josef Čermák notes that according to the poet Michal Mareš, Kafka met Klíma at the Café Edison, had known and admired Klíma from his first publications in *Tribuna,* and had even told Mareš he considered Klíma to be a "master." Čermák calls this claim "doubtful," explaining that Mareš expounds on Kafka's acquaintance with many Czech writers, all supposedly introduced to him by Mareš himself.[9] However remarkable such a meeting would have been (and it is certainly possible that Kafka had seen the pieces in *Tribuna,* and even that he discussed them with Mareš) it is perhaps even more remarkable that Ladislav Klíma and Franz Kafka shared a surprising collection of attributes—surprising because it is difficult to imagine two writers *less* similar in every other respect (aside from sharing a certain consonance of name, admittedly the kind of connection Kafka could be sensitive to). Like Kafka, Klíma wanted all his unpublished manuscripts burned; unlike Kafka, he didn't assign this task to his best friend and biggest fan, but instead burned 90 percent of his own work in a fit of self-loathing. Like Kafka, he was interested in Schopenhauer; he died much too young of tuberculosis in the 1920s; his best-known novelistic works were only published posthumously; and he tended towards aphorism. These were the only ways—besides publishing in the *Tribuna*—in which Klíma in any way resembled the abstemious, contained, dutiful Kafka, who devoted so much of his time to an office job he took seriously but never loved. Best known as a philosopher, Ladislav Klíma performed his concept of absolute will—an embodied mediation between Schopenhauer and Nietszche—by doing exactly as he wanted. He is famous for having been kicked out of the Gymnasium, and then out of *all* schools, for incredible insults against the Habsburg monarchy. He never had a job. Though extremely poor, he preferred to rely on friends and supporters than to compromise his principles and do anything he didn't want to do. His writings for *Tribuna* could hardly have contributed much to his upkeep, but his several collections of aphorisms published in the paper's feuilleton space include some comments about the Czech experience of the German language, ascribing generations of resistance to the ugliness of the Czech word for "German":

> Those who are committed to reconciliation with the Germans should, above all, strive to eliminate the curse word "Nemec." At a deep psychological level, nothing has so incited the Czechs' constant national resistance to the Germans, and consequently the Germans to the Czechs, as this disgusting word and the disdain and ugliness it expresses. It was this that awakened, in my earliest childhood, the sense that Germans were something bearish, mumbling, bestial, brutish, monstrous, a sense I have not thrown off and which to this day poisons a great portion of German culture for me. It is certain that every Czech has experienced something similar, though perhaps to a lesser degree and unconsciously. The consequences, however, are terrible. By baptizing its neighbor with a slur, the nation decided its future, perhaps even wrote its own death sentence.[10]

The passage offers an intriguing if deeply ironic counterpoint to some of Kafka's comments about the sound of Czech on German ears (and, as I argue, his representation of it in "The Burrow" and "Josefine"). Here it is not the actual sound of the German language, but the sound of the Czech word for that language that dehumanizes the German people, defining them as something animalistic, bestial. The word shapes Czech experience of German language and culture, deforming it (or worse), a twist on Kafka's sense that when the wrong kind of utterance becomes performative, the consequences can be dire to the point of deadly (as with a sentence uttered by the father in "The Judgment" ["Das Urteil"; also translated as "The Sentence"]; or, possibly, with a slur in "The Metamorphosis" ["Die Verwandlung"]—as if by calling someone a "vermin" we might turn them into Gregor Samsa).[11]

While impossible to verify, it is no stretch to imagine that Kafka would have read Klíma or indeed anyone else publishing in this newspaper, because Kafka was an avid *Tribuna* reader. It was unusual when he *didn't* read it: he tells his brother-in-law "he was not even reading *Tribuna*" in a letter from Matliary, offering this fact as testimony to how utterly cut off from Prague politics he tried to keep himself there (although other letters indicate he was not always successful in this). The formulation also suggests that *Tribuna* was basic reading for him elsewhere, as do his comments in letters to Brod and Jesenská. In contrast to the loud, vocal Czech antisemitism he would encounter on the streets or in *Venkov*, *Tribuna* presented a version of a Czech-language world that was free from ethnic slurs but replete with literary and cultural pieces that did not police its boundaries for German encroachment or bludgeon with polemics. The newspaper was in Czech, but it was run by Jewish friends and colleagues. Of course, *Tribuna* had a particular presence in Kafka's consciousness for publishing not only Jesenská's translations of him but her columns about her life in Vienna, thus providing a source of news of and textual contact with her as well.

This potential was not even restricted to print. In July 1920, obsessed by a need for news of Jesenská (who was writing at this time very regularly, but never enough by Kafka's standards), Kafka visited her *Tribuna* editor, Arne Laurin. Laurin was able to tell Kafka that "he hadn't heard of anything bad happening" to Jesenská and even telephoned the journalist Egon Erwin Kisch at another paper, asking him to make inquiries about Jesenská's well-being. In these offices, then, as a result of proximity and technology, Kafka could hear her spoken of: "So I was sitting at Laurin's, heard your name mentioned several times and was grateful to him. Even so, talking to him is neither easy nor pleasant." Kafka likens Laurin to a child, a braggart and liar, but also to a "big serious grownup when it comes to kindness, sympathy and readiness to help," and as distressed as Kafka finds himself by this combination, he hangs around anyway in order to keep hearing Jesenská's name.[12]

Tribuna's associations for Kafka were thus far from uniformly positive. There had been a suicide in the newspaper's offices—a young editor, Josef Reiner, had killed himself. In June of 1920, Kafka had received word from Max Brod that the suicide, which had happened in February of that year, was now explained: it was the result of an unconsummated affair with "a Christian, a friend of Milena Jesenská and similar to her," according to Brod—who did not yet know of the obsessive textual affair between Kafka and Jesenská. So Kafka had just learned that Jarmila (maiden name Ambrožová, later Haasová-Nečasová), a Czech Gentile friend of Jesenská's, was having an affair with Willy Haas, a German Jewish friend of Kafka's; Jarmila also translated from the German; Haas was also a writer who had trained as a lawyer. Kafka is obviously struck by the structural and demographic parallels to their situation but, as Kafka biographer Reiner Stach observes, Kafka goes "one baffling step futher" and quotes Brod's account of the tragedy to Jesenská, introducing it with the phrase "you belong to me."[13] About a month later, the day after having complained that talking to Laurin was "neither easy nor pleasant," Kafka even goes back to the *Tribuna*'s offices to see Laurin again, but misses him and instead spends the evening talking to another acquaintance—the poet Michal Mareš (who would later claim Kafka knew Klíma and any number of other Czech writers). Mareš had apparently been with the young Josef Reiner that last evening, and he sat with Kafka and told him all about it, sitting on the same sofa on which Reiner had killed himself—as Kafka reports to Jesenská in detail. The proximity could only intensify Kafka's already heightened sense of the potential parallels to his own situation, and his interactions with the newspaper staff remain charged with this trauma. On another visit, Kafka and Laurin talk about women, including Jarmila Nečasová, the woman who had married Reiner, had the affair with Willy Haas, and purportedly threatened to throw herself out of a window if Laurin himself didn't sleep with her. Clearly, while Kafka was a regular reader and sometimes, via Jesenská, even a contributor, *Tribuna* could also be a source of discomfort and concern.

For a brief time, certainly, *Tribuna* was a formidable cultural force far beyond its influence on Kafka and beyond its immediate readership in the Czech Jewish community. However, it lost Laurin to Masaryk's *Prager Presse* in 1921 and ultimately, in a fairly intense irony, lost control of its finances to the Czech Agrarian Party—which also controlled *Venkov*. Thus the newspaper founded on the hope of presenting economic and cultural news in a Czech-language context free of antisemitic feeling and rhetoric was suddenly controlled by the party of Czech antisemitism, although it continued to operate under the same name. Although this transfer took place after Kafka's death, it was typical of the kind of shifts in words, names, and their meanings—the travails of homonymy—he sometimes explores in his late writings. It was hardly the only newspaper of the period to suffer a similar change in fortune from more tolerant and hopeful beginnings.

Kmen

In many ways, the little magazine *Kmen* (*The Stem*) encapsulated both the promise and the ultimate fate of the inclusive leftist print culture that thrived for a short time in Prague toward the end of Kafka's life. When Milena Jesenská wrote Kafka for permission to translate his work, she was translating for this magazine.

The first publication to publish Kafka in Czech translation merits close examination for the way it illuminates the Czech face of cross-cultural, international modernism. In the pages and editorial offices of *Kmen*, at least, Kafka would have found the Czechs who knew "a little of the world" whom he imagined in 1911 as being "sad" at mediocre Czech theater. This small leftist Czech cultural magazine of the early 1920s occupies an almost entirely obscure yet, I argue, highly significant position in literary history. It would also go on to a future even more political than the government propagandist *Prager Presse*. In part, *Kmen*'s place in the footnotes is guaranteed by providing Kafka's fiction with its first foray into the world of the "minor literature" of which he had written in passing a decade before—now the "major" language of his "new" nation that would later be immortalized as "a faraway country about which we know nothing." If "we" outside of Czechoslovakia knew nothing of that country, however, it is safe to say that "we" knew even less of *Kmen*, and unlike the newspaper dailies discussed above, it was not in wide circulation even in its day. Yet as several references in his letters make clear, Kafka, increasingly textually obsessed with Jesenská, read *Kmen* with regularity since she published in its pages.[14] And 1920–21, the year of this intense but ultimately short-lived correspondence, was a busy year for Jesenská. *Kmen* featured Jesenská's translations not only of Kafka, but of his friend Franz Werfel; the "authentic" German worker-writer Georg Schultz; excerpts from Upton Sinclair's *Jimmie Higgins*; an essay on Russian poetry by Rosa Luxemburg (recently murdered); and a long essay on Friedrich Hölderlin by the anarchist Gustav Landauer (also recently murdered), on which it seems Kafka actively advised her.[15] As Jesenská's translations themselves attest, under the editorship of Stanislav K. Neumann, *Kmen* strove for a balance among French, German, Anglo-American, and Russian influences, all presented in Czech and appearing alongside contemporary Czech writing. Thus in *Kmen*, Kafka encountered a cross-section of contemporary European and American literature and leftist thought in translation in juxtaposition with new writing by the upcoming generation of Czech writers—notably, future members of the influential avant-garde group Devětsil—Jaroslav Seifert, Karel Teige, and Vladislav Vančura—as well as the poetry of the future socialist heroes Jiří Wolker, Josef Hora, and, abundantly, S. K. Neumann himself. On the basis of information we have, *Kmen* would have provided Kafka with his most sustained reading experience of the Czech literary avant-garde.

As with many literary magazines, most if not all of the contributions to *Kmen* by notable writers—Franz Kafka, Roman Jakobson, Jaroslav Seifert, Franz Werfel—have been published elsewhere in multiple languages, almost all of them more widely spoken than Czech. Many of *Kmen*'s most notable pieces, furthermore, appear in Czech in translation only—its yellowing pages provide neither an original, native environment nor access to the modernist quasi-aura of these works' first mass reproduction. *Kmen* was short-lived, or rather, its quality and purpose changed course radically several times before it petered out; its circulation was never large. Even were critical attention to turn to the "minor literature" Kafka actually referenced in his now-famous journal entry, *Kmen* falls short of the mark, since a primary purpose of the journal was to represent "language-of-the-masters" texts originally written in German, English, French, and Russian. Inconvenience and these arguments for its continued obscurity aside, however, there are reasons to resist *Kmen*'s continued absence from literary history. In the unknown and disappearing stories told relationally on *Kmen*'s pages, between the lines and bylines, translation credits and advertisements, *Kmen* gives us a glimpse of the mechanisms of modernism at work, how its international character was transmitted, how its internationalism signified—a glimpse not just of a Prague or a central European modernism but of an international modernist culture, emerging in tension and in tandem with strong local inflections.

Although Prague was indeed what Max Brod called a "polemical city," a city likely to amplify political tensions by literary means, it was also a small city, and young people, even Czechs, Germans, and Jews, were likely to meet—and did so, as Kafka's correspondence with Jesenská, Max Brod's translation and promotion of Leoš Janáček, and Jesenská's marriage to Ernst Pollak attest. Such figures met not only in the personal but in the public sphere as well, to important literary and political effect. Publications like *Kmen*, then, make it possible to reexamine issues addressed by Deleuze and Guattari—the relations between major and minor literatures, between language and territory—in conjunction with related issues that the French theorists do not examine—the relations between "translation" and "original" or "novel" and "excerpt"; between "nationalist" and "internationalist" or, ever vexing in a Prague context, between and among "Czech," "German," and "Jew." In reading *Kmen*, furthermore, we can view these issues from the perspective afforded by engagement with the textual traces these relations left behind.

Most remarkably—and importantly for Kafka—*Kmen*'s editorial policy demonstrated a commitment to representing not just the Czech but the *Prague* literary and cultural scene, inclusive of its German and German Jewish constituents. To this end, *Kmen* published a representative sampling of fiction and essays by members of what Max Brod would later style as the Prague Circle, including Jesenská's translations of Werfel, an essay on Catholicism by Franz Blei (a Viennese, but Kafka's first publisher in German in his magazine *Hyperion*), an essay (identified with apparent pride as commissioned) on Émile Zola by Egon Erwin Kisch, as well as a number of reviews of these writers' work.[16] Moreover, these contacts did not stop with literary translation, but crossed over into joint political action: when

Neumann published a manifesto in support of the newly founded Order of Worker Education, for example, its eleven signatories included Werfel and two other German-speakers, Hugo Sonnenschein and Albert Ehrenstein, both of whom were represented, discussed, and advertised in *Kmen*.[17] Neumann's committed socialism and the leftist leanings of this German Jewish intellectual community accounted for such contacts, but the magazine also helped bring them into being.

Thus the *Kmen* of a single publishing year—1920–21—occupied a window of tolerance, eclecticism, and literary interest of the kind that hard-line Communists, Neumann himself included, would soon rush to slam shut. While its Communist orientation remained clear, *Kmen* distinguished itself from its subsequent incarnation as a narrowly propagandist party organ by publishing a real range of perspectives. Its editorials, reviews, and articles framed lively debates about the relationship of leftist ideology to the arts; workers' participation in the arts; the constraints of nationalism on cultural development; the nature of Czech participation in a broader European modernist culture; the relationship of Communism to anarchism, nationalism, and Catholicism; and the merits of particular artistic and literary journals, volumes of poems, novels, and translations. It reached out to German Jewish writers at a time when other magazines were filled with antisemitic and anti-German venom and indeed, in the streets, ethnic tensions again boiled into violence. The magazine placed emerging Czech writers and poets in the context of an international modernism that Neumann strove to make available to Czech readers. This trend toward representation hardly means that the publication was free from tensions or prejudices, that it was without political or national program or bias, or that it was evenhanded. But it did provide certain opportunities for overlap and coincidence that many accounts of Prague culture—particularly those appearing in literature on Kafka—have tended to elide.

The magazine's Communist orientation certainly meant, for instance, an interest in intellectual and theoretical as well as political developments in newly post-revolutionary Russia. No doubt for this reason, we find that *Kmen* was among the first Czech magazines to publish the work of the young Russian Roman Jakobson, recently arrived from Moscow. Jakobson had come to Czechoslovakia in July 1920 as a representative of the new Soviet government, and as such was regarded suspiciously—Jindřich Toman reports that some believed he was a counterfeit Jakobson who had murdered the authentic Jakobson on the way to Prague.[18] Within a year of his arrival, an excerpt from Jakobson's essay on the Russian poet Velimir Khlebnikov was published in *Kmen* under the title of "Vivisection as the Nearest Goal of the Study of Art" ("Vivisekce jako nejbližší úkol vědy o umění"), a goal tantalizingly anticipated by Kafka's harrowing story "In the Penal Colony."[19] So Jakobson and Kafka, the two non-Czechs then writing in Prague who would make the most significant impact on how the twentieth century looked at literature, appeared within the space of a few months in the same magazine, both as complete unknowns. To add to this coincidence, Kafka remarked to Jesenská that "this issue of *Kmen* has the first good original piece that I've read there—I don't quite remember the name of the author Vladislav Vančura or something."[20] For Kafka to single out Vančura for praise at this stage in the Czech writer's career speaks volumes about both Kafka's sensitivity to the Czech language and his acumen as a literary critic. Vančura is widely acknowledged to have written the most innovative Czech prose of his generation, notable particularly for its range and difficulty of lexicon and its ironic manipulation of register—an appreciation of which requires a substantial knowledge of literary Czech. But despite Vančura's later illustrious career, the short piece that caught Kafka's eye—"So think about something merry" ("Vzpomeň si na něco veselého")[21]—was the first-ever publication of a completely unknown medical doctor who, rumor has it, also had a terrific crush on Jesenská during her brief sojourn in medical school. Prague was not, after all, a very large city.

From the perspective of someone unfamiliar with Prague culture and its dominant narratives, such coincidences seem mild, and only to be expected. Why should a radical literary-innovator lawyer and a radical literary-innovator doctor *not* fall for the same "New Woman" writer in a small city? Why would a journal committed to innovative writing *not* find and publish the most significant work being done in its city—even by virtual unknowns like a recent Russian immigrant academic, an obscure German Jewish lawyer/fiction writer, and a Czech avant-garde doctor? Yet Prague's peculiar ethnic and political climate renders *precisely this* combination of writers quite surprising, and marks the journal as bucking more than one trend of Prague intellectual life.

Kmen and materials like it are invaluable in recovering a Prague history that was small in scale but large in intellectual, literary, and cultural importance: the history of intercultural exchange in Prague in the teens and twenties. Precisely such small-scale activities can have great impact on literary, artistic, and theoretical developments. For the various strains of modernism that flourished in Prague during this period, these contacts were made and exerted an influence as yet unaccounted for by contemporary scholarship, as examination of long-buried and ignored cultural artifacts like *Kmen* amply illustrates. Anyone who came to know Prague culture of the day through magazines like *Kmen*, its sister publication *Červen* (*June*), and, before World War 1, *Umělecký měsíčník* (*Art Monthly*) would find a far less polarized picture than has been presented thus far, either in memoirs colored by history and politics or in scholarship. Simple coincidences such as those we find in *Kmen* themselves do much to dispel the sense of mutual and inviolate isolation that was long seen to characterize Czech and Prague German intellectual developments. And *Kmen*, furthermore, is evidence of what such histories have taught us was even rarer than German interest in Czech culture—that is, interest flowing in the opposite direction.

The man who brought such diverse strains of Prague culture together, the editor Stanislav Kostka Neumann (1875–1947), deserves attention as well, not least because his life work was so telescoped and politically tidied by subsequent generations of Communist biographers (including Neumann himself). Quite possibly, an eclectic magazine like *Kmen* would itself have been impossible had its editor not lived through quite so many literary lives. Indeed, one factor that renders the magazine's heterogeneity so surprising is the fact that its editor soon went on to ardently oppose the aesthetic and literary orientations of many of *Kmen*'s contributors—and of his own previous incarnations. Neumann's career spans many decades and literary movements, most of which he seems to have found a way of participating in. As a figure in the Czech Decadence, he contributed to the influential *Moderní revue* (1895) and, in 1897, founded his own magazine, *Nový kult* (*The New Cult*), although Neumann and his later Communist rehabilitators made considerable efforts to distance this important party voice from his early work: "He paid his dues in so called 'Czech Decadence.' But of course, in reality, he was no 'decadent' or 'neoromantic.'"[22] Neumann's books of poems from this period—*Nemesis, bonorum custos* (1895), *I Am the Apostle of the New Life* (*Jsem apoštol nového žití*, 1896), *Satan's Glory among Us* (*Satanova sláva mezi námi*, 1897)—suggest a rather different reality. His enthusiasm for the Decadence, however, did not hold him back from a simultaneous interest in anarchism that did soon develop into the "anarcho-communism" his later rehabilitators quickly stressed. His journalistic, political, and critical writings are far too extensive to go into here, but a few more book titles give a much-condensed idea of his rather wide-ranging development: *Czech Songs* (*České zpěvy*, 1910), a nationalist phase; *The Book of Waters, Woods, and Hillsides* (*Kniha lesů, vod a strání*, 1914), a vitalist phase; *New Songs* (*Nové zpěvy*, 1919), a Futurist phase; and *Red Songs* (*Rudé zpěvy*, 1923). Throughout these phases, the poet, critic, editor, and translator S. K. Neumann was one of the critical forces setting the courses for Czech modernism from his days as a young Decadent on, and his editorship of *Kmen* proved no exception.[23]

Little magazines like *Kmen* have long been interesting for "providing context" for the canonical writers who published in their pages, but what besides footnotes to more widely recognized forces on the modernist scene has *Kmen*'s independent and idiosyncratic editor left to posterity? As Adam McKible has argued of little magazines more generally, publications like *Kmen* should be read as texts, as documents in their own right: little magazines as such "offer ways of reading modernism that are unavailable through studies based on collections, selections, or single authors: these publications provide insights and points of contact that canonizations and institution building have often obscured."[24] On this logic, *Kmen* offers more than a conglomeration of translated, excerpted, or otherwise reproduced and altered texts, interspersed with the odd "Original-Stück," as Kafka called the items of new Czech writing: it is itself a text that is at once Czech and not Czech, simultaneously nationally bound and internationally aspiring. The magazine poses challenges to notions about what might constitute an "original" work—even one, like Kafka's "Stoker," that appears as a republication *in a magazine* and *in translation*.

The most compelling reason to read *Kmen* or consider its provocations is not divorced from the issues of reconstructing lost elements of Prague culture by any means, but neither is it limited to such a project. *Kmen* has a great deal to tell us about the international character of modernism, and how that very internationalism can be, at the same time, extremely local. *Kmen* shows how translation—not just linguistic, but cultural translation, manipulation, and appropriation—was central to constructing a modernism that was international at the conceptual level. It also illustrates, however, how translation was central to constructing local modernisms, different modernisms: even those constructed with and around the same texts by Apollinaire, Bergson, or Kafka. The same texts are not the same texts when they appear in another magazine, in another language—with a different article on the page before, and a different advertisement below it.

This phenomenon is confirmed and amplified by the experience of reading Kafka's story "The Stoker" ("Der Heizer," "Topič") in Czech—and in near isolation—in a Communist magazine. *Kmen* devoted an entire issue to Jesenská's translation of the story, accompanying it only with a negative review of a film about the mythical Rabbi Löw (supposed conjurer of the Golem) and a brief editorial note explaining the decision to run the story.[25] In his note, Neumann singles out Kafka as one of the best German prose writers of the day and explains that he thought it was better for readers to have the story all at once, rather than serializing it (although he also explains that this made it a bit easier on the editor, whose life, after all, was hard). Nonetheless, whatever the editorial expediency involved, "The Stoker" is the only text so distinguished in all the issues of *Kmen*, and if we are looking at *Kmen* as a cultural artifact with its own integrity and logic, then this choice clearly sets Kafka's story apart from the rest, singling it out for special emphasis.

In this way, "The Stoker" stops being a fragment of a novel, which it eventually became, or a story in German, or even, entirely, a story by Kafka. Its appearance in *Kmen* suddenly brings it into conversation with a number of other stories distinct from the novel of which it would eventually form a part. From the outset, when we see Kafka's tale in the pages of an actively pro-Communist, pro-revolution magazine, we already begin to see it in the light that S. K. Neumann might have viewed it. We are primed to see it as a pro-worker allegory of the unhappy manual laborer who unsuccessfully takes his grievances to the captain of the ship and whose case is unsuccessful in part, the young bourgeois Karl Rossmann believes, because he is lacking the necessary rhetorical skills. The editor, after all, was an agitator for the cultural and literary education of the proletariat, and his manifesto had recently been signed by the author's friend. But we also see that when Karl, the well-meaning bourgeois, tries to intervene on the stoker's behalf, the whole scene is diverted from the concerns of the stoker by a Dickensian coincidence of a reunion with Karl's long-lost American uncle, now become a senator (with a new, less culturally specific name). As Karl leaves, reluctantly and regretfully, he worries that his relationship with his newfound powerful uncle will not replace the friendship he found with the stoker, but he also worries that the stoker has ceased to exist. As we see this story's ending next to the advertisements for Petr Kropotkin's *Anarchist Morals* (*Anarchistická morálka*), Dr. Emanuel Vajtauer's *Socialist State* (*Socialistický stát*), or Josef Hora's poetry volume *Working Day* (*Pracující den*), these visual items accentuate and reinforce Marxist readings: like any story by Kafka, "The Stoker" itself suggests many other, equally plausible narratives, but this particularized context will teach the *Kmen* reader to remember this one.[26]

Another aspect of the story, too, comes in with greater force, complexity, and ironic bite in translation: Karl Rossmann sides strongly with the stoker as one who has suffered great injustice. But the primary injustice the stoker feels is nationalist resentment—the alliance between the two men is based on the fact that they are both "German" (Karl is afraid of meeting Irishmen in the new world), and the stoker complains that on a German ship, there are too many Romanians who are treated too well. Prague language tensions lend this whole passage about German-German sympathy rendered in Czech a certain irony; similarly, a passage in which Karl relives his suspicions about his Slovak cabin mate resonates differently when it appears in Czech in the context of a newly established Czechoslovak state than it does in the original German. In the end, the stoker's plight seems a clear case of nationalism interfering in the solidarity of the working people—of false consciousness—and Karl's failed attempts at sympathy and help are the inevitable failure of well-meaning bourgeois intervention to do anything but maintain the status quo, or possibly make things worse. Such is the story that the surrounding context shows us.[27] This is not to suggest that these elements are alien to Kafka's original text, but publication in the Czech magazine has amplified them and, in a sense, appropriated Kafka's text as an item of Czech propaganda for the "anationalist" international socialist modernism that Neumann used his magazine to construct and promote.

A July 1920 position piece arguing against "anationalism" (published in response to an essay by Vlastislav Hofman in the journal *Služba* [*Service*]) demonstrates just how live an issue this was, and how central it was to *Kmen*'s project.[28] This exchange also brings into focus another familiar constituent in Prague polemics generally: the rhetorical manipulation of antisemitism. In this convoluted rhetorical and logical exchange, Hofman (as cited in *Kmen*) has attacked the "a" of anationalism on the grounds that "many Jews, for example, like the idea of a cosmopolitan, universal humanity not subject to national borders but themselves remain nationalist out of racial instincts" ("mnoha židům např. se líbí lidství kosmopolitické, všeobecné, bez hranic národnosti ač sami zůstávají nacionálními již z rasového instinktu"). The *Kmen* writer, identified as "*jeel*," seems absolutely beside himself that this dynamic should be inserted into a debate about socialism:

> I'm at a loss as to how it's possible to have a real argument with someone who drowns the humanitarian ideal of socialism in coarse antisemitic invective; who considers international socialism as a suggestion about the specific creative potential of an entire nation; who thought that a nation as a cultural unit was identical with political nationalism and on the basis of this substitution attacks "anationalism."[29]

The reviewer refers Hofman to the previous issue of Neumann's *Červen* in which, *jeel* claims, Neumann makes clear that

> anationalism is a *political*-cultural program that asks art to respect the socialist current of our day and to resolve cultural questions in the socialist sense, that it is a calling for a new tendency directed against the old *political-nationalism*. That an attack on "anationalism" is an assault on a tendency in art overall, and that only in those terms should it be conducted.[30]

This exchange attempts to make clear the editorial position on "anationalism," but we begin to see how locally inflected this particular construction of the idea is and how clearly fraught with the familiar tensions of Prague cultural life it is. Certainly pro-"Internationale," *Kmen*'s editors and writers nonetheless debate at some length the possibility of healthy, socialist-friendly forms of nationalism—national cultural identity—as opposed to the bad old capitalist, petit-bourgeois model that brought on the world war, kept workers down, and so on. A subsequent defense of Hofman argues that he had other alternative, even more spiritual, collectives in mind. One writer even suggests that "nationalism can be a holy thing" if it leads in the right direction. Besides, he continues, why upset "Czechness" with "nationalism" when "a man stays a man, a woman a woman, a Czech a Czech . . . it would be perverse any other way. And hermaphroditism is against natural law."[31] And indeed, the magazine's relationship to nationalism, and to Czech nationalism in particular, is by no means homogeneous. When Neumann reviews a new publication called *Musaion* (*Museum*), however, he makes this distinction again, opposing the "narrow-minded nationalism" that interfered with the progress of art with the "inner strength of the new Czech art" which was "tenacious and authentic enough to wait out the disruption and ignore the superficial claims of the 'identity' crowd"—and as a result, has produced work that "stands up in competition with the modern art of other nations."[32] This passage's message—that by *resisting* Czech identity and nationalism, it has *gained* a Czech identity strong enough to "stand up" and "compete"—is rather conflicted, and not quite in keeping rhetorically with a socialist logic. What it does make clear, however, is that part of Neumann's project is to claim *territory* for Czech art—international territory. And one sign, he suggests, that this Czech art is now strong enough is that it no longer needs to fear contamination by coming into contact with other (foreign) forms.

It may be that Neumann's project in *Kmen* enacts a similar argument. *Kmen* presents a European, even transatlantic modernism *in Czech*—a language that had only recently (in the previous century) regained currency as a recognized literary language. The magazine's internationalism in fact turns our attention to another central Prague truth—a truth not peculiar to Prague by any means, but rendered highly legible by the city's tightly wound and compressed ethnic tensions: language itself signifies.

This hardly sounds like news, of course, but in a Prague context, the phrase takes on surprising connotations. In Prague, the question of language—*which* language, spoken or written *by whom*—often signifies more, and more materially, than anything the language ostensibly references. For German-educated Bohemian writers during the first part of the nineteenth century, for example, the very act of writing in Czech itself signified first and foremost the kind of politically motivated cultural nationalism that the *Musaion* reviewer seems to rail against. Here, the fact of a Prague German writer translated *with permission* and *by a Czech woman*, as Jesenská's translation explicitly and prominently announces, is itself a story. And this story—the story that unfolds in the byline alone—suggests how much things have changed in terms of the literary-cultural balance of power in Prague—for instance, the mere fact that German has been translated into Czech in a literary magazine asserts that not every educated person who reads Czech can read German, that Czech has become a first, and for many, an only literary language. Thus *Kmen*, too, *by virtue of translation* commits a kind of cultural-nationalist act: it announces that Czech culture has arrived as an international player. It can stand up with *and translate* all the great works of international modernism—including even those written in German, in Czech's own (political, cultural) territory. This presentation of an international modernism in Czech differs radically from the presentation of the same source-texts in, say, English, French, or German, or any other language that already *itself* can assume and confer an international status. That is, when a French magazine devoted to international modernism translates a Czech text, it is not claiming for itself but rather granting international status. When it prints a translation from the German, it is not "standing up to" a German text, but simply making it available in French. In *Kmen* and in Czech, however, it is a different matter.

Such juxtapositional, translational, and transnational logics play out in and among the ghosts of languages that do not appear on the pages of *Kmen*. The Czech language that does appear—exclusively—thus lays claim to its own centrality even as it guarantees the magazine's ultimate marginality on the broader European stage. *Kmen*'s leftist move to the center—a tenuous and sparsely occupied cultural no-man's land between German and Czech—placed it even more firmly on the margins of history, since any collaborative efforts could only be overshadowed by the narratives of annihilation that were to come. What is more, *Kmen*'s attempt to lay out a kind of verbal exhibition space for "the new"—on the theory that revolution is more likely to come about through cultural dialogue, contact, and ferment than through strictly enforced adherence to ideological and representational norms—seems almost tragically quaint in the wake of the Slánský show trials in the early 1950s or the crushing defeat of the Prague Spring in the late 1960s. These "grand narratives" could not be doubted away by any amount of postmodernist skepticism because the body counts are too large. Analogously, the Czech-Marxist-female-mediated Kafka is not going to supplant the visionary loner whom the world's imagination continues, by and large, to embrace. Despite all these ghosts, the optimism of these pages so effectively silenced by history gives a face to modernism, as Mark Morrison has argued of other such publications, that "major" single-authored modernist texts like *The Trial* or *The Waste Land* do not show us.[33] In Prague, this aesthetic and cultural eclecticism aspires to do what Morrison sees similar, more widely known publications in Britain (*The Little Review*) and the United States (*The Masses*) attempting: the creation of a counterpublic sphere that would challenge the primacy of the dominant spheres of discourse—where, in Prague, the splintering voices of nationalism, antisemitism, and cultural chauvinism still reigned or even where they gave way to less strident but still overpowering voices of ascendant liberalism and bourgeois capitalism that found confirmation in the newly formed, industrially successful Czechoslovak Republic. Given the future of Communism in this "faraway country about which we know nothing," it is worth remembering that it was not always a foreign-imposed unilateral and brutal power, but that at one time, it functioned as the inspiration for an eclectic forum for dissent, one that encouraged pluralism and dialogue in aesthetics and politics alike. It was this version of Communism, under the literary-critical guidance of S. K. Neumann, that first introduced Kafka to Czech readers, and his choice implies a recognition of ideological as well as territorial common ground. In keeping with Deleuze and Guattari's claims about the disruptive potential of what they call "minor literature," Neumann clearly saw a literature of political dissent in Kafka, albeit one quite differently configured. "The Stoker" was translated in Czechoslovakia but written before that country's existence. In appearing in those pages, this early story with its worker-character clearly enters into conversation with the concerns of the magazine, but its presence there should also alert us to the extent that other concerns of the magazine—questions of identity, to what extent it may be flexible or fixed, how it intervenes in both political *and* aesthetic judgments, and whose interests these interventions serve—were also central to the fiction of Kafka's "Czechoslovak period."

Chapter 3

✦

Language Territories

> For everything external to the sensory world, language can only be used allusively and not even with close approximation, since with respect to the sensory world, it deals only with property and property relations.
>
> —Kafka, aphorism, 1918

> *"Dieses Dorf ist Besitz des Schlosses . . ."*
>
> —first words spoken in *The Castle*

The divisions of Prague life and indeed much of the former Habsburg Empire—divisions of property, territory, and a variety of social and even aesthetic identities—long relied heavily on distinctions drawn within and between languages. Germans and Czechs had vied for cultural and political dominance throughout the Czech lands on and off for centuries. The conflict was settled, seemingly decisively, nearly 300 years before Kafka's lifetime, with the crushing defeat of Czech forces (the Protestant rebel Bohemian Estates) at the Battle of Bílá Hora (White Mountain) in 1620. That battle led to a long period of German political, linguistic, and cultural dominance during which German was the vernacular language of letters and wealth (though Latin continued officially as the language of state until 1780) and Czech was the language of (many) villagers and peasants. In the late eighteenth century, the movement that would become known as the Czech National Revival began to challenge that dominance, at first linguistically, then culturally and politically. This Czech Revivalist movement coincided, however, with efforts to consolidate imperial power around the German language, and so Revivalists were working at cross-purposes with the empire's linguistic and political aims. Benedict Anderson argues in *Imagined Communities* that Emperor Josef II established German as the language of state for the Habsburg Empire not in an act of German nationalism but rather in the interests of uniting the empire under a single vernacular language—a triumph over Latin, that is, rather than over Czech, Hungarian, or any other language.[1] In practice, the establishment of German as the official language of state led to a campaign to ensure that the empire had as many German-speakers as possible, in the interests of legitimacy, cohesion, and loyalty. Language and education reforms ensued throughout the empire. Importantly for Kafka's own linguistic heritage, the Germanization of Bohemian Jews—so influential for Prague cultural history—was engineered as part of this large, complex project of expanding the empire's base of German-identifying subjects within its territories—again, as historian Peter Bugge has also argued, less in the interests of German nationalism than of consolidating and facilitating imperial rule.[2]

This project, whatever its intentions, had a profound impact on Jewish lives, linguistic affiliations and, in turn, political positions—and it would continue to reverberate when Kafka was born a century later, and indeed, throughout his lifetime. When in 1782 Emperor Josef II issued the Edict of Toleration, which in name and law if not always in practice removed the legal and physical barriers that kept Jews segregated, he also "mandated the adoption of German names and surnames, [and] required the use of German in all legal documents such as birth and marriage certificates." The law opened secular higher education to Jews, but also mandated the establishment of German-language Jewish elementary schools.[3] Jewish equality and integration—physical and civic—went hand-in-hand with German language adoption. The disappearance of one set of physical and legal boundaries thus erected a new set of boundaries in their place, these designed to absorb rather than segregate, to increase imperial hegemony by creating German-identifying political subjects bound by language, education, and gratitude to the empire and *its* boundaries. And language was a *primary means* by which these economic, political and, subsequently, physical and even architectural boundaries were drawn.

Throughout the nineteenth century, the Habsburg Empire continued to reform laws governing how and where Jews lived, abolishing the Prague Ghetto in 1852 and granting civic equality to Jews in 1867. These liberalizing measures hardly meant that ethnic Germans embraced Jews as their own, it should be emphasized. But for a burgeoning Czech nationalism that increasingly defined itself in terms of the equation "Czechness = non-Germanness," the increasing assimilation of Bohemian Jewry to the German language and culture only fueled Czech antisemitism on nationalist grounds, leading to Czech nationalist axioms such as Karel Havlíček's "He who would be Czech must first stop being a Jew."[4] Indeed, Havlíček's stinging rejection of the first collection of Czech Jewish poetry (*České listy/Czech Leaves*, 1846) is sometimes credited with all but single-handedly crushing Czech Jewish literary aspirations for at least a generation. This verse collection by Siegfried Kapper intersperses romanticized depictions of the Czech countryside pitched to evoke nationalist gratitude and belonging with visions of Jewish inclusion and emancipation, all alongside darker poems more evocative of the poet's major influence, Karel Hynek Mácha, whose great poem *Máj* Kapper was the first to translate into German. It is an unusual, even arresting juxtaposition, but sadly, Havlíček's review was long better known than the poems themselves, and Kapper stopped writing in Czech for nearly twenty years. By the 1860s, however, Kapper had returned to lecturing and writing in Czech and despite this earlier rejection continued to advocate for Bohemian Jews' Czech identification and assimilation, work that ultimately helped inspire the Czech Jewish movement. Kapper's late nineteenth-century translation and critical activity also looked forward to the leading role that Max Brod and other Jewish writers played in presenting Czech culture to a German audience. Still, he was far from the norm. The majority of the Czech lands' educated urban Jews, at least, wrote and spoke in German and paid little attention to Czech literature and culture. Nonetheless, a substantial minority of Jews, particularly those in rural Czech-speaking villages—among them Kafka's father's family—did speak Czech. But even when, after 1870, the Czech Jewish movement actively promoted Czech identity as an assimilationist platform, they were hardly consistently embraced by other Czech patriots.[5]

Some of the worst language-related conflicts in the region's history broke out in 1897, when new language ordinances required regional civic and government officials to conduct their work in both Czech and German and made Czech the official language of the Czech lands (Bohemia and Moravia). While educated Czechs holding civic posts would know German, anything but a rudimentary knowledge of the Czech language was still rare among the country's German population, and this population objected to these new laws polemically and violently. The unrest was profound enough to catch the attention even of Mark Twain, who was traveling in the region at the time and wrote about the conflict over the language ordinances for *Harper's*:

> The recent troubles have grown out of Count Badeni's necessities. He could not carry on his Government without a majority vote in the House at his back, and in order to secure it he had to make a trade of some sort. He made it with the Czechs—the Bohemians. The terms were not easy for him: he must issue an ordinance making the Czech tongue the official language in Bohemia in place of the German. This created a storm. All the Germans in Austria were incensed. In numbers they form but a fourth part of the empire's population, but they urge that the country's public business should be conducted in one common tongue, and that tongue a world language—which German is.[6]

Twain goes on to describe with real horror what happened in Parliament—a violent outburst, a fight among opposing representatives, and then, to Twain's astonishment, the police suppression of the Parliament and ejection of some of its members, and the ensuing nationalist and ethnic violence:

> Some of the results of this wild freak followed instantly. The Badeni government came down with a crash; there was a popular outbreak

> or two in Vienna; there were three or four days of furious rioting in Prague, followed by the establishing there of martial law; the Jews and Germans were harried and plundered, and their houses destroyed; in other Bohemian towns there was rioting—in some cases the Germans being the rioters, in others the Czechs—and in all cases the Jew had to roast, no matter which side he was on.

Despite the shifting political fortunes of the various parties, the basic structure Twain identifies—unstable boundaries with Jews caught in the middle—remained a constant throughout Kafka's life.

With the shifting politics of the early twentieth century, the question of Jewish cultural and linguistic alignment grew increasingly delicate, and was complicated by class lines as well as politics. Kafka's father, for example, the son of a village butcher, had grown up in a Czech-speaking Jewish family, but on marrying and settling in Prague, Hermann and his German-speaking wife joined the ranks of bourgeois Prague German Jewry. Prague Jews most often identified with German culture, and were the subject of much Czech nationalist anger and prejudice because of it. Like many Bohemian Germans of the era—among them Gustav Mahler (Jewish by birth, converted to Catholicism), René (later changed to the more German-looking Rainer) Marie Rilke (of Jewish heritage on his mother's side), and Robert Musil—and Bohemian German Jews such as Sigmund Freud and Franz Werfel, the Kafka family relied on Czechs as employees and domestic servants. Young Franz and his siblings grew up speaking Czech with these servants. Thus German Jewish families in some respects—though not in others, since antisemitism was long common among the city's and the broader empire's ethnic Germans—enjoyed the privileges of the ruling classes and therefore a class-determined relationship with many of the Czech gentiles in their daily lives. Influenced by both gratitude and relative privilege on one hand and hostile Czech nationalism on the other, Bohemian German Jews sympathized overwhelmingly with Austria in the First World War.

The Czech majority, however, was on the rise long before the war ended, and it was Hermann Kafka's practice of speaking Czech with customers along with the Kafkas' morphologically Czech family name that spared the family dry-goods store from the antisemitic and anti-German riots in 1897. This effect continued after the war. With political, ethnic, and linguistic affiliations so complex and intertwined and with the map of Europe being redrawn along these twisting lines, it seemed a matter of great urgency to measure who exactly should be counted in which group and what precisely they owned or owed on that basis.

Surveying—in the sense of land surveying, the purported work of K. in *The Castle*—was one way in which national property boundaries might be mapped; the census—with its questions about language determining an area's civic administration, schooling, access, and representation—was another. Both land surveying and the census determined and delineated the relationships of complex, diverse, and unruly entities—people, land—to the state. Both functioned to parcel out these entities into categories rather than particulars—land became property, people became citizens, recipients of services, and the like. In order for these measuring systems to work, they had to employ commonly held units of measure and definitions, and they had to be clear about what exactly they were measuring and how.

A 1920 article in the widely read newspaper *Lidové noviny* (*The People's News*) gives a good idea of how deeply embedded in quotidian life these issues were, explicitly illustrating how issues of nationality, identity, and language—specifically, the "language of everyday use" (*Umgangsprache*)—played out in the textual corollary to everyday language: the newspaper daily. Language statistics had already been used to help determine (Czechoslovak) territory; here, we see, they will be used to determine rights, privileges, and the linguistic makeup of public governing bodies and offices. As the front-page article remarks, the occasion of the first Czechoslovak census once again brings this difficult tangle of issues to the forefront of public consciousness. The empire's conflation of "everyday speech" with national identity—a policy the Czechs had long seen as an artificial way to inflate the ranks of German-identified citizens—still rankled. The newspaper recalls its role in (ultimately ineffectively) resisting this policy before the last imperial census in 1910:

> We remember how at that time we wrote promotional brochures to send abroad, to make the methods of the Austrian government known and to expose how by such means the ever-obliging German statistical science tried to multiply the number of citizens of the ruling nationality. We remember the well-known resolution of Dr. Kramar . . . to amend the question to identify mother tongue or nationality rather than everyday speech, but it was all in vain. Austria remained statistically faithful until the day of its death![7]

The paper points out that it is now up to the new Czechoslovak state to decide how it wants to record the nationality of its citizens, and remarks with rhetorical surprise that there is no easy accord on the question of how nationality should be determined. Even those who favor a strictly linguistic determination of national identity do not agree: the question of whether the criterion should be "mother tongue" or "everyday language" is remarkably charged, even polarizing. The newspaper, however, advocates a question asking directly for national self-identification—arguing, essentially, that national identity should be a matter of national "feeling" rather than birthright or the by-then infamous "language of everyday use" favored by the former empire:

> Opponents of the "nationality" question object, as they did in the old Austria, on the grounds of its purely subjective character; that it is

> objectively uncontrollable, and that subjective feelings of the population . . . cannot be subject to a statistical survey. In the first instance they are right, but not in the second, which as a position ranks among the unchallenged (but also unproven) truths of official Austrian statistical science. The fact that a statistical survey usually measures only objective characteristics and traits, and that in Austria and elsewhere subjective characteristics are not surveyed, is not, in our view, sufficient evidence that these characteristics are not statistically measurable. It should be borne in mind that those who advocate that a question about native language be used to determine the national identity of the population are risking a dangerous contradiction in all cases where the mother tongue and the nationality of the individual do not coincide (when, for instance, an individual spoke German as his mother tongue and now feels Czech or vice versa; those wanting the mother tongue to define nationality will now force that individual into an untruth).

The article presents a situation in which questions about language determine questions of identity—or, at least, they have done, and perhaps will do so again: the status of these questions is itself in question. As the article's ambivalence about linguistic identification accentuates, however, the problem of *which* language, *when*, *what* question, and *when*—as well as what additional official meaning and political ramification questions about language would carry—was far from clear-cut. At any given time, though, for any given census, the questions, answers, and their meanings would be fixed and would in turn fix other statistics that would shape the representation, education, and economic benefits conferred on national groups. Specifically, for the 1920 census, these questions affected representation and the linguistic accessibility of state and local offices. The specific question determining these results, however, might stay the same while the stakes behind it might change; or, for that matter, the question might change while the stakes remained the same. The language—in the sense of the terminology of the question—may change and, since the question is being asked by the state, it is crucial that the official language of the *state* has also changed.

Furthermore, typical of what Marek Nekula decries as "Czech/German polarization" and the "monolingual interpretation of the world," at no point does either the Austrian or the proposed Czechoslovak model include an option for bilingualism or binationalism—even though this was, after centuries of living in close quarters and intermarrying, a common enough situation for both individuals and families. Bilingualism was even sought after as an advantage, often pursued by school or family exchanges.[8] As we see below, however, a stipulation in the law required bilingualism of the *state*—depending on the single primary language indicated (by whatever question) by the same individuals from whom bilingualism as a status was withheld:

> The most serious objection to a question asking after nationality, however, was a reference to a law which, it is said, clearly requires a statistical investigation of the ratio of speakers of various languages relative to the general population. Compare section 2 of the language law providing for bilingualism in public offices in districts where at least 20 percent of the population share a common language other than Czechoslovak. There is, of course, the question of whether this use of the term "language" has the sense of "mother tongue" in the way its statistical supporters conceive. Surely it was not the intention of the language law that the linguistic ratios of public bodies be determined by the native language of people who, in some cases, have forgotten their mother tongue entirely and speak (converse in!) a completely different language. Are we not now approaching, however, a sense of "language" precariously close to the famous "everyday language" that had been defined as the language predominantly and ordinarily spoken by the population regardless of whether it was a "mother tongue"? Accordingly, if we take seriously the concept of "mother tongue" as the most important, decisive indication of nationality, then we must conclude that the language law and its provisions for "citizens of the same language" meant by this citizens of the same nationality in the political sense, no matter what is (or was) the language commonly used and predominantly used in public or private life.

These unstable definitions of nationality and language were *central* to the makeup of state offices, the distribution of services, and the classification and identification of citizens. Complicating further these already complicated interrelations was the case of Jewish identity, which is never, as we see, a question relevant only to Jews:

> In most cases, a person of nationalist consciousness will profess as either his mother tongue or everyday language the language of the nationality in which he self-identifies. However, what of cases where the nationality in question has no living language but where, as in the case of the Jews, there are claims to a consciousness of ethnic cohesion, as with, for example, Zionist political parties? Here we come to the most serious and politically most important consequence arising from the choice between questions about nationality or native language. Proponents of directly questioning nationality recognize that without fail the Jewish-born self-identifying Israelite (Zionist) would be able to enter Jewish nationality on the census sheet. Opponents argue: how then will the section of the language law discussed above be carried out? Suppose (although this is unlikely) a district with a 20% Zionist minority. What then? or say (which is much more

> realistic) that a district will number 80 percent Czech, 12 percent German, and 8 percent Zionist, a population whose language is German without exception. In this case, how should public offices be administered (in one language or bilingually)? From this example, it is clear that Germans have a political interest in ensuring that Jews not be allowed to indicate Jewish nationality, but rather be required to give their mother tongue, which must necessarily be one of the living languages. In this way, the German minority would achieve the 20% linguistic minority status and gain all the attendant legally established provisions.
>
> If we recognize on principle the notion of political-national self-identification, then it would be manifestly unjust if we wanted to withhold this opportunity from nationally conscious Jews when Zionist currents among them are undeniable. But whether we should exclude any activity by which they can through the census process, in accordance with choices freely made, help shape the linguistic makeup of public offices in the areas where they live—that is a different question. In the case mentioned above they would influence these outcomes just the same, not freely and directly, however, but merely indirectly, generally in favor of the Czech and to the detriment of the German element.

Whatever the Jewish citizen gained by the inclusion or exclusion of a particular question, he gained something not only for himself, but for one group at the expense of the other. In the eyes of a nation-state that privileged linguistically based definitions of ethnic nationality, there was no legitimate nation status for Jews: they had no mother tongue. Whichever language question was asked, then, would gain or lose population with one side or the other: no language question at all, however, would only shrink the ranks of both populations, but not equally. There could be no neutral position—and in fact, the census had an enormous effect on the official population statistics of the new state, with substantial decreases in the German population (in some areas by as much as 50%), in some part attributable to forced affiliation because of the insistence on single-language identification by (verified) mother tongue.[9] One brief foray into the newspaper thus illuminates how linguistic "minority" status made demands on the new Czechoslovak state, required changes of the state in terms of its own functioning and makeup. Minority status, in short, was an officially recognized status to which small populations would aspire. In this light, particularly, we must remark that in the Castle realm, K. speaks intelligibly but "as a stranger." The foreign quality of his speech suggests that his "language of everyday use"—at least insofar as we see him use language in the world of the Castle—may not be the same as his mother tongue. In terms of Habsburg census policies, K.'s "everyday use" of the common Castle tongue would have him counted as a member of the Castle community, regardless of mother tongue or feeling of belonging; if, however, membership was determined by "mother tongue," as with the new Czechoslovak census rules, K. would *never* be eligible, because he would never be native. In the world outside the novel, this linguistic otherness could also raise the question of minority status, which language also determined, but minority status required a minimum population threshold, while in the Castle world, there seem to be no other foreigners.

The eponymous "Schloss" (castle) focuses Kafka's most sustained consideration of language, property, and power relations. The governing figure of the novel as well as the governing structure of the depicted world is architectural, but it never leaves the question of territory far behind even as the status, identity, and boundaries of such a territory remain remarkably nebulous as to its material status, which is purportedly fixed but apparently open to flux. Readers are never allowed to forget that the novel's protagonist is (maybe) a Land Surveyor, K.—whose title perpetually inscribes the sign "Land" into a novel which actually never represents *arable* land of any kind. What, exactly, would a Land Surveyor be surveying, were he ever to be established as such, and what bearing would such a job description have on any territory that might be surveyed in *The Castle*'s depicted world? The opening of the novel is the closest we get to any vista of land, but there is none visible, while all the named objects are manmade structures:

> Es war spät abends als K. ankam. Das Dorf lag in tiefem Schnee. Vom Schloßberg war nichts zu sehn, Nebel und Finsternis umgaben ihn, auch nicht der schwächste Lichtschein deutete das große Schloß an. Lange stand K. auf der Holzbrücke die von der Landstraße zum Dorf führt und blickte in die scheinbare Leere empor.[10]

> It was late evening when K. arrived. The village lay under deep snow. There was no sign of the Castle hill, fog and darkness surrounded it, not even the faintest gleam of light suggested the large Castle. K. stood a long time on the wooden bridge that leads from the main road to the village, gazing upward into the seeming emptiness.[11]

The hill is invisible here, but its presence as a geographical feature seems established (it must be there to be obscured by fog). Lexically, however—morphologically—this hill is presented in a compound, *Schlossberg*, a geographical feature with a specifically human, constructed use. Similarly, "Land" first appears as part of a compound, "Landstrasse" ("road"), that stresses human use. In fact, "Land" as a sign in the novel most frequently appears in the compound *Landvermesser* (Land Surveyor), object of *vermessen*, or "measuring": a specifically human activity, and most often used to name a man (K.) rather than to signify land at all. From the outset, the world of *The Castle* is presented as almost entirely socially constructed, even architectural.

This early passage also cannot help but reveal K. as an observer without much technical or even perceptual acumen in evidence: his gaze seems as empty as the landscape. It is certainly an inauspicious prelude to surveying, as any land that may be there is invisible and the surveyor is content to gaze at emptiness—but at this point, K. is not identified as a surveyor, so this initial scene provides an irony we must initially be blind to, much as K. is blind to the landscape. Furthermore, throughout the novel, the physical world behaves as if unfixed—streets turn without notice and seem resolutely to refuse to bring K. toward the Castle—and indeed it appears *not* to be fixed, at least not on a map: the villagers claim to understand their property boundaries but no documents are produced to such effect, and no cartographical fixing forms any part of K.'s activities. While it emerges that he (possibly) has been summoned as a land surveyor, this order may be nothing more than a bureaucratic error, and there is a further question about whether, if indeed such a person had been summoned, K. could actually be the Land Surveyor in question. The villagers are initially very suspicious of K., and first believe him to be a tramp.

The novel calls these villagers "Bauern" or, literally, "farmers," but this term includes the village tradespeople, so the link to the land is rhetorical or lexical only—just as "Land" as a sign most frequently appears as part of a compound that distances it from signifying any actual land. The word "Land" on its own appears three times, of which one is figurative; "Landstrasse" appears six times; "Landstreichermanieren" ("tramplike manners") and "Landstreicher" ("tramp") appear once each, while "Landvermesser" (land surveyor) appears 104 times in total. Although K.'s status and expertise are in question, he *is* referred to throughout the novel as "Landvermesser," with the result that this job description is thus the primary means by which "land" enters the discourse of the novel at all. "Landvermesser" functions as the novel progresses more as a proper name than a professional title, but it nonetheless provides a scripted reminder of "land" not as such, not as material, tillable, walkable ground, but as something to be named and governed. "Land" accompanies almost exclusively the possibility of its precise measurement, its parceling into property, and the clear, legible documentation thereof that the novel and its represented world never attain or even aspire to—yet nonetheless through their unwelcome visitor constantly evoke. The compound "Landvermesser" refers to the hapless and confused protagonist while suggesting the promise of a clarity the novel itself certainly never provides.

What is the referent for this activity constantly named but never represented, in a novel that consistently withholds other references to both land and measurement? A "Landvermesser," as it turns out, performs a particular kind of surveying—not simply the measuring and documentation of geological features, but the measuring and recording of property lines, usually

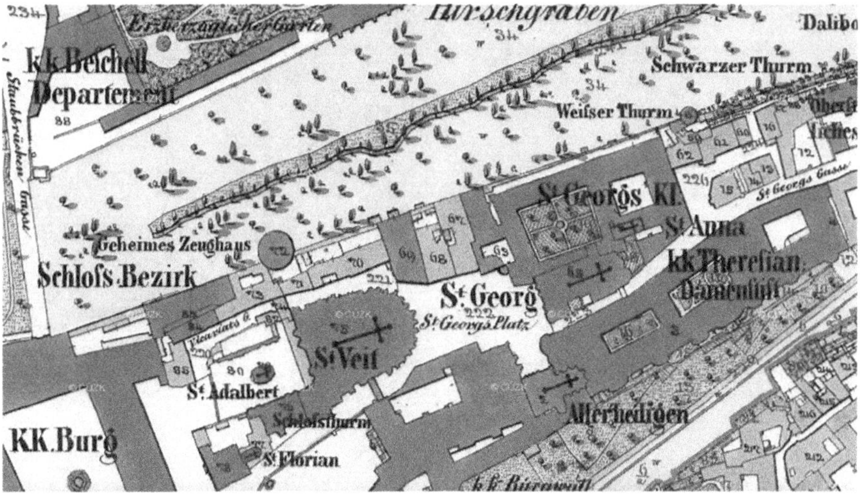

Figure 4. 1842 Cadastral map of the Castle district in Prague. Císařské povinné otisky stabilního katastru [Imperial Imprints of the Stable Cadastre] / 1:2880. Ústřední archiv zeměměřictví a katastru/ Central Archives of Land Surveying and Cadastre.

for state purposes—taxation, for example, but also settling property disputes. Cadastral surveyors, as they are also known, rely as much on ledgers and public and private records as they do on the measurement of actual land features, and they produce, essentially, maps of property lines, or cadastral maps.

But K. never receives the explicit recognition of his position or confirmation of the need for his services that would be necessary to *be* a Land Surveyor, since a cadastral surveyor's job is to produce records which would be officially recognized and carry the weight of law. A Land Surveyor of this kind can *only* exist via official recognition, and his surveying work is performative of official status, and conveys it. This work would require not only access to physical land, but also, and equally importantly, to previous official documentation as well as any local records. Yet K. can't get into the Castle, the seat of local government where presumably such things would be stored. Furthermore, we learn early on that everyone in the village understands the boundaries *except for K.*:

> The boundaries of our small holdings have been marked out, everything has been duly registered, the properties themselves rarely change hands, and whatever small boundary disputes arise, we settle ourselves. So why should we have any need for a surveyor?[12]

This passage marks one of the only times in the novel when relationships are presented as clear, and it describes relations between landholdings and

Figure 5. The Ethnic Groups of Austria-Hungary, 1910. Map from Wikipedia Commons. Based on "Distribution of Races in Austria-Hungary," *The Historical Atlas*, William R. Shepherd, 1911.

people to which K. has no access and on whom he has no influence. They do not need him; they are a closed system. What a perfect nation-state the Castle world would be: a collective so unified in its mutual, internal comprehension and so incomprehensible to its only outsider that its exclusionary nature and autonomous self-governance seem to preclude any alternative. Even the stratifications of class that (apparently) divide its internal territory fail to trouble the residents of this realm. In this way, the Castle realm resembles the newly formed Czechoslovak nation-state in absolutely no respect.

When Kafka began chronicling the misadventures of his superfluous Land Surveyor, his new linguistically defined nation had already fought a war with Poland over how borders should be determined: by historical sovereignty? By ethnicity and language (in keeping with the logic of the nation-state)? By geographical features? By the necessity of railroad access? By the political desires of more powerful allies? The problem with divvying up land into new states like Czechoslovakia or into new administrative districts within that state was in part that the people who lived on the land and inhabited these territories spoke different languages (from one another, and with one another) in ways that didn't map tidily in the *slightest*, as shown in figure 5.

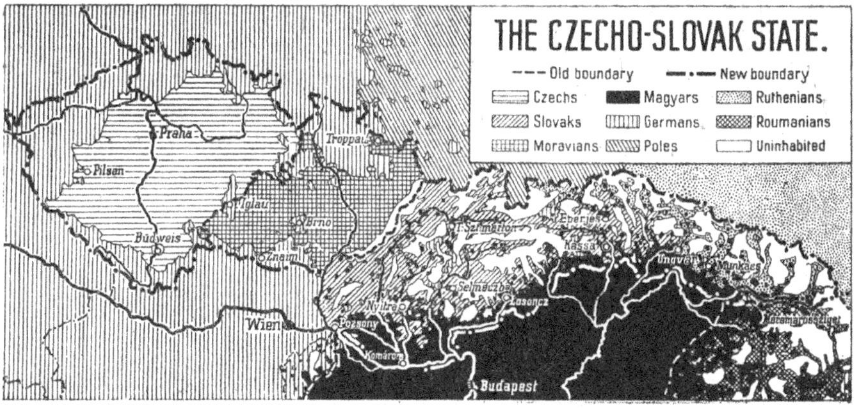

Figure 6. Languages and boundaries, Czechoslovakia, 1920. Francis Fodor, *The Geographical Impossibility of the Czech State* (London: Low, W. Dawson & Sons, 1920), 11. Accessed via Hathi Trust.

The lighter-shaded portions of Bohemia and Moravia shown on the map in figure 5 represent the majority Czech–speaking lands; the darker-shaded lands surrounding them, the German-speaking. German-speaking majority "islands" formed even in the Czech territory, in and around cities such as Brno, and the Czech region is all but entirely surrounded by a ring of German speakers. Even this ring of German language, however, is by no means so monolithic as William Shepherd's 1911 map of "races" suggests, since those designations refer only to the majority of language speakers: some "German" areas are 25 percent Czech, while an area that was only 51 percent Czech would still count as majority-Czech. But borders cannot be more or less dense depending on population. Furthermore, the region's populations had various understandings of ethnicity and tradition and what these meant for property rights and national affiliations—different from one another, and different also from the codifying, normalizing forces of the new state. If national tradition and ethnic heritage were to be contributing factors, whose national tradition? At what point in time would that map be taken from? If territorial integrity and viability from the point of view of, say, defense were to be consulted, that would be another set of concerns that did not, as it turned out, map tidily onto linguistic and ethnic boundaries. Different political aims would map the region differently—but still (purportedly) on linguistic and ethnic grounds—or, as Dr. Francis (Ferenc) Fodor claims should be done, in accordance with "national energy." This geography professor and author of the 1920 Hungarian propaganda pamphlet *The Geographical Impossibility of the Czech State* has yet another map to present in support of a very different agenda (figure 6).

The map is difficult to read; this is intentional, and is precisely the point Fodor wishes to illustrate. He minces no words, as his title might suggest:

> New lines have been drawn on the map of Europe, lines that are soon to become political frontiers. Yet the draughtsman's hand displayed an entire ignorance of geography. The lines seem to have been drawn in the air, but when brought down to the surface of the earth, they would cause the greatest mischief in economic conditions. The drawing hand seems to have perceived but one geographical object in the misty depths below, man, and him but in his nationality and language, without his economic background.[13]

This draftsman seems less equipped to draw maps than K., and the lines he does draw not only misrepresent the surface they map, but actually disrupt it. The lines in the air and the mist produced by this "draughtsman" eerily anticipate K.'s initial approach to the (then invisible) Castle, while Fodor is as concerned about this incompetent mapper's effects on local economic units as the Castle denizens will seem to be suspicious of K.'s efforts. Fodor then goes on to argue on the basis of geography for the natural separation of the Hungarian basin (including parts of Slovakia) from the Czech lands, whose politicians do not respect the role of mountains and rivers in their history and character.

Such broad, national issues were hardly the only land issues in the early days of postwar Czechoslovakia. Individual property lines were of tremendous concern. In 1919, the Land Control Act limited the ownership of arable land and determined that any excess be confiscated and redistributed (with compensation) from (mostly ethnic German and Hungarian) large landholders to the (mostly ethnic Czech or Slovak) small farmers and returning veterans. Borders—internal and external—were disputed intensely and were often front-page news, and in actual fact, land surveyors had already been advocating for their own increased cultural and civic importance. Even before the war, in 1912, the surveyors' society had campaigned for more schooling, increased state recognition, and higher position as public servants. And in the new Czechoslovak Republic, there was great need for their services.

By contrast, the internally comprehensible (to its inhabitants) yet coercive and perplexing (to K. and to us) Castle world has no such need. The Castle is not confronted—as Czechoslovakia was—by Poles or Germans with competing claims to any of its territory. The Castle has territorial integrity and apparent ethnic purity. It has "no custom of hospitality"; no outsiders are welcomed. But does this make it more vulnerable to the effects of unwanted strangers? When this linguistically and territorially pure state miscommunicates with the radically othered outside world and mistakenly ends up with a Land Surveyor, could K. as a minority of one end up being disruptive? By failing to integrate him into a civic role—a role such as the surveyors had campaigned for in living memory, and as all ethnic groups were campaigning for in the new Czechoslovak Republic—does the Castle fail to subsume K.'s potential disruptive force? Can the Land Surveyor be read as a potential site of resistance against state power? Wilhelm Emrich saw surveying as potentially rebellious, aligning it with a redrawing of borders that would weaken the status quo of the ruling (Austrian/German) power. More recently, John Zilcosky has taken a different view; in *Kafka's Travels: Exoticism, Colonialism, and the Traffic of Writing*, he discusses the importance of surveying in a colonial context, drawing on Kafka's beloved travel literature for children, the *Grüne Bandchen*, which details the lives of adventurous Europeans who do well in the holdings of empire—often working their way up through a series of positions, including that of land surveyor. On the one hand, Zilcosky sees the activity of surveying in this literature as reactionary, colonial, a part of the conquest and co-optation of property; and on the other, as a process of individualistic self-discovery by means of the vista (arguing also that individualism and imperialism often have such ideological reciprocity in period literature in a variety of national traditions). It is plausible to imagine K. seeing himself aligned with either of these potential goals and perspectives—plucky renegade or brave colonial entrepreneur. He would love a narrative that allowed him to discover himself, solidify his position, take control of land, disrupt the status quo. While his presence is disruptive to the Castle world in some respects, however, it is difficult to see this disruption as in any way linked to the actual activity of surveying simply because he fails to do any of it. His disruptive force may, on the other hand, be linked to his *name* as Land Surveyor, or to assumptions people have about his *identity* as Land Surveyor—as the novel asserts, the redrawing of property is of intimate concern to farmers, and they are likely to view such a person with suspicion. And they do.

The anthropologist and political theorist James C. Scott—writing not on Kafka, but on failed projects of statecraft—sees surveying as aligned with a host of state attempts at taxation, control, and regulation undertaken in tension with or opposition to local practices of measurement and understanding: local rather than state interests, which are internally and locally comprehensible but "illegible" to the universalizing state.[14] Throughout the early modern era, he argues, local custom and use were at odds with state forces of legibility and standardization, among which he includes "processes as disparate as the creation of permanent last names, the standardization of weights and measures, the establishment of cadastral surveys . . . the standardization of language and legal discourse, the design of cities."[15] Early modern European statecraft, then, is devoted to "standardizing what was a social hieroglyph" and producing simplifications that function "rather like abridged maps."[16] These official surveys did not successfully represent the actual activity of the society they depicted, nor were they intended to; they represented only that slice of it that interested the official observer. They were, moreover, not just maps. Rather, they were maps that, when allied with state power, would enable much of the reality they depicted to be remade. Thus, a state cadastral map created to designate taxable property holders does not merely describe a system of land tenure; it also *creates* such a system through its ability to give its categories the force of law. A cadastral map is *performative*—a quality of utterance already of great interest to Kafka, as demonstrated in earlier works such as *The Trial* (the performative quality of legal utterance), "The Judgment" (the potentially performative quality of a "sentencing"), and *The Metamorphosis* (what if figures of speech were performative?).

Land surveys, then—much like the language surveys that apportioned government recognition, representation, services, and schooling, and which also made front-page headlines in Kafka's day—did not and could not reflect the complex reality "on the ground." Following Scott's logic, however, because these surveys were officially invested, because they created law, they nonetheless affected the facts on the ground and began to be performative, to create the reality they imperfectly represented in their own image. If K. is aligned with *these* forces, the local Castle world itself is the site of resistance to state regulating control as opposed to local custom—which was also a live issue in Kafka's world, which seems to be roughly contemporaneous with the world of the novel. The Castle is first presented as the *property* of a Count Westwest, but it also has telephones—this is not a feudal time period. Is this world—created by Kafka in 1922 and never finished—subject to the 1919 land law? Would these land parcels be redistributed to speakers of a different language? For large landowners, the answer would almost certainly be yes. No wonder the locals don't want to let K. in.

In the Czechoslovakia of Kafka's last years, lines of property, territory, and belonging were being drawn, redrawn, and crossed. Buildings, architectural styles, even building materials all took on ethnic and national meaning. Textual territory was parceled out in print as lines were drawn between and among and within newspapers and journals. Lines in the form of street signs and their names were drawn between and among neighborhoods and the people who lived in them. The boundaries of gender and sexuality were also being reconfigured—in part *by* the nation-state and its project. Officially—as government policy—many of these lines come down to language. One key insight of Kafka's late work, however, is that language will not, ultimately, toe these lines for long. Language crosses them: as in transgression, betrayal, cross-breed, crossed wires. Kafka yearned for a writing that would transcend the world, be free of its referents. Or at least he did—and then he started work on *The Castle*. This novel is arguably the most specifically autobiographical and locally referential text of Kafka's maturity, as well as among the most self-consciously linguistically driven, and it turns on this question of boundaries as well, asking with great insistence at an astounding number of levels: where is that boundary, and what exactly is it the boundary of?

Chapter 4

✦

"Is There a Castle Here?"

An Architecture of Disappearing Lines

> *Ist denn hier ein Schloß?*
>
> —K.

> It is torn to pieces by its own elements, a fate it richly deserves. Of course there's no more beautiful fate for a story than for it to disappear, and in this way.
>
> —Kafka, letter to Milena Jesenská, July 1920

> You see, it is as if my life task had consisted in taking possession of a house.
> —This, too remained unfinished.
>
> —Kafka, letter to Max Brod, January 1921

"Diese ganze Literatur ist Ansturm gegen die Grenze" ("This entire literature is an assault against boundaries").[1] So Franz Kafka wrote in his journal shortly before beginning work on his last novel, *The Castle*, a work this earlier journal passage might well describe. The novel indeed pushes at the boundaries of narrative as it charts the unlikely pilgrim K.'s lack of progress through its strangely structured world. An important distinction arises at the level of plot, however: boundaries may be crossed, but they are not successfully stormed. Storming boundaries entails an intention successfully carried out, by force, and for K., boundaries when crossed are crossed in error. Even in retrospect, their location can be difficult to chart. This difficulty soon emerges as a (potential) professional problem for the novel's protagonist, because K. is (ostensibly) in the Castle realm as a Land Surveyor (although he fails to establish even this much). The identification and delineation of boundaries is his métier, yet K. never draws a single line. The novel itself ceases midsentence, its own last line unfinished; little progress has been made in K.'s quest, no threshold has been crossed: the Castle remains inviolate and K.'s position in its world unclear. We are left hanging, with intimations only of the peculiar and apparently unchartable topography of the Castle realm.

Kafka's late 1921 journal entry makes no reference to his next long narrative project, but it does identify a type of literary relation that resonates strongly with K.'s experience in the Castle world, as does the passage that directly precedes it:

> Pursuit, indeed, is only a metaphor. I can also say, "assault on the last earthly frontier," an assault, moreover, launched from below, from mankind, and since this too is a metaphor, I can replace it by the metaphor of an assault from above, aimed at me from above.[2]
>
> "Jagd" ist ja nur ein Bild, ich kann auch sagen "Ansturm gegen die letzte irdische Grenze," und zwar Ansturm von unten, von den Menschen her, und kann, da auch dies nur ein Bild ist, es ersetzen durch das Bild des Ansturmes von oben, zu mir herab.[3]

The passage gestures toward a frame of reference far removed from the contingent, quotidian Prague that Kafka sometimes cited as a distraction from his writerly work. Here, Kafka's own critique of what he will name only as "this literature" anticipates the very kind of highly rhetorical readings that long preoccupied the critical literature devoted to his work. Kafka was suspicious of metaphor, and the deformative power of rhetoric often produces dramatic and tangible consequences in Kafka's fiction. Gregor's transformation into a vermin in *The Metamorphosis*, for example, has been read as a transfer of the wrong constituents of the metaphor employed in "calling names"—Gregor is not just lowly or parasitic, as habituation would dictate we understand the implied insult (the cleaning woman calls post-transformation Gregor a "Mistkäfer," or "dung beetle," literal in this case but otherwise a common insult), but rather acquires all the physical characteristics that convention would have us bracket from the equation.[4] Alternatively, we might imagine that Gregor's fate is what would happen if these idiomatic metaphors were performative utterances.[5] Here, however, metaphor deforms somewhat differently. Kafka seems to take it for granted that metaphor introduces a radical instability in categories that name necessary opposites: "pursuer" or "pursued"—a qualitative distinction if there ever was one, not easily dismissed as "purely rhetorical," and a distinction fundamentally necessary to be understood by the individuals in question.

Publishing and in residence in Prague in 1921 as well, the young Roman Jakobson gives "metamorphosis" as "the projection of a literary device into artistic reality, the turning of a poetic trope into a poetic *fact*, into a plot element."[6] Despite the fact that Kafka in the passage quoted above restricts "pursuit" ("*Jagd*") firmly to the realm of metaphor, the dynamics of the passage suggest that the destabilizing qualities Jakobson associates with "metamorphosis" are close at hand. Spatial relations, direction, origin, and even moral authority shift here with astounding fluidity. Metaphor becomes hollow structure, a formal or structural constant in which infinite internal shifting of content is possible, with the terms and their interrelations subject to constant change. This shifting destabilizes the categories "pursuer" and "pursued," a qualitative distinction if there ever was one, not easily dismissed as "purely rhetorical," particularly by the individual in question who really needs to know whether he should be running towards or away from his opponent. Yet "above" becomes "below"; "assault" stands in for "pursuit" without difficulty or warning. Each successive term interacts with the trace left by its precursor—we still remember we were in pursuit even as we run from what we had been chasing; as we scan our trajectory from the depths to see where we misstepped, our supposed quarry descends on us from above.

In Prague, as we have seen, language was a contested territory, and the combat was not restricted to a question of rhetorical modes. The question of language—which one? when?—determined, at various times, questions of property, employment, whether one's house and business would be destroyed or left standing, whether one was in the minority or majority, aligned with the governing or with the governed—but this very alignment too was subject to change. Boundaries—which the journal passage identifies as under assault—by their nature delimit territory, but what kind of territory does "this literature" assault? The territory of a particular trope, as the journal passage itself goes on to explore? Or questions more akin to the redrawing of districts, property lines, and state boundaries, a process which in both pre- and post-Habsburg Bohemia intensely and explicitly relied on language to provide the crucial dividing lines? Is the kind of language that concerns Prague School theorists really the same language that determines census results or causes unrest on Prague streets? What do literary-theoretical arcana possibly have to do with messy streets? Prague School concerns may seem far from the apportioning of bilingual post offices and, for that matter, from fictional land surveying, but they are more obviously pertinent to the way Kafka's late fiction figures language by means of structure and social use. Bringing these two spheres—Prague linguistics and politics—into proximity makes clear that they both engage the very issues and rhetorics of territory and structure that Kafka also addresses in his fiction.

The structure identified by the words "above" and "below" in Kafka's journal passage on metaphor and pursuit is less that of territory than of hierarchy, but a hierarchy that is strikingly subject to change. The rapid, arbitrary substitution ("pursuit" for "assault" and "assault aimed at me from above" for "assault from mankind") supplies no rationale for the succession: metaphor, apparently, allows for infinite shifting along its vertical axis. Kafka's text implies a layering of effects, less a series of replacements than a stack of metaphors in which each layer retains a basic structure but in which the terms and their interrelations are in flux. This metaphorical state of affairs finds a material analogue in the political situation in Prague, especially that of its Jewish population. When Czechoslovakia attained its independence in 1918, some Germans, including German-identifying Jews, feared finding themselves suddenly second-class citizens, subject to the people whom they had come to see (for German-speakers, even Jewish ones, had enjoyed the privileges of the ruling classes) as an excellent source of household servants. The rules had changed—a change that might well be interpreted as "assault from below" becoming "assault from above." That is, this apparently abstract passage about figurative language and the nature of literature also describes the very real, concrete fears of Czechoslovak politics, which also naturally concern boundaries.

Alternatively, and firmly situated in rhetorical analysis, Kafka's journal passage about metaphor evokes the spatial axes (vertical and horizontal) along which rhetorical modes will later be plotted (as in graphed) by Kafka's Prague contemporary Roman Jakobson. For Jakobson, metaphor governs vertical substitutions, as Kafka here also implies, while metonymy relies on horizontal contiguity.[7] In Kafka's journal, however, rhetoric seems to be spinning on these axes. The uncertainty of spatial and hierarchical relations that characterizes the journal passage, furthermore, serves as a plot summary of *The Castle*. The problem for K. as the "pursued"/"pursuer" of Kafka's fiction is that these shifts that Kafka here associates with metaphor affect the horizontal, prosaic axis along which K.'s course is to be plotted, a course as deformed and unpredictably behaved as the snowy village roads by which K. tries and fails to reach his Castle destination:

> The street he had taken, the main street in the village, did not lead to the Castle hill, it only went close by, then veered off as if on purpose, and though it didn't lead any further from the Castle, it didn't get any closer either. K. kept expecting the street to turn at last toward the Castle and it was only on this expectation that he kept going.[8]

Indeed, it often seems throughout the novel that it is only the expectation of a plotted course that keeps K. going, rather than any actual plot that guides him. The novel is almost without plot—or rather, its plot, like K.'s trajectory through the village, derives from a groundless expectation (that K. will enter the Castle) which never comes to fruition. The street, in other words, never turns. Furthermore, while this passage from the novel describes physical, geographical relations between Village and Castle and the uphill streets that must connect them—describes relations, in other words, of contiguity—the road seems to shift in directionality with the same ease that Kafka in the journal identifies with metaphoricity. In setting out for the Castle, K. begins on a path upward, but his status as pursuer, as the agent taking the streets *up* to the castle (along the vertical trajectory Jakobson associates with metaphor), shifts such that soon, the streets are literally "taking him" along a course perpendicular to the Castle, neither advancing his cause nor sending him below. K.'s exhaustion proves the only measure of his progress; he moves along the street only by virtue of his inability to break free of it, and when he finally does break away from the "clinging street" ("festhaltenden Straße"), his progress stops entirely. He was not taking the street, but being taken by it, as the spatial and hierarchical relations "pursuer" and "pursued" shift along their axis. This passage is but one of a number of allegorical mise en abîmes that encapsulate the "plot structure" (such as it is) of Kafka's unfinished novel; all seem to support Brod's claim that Kafka intended the book to end with K.'s death from exhaustion, surrounded by villagers but no nearer to the Castle. The linear progression (plot), however, here exhibits the very characteristics of metaphor as Kafka seems to define them in his journal. Thus the novel projects figure into plot in the manner of Jakobson's "metamorphosis," but also vice versa. Similarly, the novel seems to insist on complex relations between *syntax* and figure—to the extent that K.'s journey resembles that of the reader being carried along the contiguous, unidirectional paths of sentences all the while struggling to obey the Castle's implied command, a command identified by Theodor Adorno as the siren call of Kafka's work generally: "interpret me." Indeed, the passage depicting K.'s walk begs the question of whether the Castle is contiguously related to the Village at all, or if it resides in some metaphorical "above" or "beyond," inaccessible by simple streets.

Other aspects of K.'s relation to the Castle world are subject to similar shifts, as when he attempts to chart his position in the socio-political power structure:

> K. almost concluded that his situation was quite satisfactory, though he always told himself quickly after such fits of satisfaction that this is precisely where the danger lay. Dealing directly with the authorities wasn't all that difficult, for no matter how well organized they were, they only had to defend distant and invisible causes on behalf of remote and invisible gentlemen, whereas he, K., was fighting for something vitally close, for himself, and what's more of his own free will, initially at least, for he was the assailant, and he was not struggling for himself on his own, there were also other forces, which he knew nothing of, but could believe in because of the measures adopted by the authorities.[9]

Here, the positions charted are less obviously physical, but K.'s certitude about his position as "assailant" ("*Angreifer*," from "*greifen*," to grab, grasp, or snatch) nonetheless stems from a sense of its tangibility, its literality: it is grounded in immediate concerns, in self-interest and free will. This tangibility, he assumes, renders his position superior to those whose struggle is guided by remote, perhaps even esoteric concerns—the assault from below trumps the assault from above. The shift in the differential occurs, however, immediately with the introduction of the very tangible word "Angreifer" which then introduces analogous "other forces" who fight on K.'s behalf, forces equally remote and indeed intuitable only by virtue of the reactions of the remote authorities who were just (K. thought) put at a disadvantage by the immediacy of K.'s concerns. The sentence in question turns on the term ("Angreifer") that names the position K. believes his immediacy confers, the term K. believes to firmly define his relation to the authorities. Before he names this position, K. presents himself as having the upper hand by virtue of the advantage that groundedness and immediacy enjoy over remoteness; after the term "Angreifer" appears, however, the nature of his advantage shifts so that now it is K.'s intuited alignment with esoteric "other forces" that confers superiority. Not surprisingly, then, K.'s certainty in his position as "assailant" begins to crumble as it emerges that the very ease that marked his relations with the authorities may be their most potent weapon:

> By mostly obliging him from the start in some of the more trivial matters . . . the authorities were depriving him not only of the chance to gain a few easy little victories but also of the corresponding satisfaction and the resulting well-founded confidence of other, greater battles. Instead they let K. wander about as he wished, even if only in the village, spoiling and weakening him, barred all fighting here, and dispatched him to this extra-official, completely unclear, dull, and strange life. If this went on, if he weren't always on guard, he might one day, despite the friendly attitude of the authorities, despite his meticulous fulfillment of his exaggeratedly light official duties, be deceived by the favor seemingly granted him and lead the rest of his life so imprudently that he would fall to pieces, and the authorities, gentle and friendly as ever, would have to come, as though against their will but actually at the behest of some official ordinance of which he knew nothing, in order to clear him out of the way.[10]

As with his physical wanderings, K.'s seeming pursuit of a goal ends in stasis, and the pursuer is now in pieces ("zusammenbrach") that recall the physical character of the Castle elements themselves—the architectural materials—as K. initially perceived them: "pieced together from village houses" ("aus Dorfhäusern zusammengetragen"); "the paint had long since flaked off, and the stone seemed to be crumbling"[11] ("der Anstrich war längst abgefallen, und der Stein schien abzubröckeln").[12] K. has now assumed the position in which he had perceived (much to his disappointment) the Castle buildings, while the authorities—at the behest of an unknown order, analogous to the one from which he had so recently believed he might derive strength—now come after him, rendering him not assailant, but assailed. Both passages from the novel, then, follow the pattern outlined in the journal entry as being particular to metaphor, and both involve the hierarchical structure—Village to Castle—readily identifiable as the determining metaphor of the novel. Both also, however, stress the material and the tangible: shifts within metaphor, then, affect literality and linear progress.

Yet the nature of the rhetorical structure responsible for the novel's governing uncertainty is likewise less than clear. The Castle is not, after all, "only a metaphor." Pursuit, one could argue, has far more to do with a different rhetorical mode: that of the traditional allegory. Structurally the novel resembles the paradigmatic allegory, Bunyan's *Pilgrim's Progress*, or, as the Czech critic František Kautman has suggested, the Czech allegory by Comenius, *The Labyrinth of the World*. And indeed, a good deal of debate has arisen as to whether the dominant rhetorical mode of the novel is metaphor, symbol, or allegory. Early allegorical readings include those by Max Brod (who edited the novel with his reading in mind) and Thomas Mann, who both present *The Castle* essentially as religious allegory in their forewords to the 1926 (Brod) and 1954 (Mann) editions of the novel. Erich Heller argues against this tradition in favor of a reading that gives precedence to the symbolic mode,[13] while Charles Bernheimer takes issue with Heller's recuperative symbolic reading, applying Walter Benjamin's theory of allegory as ruin, as "unending decay," to Kafka's text. *The Castle* is thus an allegorical structure wherein the stable truth to which signs refer is absent—in Adorno's reformulation, a parable "for which the key has been stolen."[14] Benjamin critiqued Brod's work on Kafka, particularly on *The Castle*, arguing that it overemphasizes theological and redemptive narratives and relies too heavily on symbolic wholeness and suggesting, too, that Brod misses something essential in Kafka's tone. He goes on to identify a tradition of which Kafka's work represents the inverse: "Wisdom has sometimes been defined as the epic side of truth. In this sense, wisdom is characterized as tradition; it is truth as haggadic consistency."[15] Kafka, however, confronts us with a world in which precisely this consistency of truth based on tradition (which we might, although Benjamin does not, call the "consistency of a common language") has been lost. Kafka's genius, according to Benjamin, is that "he gave up truth to cling to transmissibility, to its haggadic element," becoming, essentially, Haggadah (the story or parable) without Halakah (the law or truth).[16] Stanley Corngold characterizes the relationship of rhetorical modes in Kafka as one of "priority": "the priority of literalness and play over meaning in the story is the statement of the priority for Kafka of literature as allegory over literature as symbol, but this priority is one that has to be perpetually reasserted."[17]

To read the vermin in *The Metamorphosis*, then, as a study in the function of a figure or metaphor *to the exclusion of literality* is to bracket off the realistic wriggling of his unwieldy little legs, to dispel the impact of the insistent realism with which the thin brown liquid gouged from Gregor's mandibles in his attempt to open his door is described. The story may not be a predominantly realist exploration of the plight men face when turned into insects, but Kafka's interest in the nineteenth-century Realist tradition (as exemplified by his fascination with the novelists Flaubert, Dickens, and Němcová) argues that Realism is a mode that should not be taken lightly in his own fiction. Corngold goes on to define the relationship in Kafka's fiction between opposing interpretive modes as one of "combat," a combat in which allegory consistently retains "primacy," but only through struggle.[18] And of course, since "combat" is "only a metaphor," "primacy" may instead indicate at any time a minor, secondary status. Kafka's texts exhort us to read them in both modes simultaneously, or at least in fast succession, although—or rather because—each mode will violate and deform the other. Roman Jakobson, publishing in Prague just prior to Kafka's journal entry on metaphor and boundaries, writes that "the abrogation of the boundary between real and figurative meanings is characteristic of poetic language," thus offering a definition in terms of which Kafka's fiction emerges as intensely poetic.[19]

The somewhat later Prague School formulation that defines poetic language as that which "violates the norm radically" relies on a palpable norm against which a violation can be perceived, while in Jakobson's earlier discussion, poetic language blurs or does away with at least one such norm or boundary. The certainty of a *known* norm against which transgressions *or* compliance can be judged is a near impossibility in *The Castle*, at least from K.'s perspective (to which readers are constrained), just as the law and the nature of Josef K.'s infraction remains obscure in *The Trial*. Indeed, it is characteristic of Kafka's fiction generally that we can be certain of where we are—in what genre, in what rhetorical and fictional mode, in what, if any, frame of reference—only at our peril. The move to decide between metaphor and allegory risks oversimplifying a fictive structure in which the indeterminacy of rhetorical modes is a primary, even a constitutive feature. *The Castle*, however, frequently frames this uncertainty in terms of K.'s "strange" or "foreign" status, and connects this strangeness explicitly with language, perception, and therefore with the navigation of its social and material spaces.

Assault on Which Boundary? K. as Frustrated Structuralist

> Here we have the projection of a literary device into artistic reality, the turning of a poetic trope into a poetic *fact*, into a plot element.
>
> —Roman Jakobson

Everyone in the Castle world understands how the property lines are drawn: "what use would [they] have for a surveyor?" But what if K. imagines a function for surveying beyond "use"? Certainly Kafka has a sharp awareness of the way writing has both a bureaucratic and a literary or aesthetic function.

K.'s potential surveying lines might have a similar duality. K.'s interest in clarity of line is not exclusively professional or pragmatic; it several times takes on an aesthetic, even a compositional dimension. And furthermore, his interest in lines seems to hearken back to earlier times when distinctions were drawn more clearly, in memory at least. In *The Castle*, lines acting as boundaries mark out the forbidden and in so doing pique K.'s interest and focus his desires. This fascination with boundaries for their own sake (rather than for the sake of what lies beyond them) finds explicit illustration in one of the few passages that narrates a clear memory from K.'s shadowy former life. When K. believes himself to be approaching the Castle with the aid of the messenger Barnabas, this experience evokes memories of his childhood assaults on the cemetery wall, which fascinated him despite the fact that "the cemetery no longer held any secrets for them, they had often enough gone in through the small, wrought-iron gate and had merely wanted to conquer the smooth high wall."[20] Sanctioned entry held no charms, and the cemetery was a known quantity, but the wall provided a prohibition to violate, a challenge by which to prove his mastery, and hence a source of pleasure. In the realm of K.'s remembered life, lines are straight and walls are firm: a wall clearly marks inner from outer, sanctioned from unsanctioned; towers look and act like towers, and women and children stay at home. The only specific information we are given from this life—his recollections of the church tower in his "Heimat" (home); his mysterious reference to having a "Frau und Kind" at home to support—establishes these distinctions.[21] When K. sets out to codify the structure of the Castle world, however, to render it comparably clear in his mind, the world resists his every attempt. K. can never enter the Castle—either surreptitiously or overtly. He can neither follow the rules nor break them consciously to achieve an end: he would have to know them first, and this seems increasingly impossible throughout the novel—nothing in the strangely shifting Castle world is so conveniently static as a cemetery wall and the stationary stones and silent dead it encloses. And while defiance of a known rule is empowering, unwitting trespasses offer no such salubrious effect.

If we overlay *The Castle* with the work of the "other" Prague Circle, and see the novel in terms of a structuralist model of composition and reception, K. as Land Surveyor or line drawer can easily be read as a writer figure, while his difficulties in perceiving and judging the Castle suggest the travails of reading. Prague structuralism presents a model in which acts of reading and writing take place against a ground of agreed-upon usage—they call it "standard language," but in light of period census debates, it is tempting to call it "everyday language" or a "language of everyday use"—which the writer either upholds (communicative language) or disrupts (the poetic mode). If the text conforms with current usage and norms, it communicates to us; if it does not conform with these standards, it seems strange to us, and communication is disrupted as this strangeness itself draws our attention. As readers we can train ourselves to identify the source of this strangeness with relation to the ground of the standard language. This is Prague School poetic theory in a nutshell.

Viewed in terms of such a system, K.'s inability to draw lines—to inscribe, to follow the writer analogy—derives from two states of affairs. (1) The villagers already agree on property lines (norms) and thus have a system of usage to which K. is "not privy," so K. cannot speak communicatively (that is, unobtrusively) with complete success (he speaks "wie ein Fremde"). And (2) he cannot flout the system (*intentionally* innovate, write poetically) because he cannot fully comprehend its rules. Since for the greater part of the novel, the reader shares K.'s perceptions and has no other source of information about the world he views, as readers we, like K., are faced with the task of perceiving the novel's world in relation to a rhetorical and referential ground that is unstable or at least incompletely known. Thus we will not be able to distinguish between "communicative" and "poetic" modes of writing. According to Prague School theory, the stronger the communicative norms of the language, the greater the potential for poetic deformation—but you'd have to know the norms to tell. Is it possible to ask questions to determine such norms? How could such questions avoid the fate of the "language question" in the census: if the process responsible for determining the linguistically based identity of citizens cannot rely on a common understanding of what it means to have a language, how stable can the notion of a common language—the notion on which both the nation-state and the Prague School definition of the literary rely—truly be?

We must also recognize this instability in the Castle world as potentially double in nature. The natives think K. is strange; he (and therefore readers) think the world is strange. The scenario begs a simple question: which of these perspectives is correct? The responsibility for distortion may rest with K.'s faulty perceptions or with the realm he regards. Readers share K.'s perspective, but the novel offers abundant evidence that it is flawed. K.'s expectations based on his prior life experience, which form the ground of his perception, are singularly inappropriate throughout, as the Castle natives rarely fail to remind him. "Strangers," apparently, "never like the Castle" ("Keinem Fremden gefällt es"[22]), the village teacher explains to K. "Only a total stranger could ask such a question" ("Nur ein völlig Fremder kann Ihre Frage stellen"[23]), the village chairman complains, linking stranger-status explicitly with problems of reading: "all this is utterly clear to anyone capable of reading official letters and therefore still better at reading unofficial ones; that you, a stranger, cannot make this out doesn't surprise me" ("Für einen der amtliche Zuschriften zu lesen versteht und infolgedessen nichtamtliche Briefe noch besser liest, ist das alles überdeutlich; daß Sie, ein Fremder, das nicht erkennen wundert mich nicht.")[24] We know very little of K. (he lived somewhere where there was a tower; he claims to have a wife and child, to have had assistants, and to be a surveyor), but what we do know is that he is no native of the Castle realm. At the same time, the customs and behaviors of the villagers and Castle officials cannot fail to strike us as strange and inconsistent, like the weirdly shifting physical architecture of the Castle buildings and village streets. But since we have only K.'s perceptions to go on, we must also take into account the possibility that there is some consistent system of relations that K. simply misses as a result of his inappropriate perceptual expectations. For the most part, I follow this tack, imagining that the Castle world operates in terms of an internally coherent structure whose rules are simply illegible to K. Despite this project, however, the either-or structure that the logic of argument seems to demand is fallacious: just because K. is delusional does not mean that what he views is rational or consistent.

The Castle's potential for this "dual asymmetry" prefigures the Prague structuralist and Saussure student Sergei Karcevskij's critique of the doubly asymmetrical linguistic sign—uncertain as to both synonymy and homonymy.[25] In terms of the census language question dear to the heart of the editors at *Lidové noviny*, double asymmetry would mean that not only can questions about language (*jazyk*) have multiple meanings, but they could also be talking about the tongue (*jazyk*) in your mouth. In terms of the novel's title, on the one hand, we might ask whether the *Schloß* (castle) has more in common with a *Prunkbau* (mansion) or a *Ritterburg* (fortified castle), as K. will later consider, while on the other, we might ask of the word *Schloß* in isolation (as it appears in the title) whether it refers to a building or a lock. Analogously, K.'s failures as reader and writer may stem from the illegibility of the norms he confronts or from his myopic stranger status—or from both at once. Whatever the source of his difficulties, K.'s consternation and inability to enter the Castle or act as surveyor derive from his failure to "read" a social structure that is also an architectural structure—both of them, at multiple levels, linguistically constituted. Based on K.'s perceptions, however, it would seem this is a Castle—a social structure, an architecture—without a grammar, or at least, K. is without a grammar book.

Structuralist Buildings: Architecture as Language

The Prague School theorist Jan Mukařovský's 1940 essay "On the Problem of Functions in Architecture" describes architectural problems in terms that almost exactly replicate his earlier writings on language. Mukařovský argues that architecture—like language, although he does not make the connection explicit—depends on agreement among a social collective not only for its functionality, but for its form. Architecture is first and foremost the delineation of social space; if we do not understand the social context of a building, not only will we fail to understand its function, but we will fail to *see its form*. He first considers the nature of functionality in the abstract, and although he nowhere here refers to language, the notion of function in the abstract sounds identical to the structuralists' quasi-Saussurean notions about the functioning of language as a synchronic system of arbitrary signs. Function in the abstract, then, also emerges as dependent on a social grammar of agreed-upon usage: "the notion of function means that we commonly use the object . . . for such and such a purpose. Custom, repeated usage, is a necessary precondition of a function."[26] The use pattern of a given individual is not sufficient to define such a function; function "must be spontaneously comprehensible to every member of a given collective." The understanding of an object's function orders our understanding of the object as sign, since an object "not only performs but signifies its function." Our understanding of its function furthermore colors not only our comprehension but our apprehension of the object: "its sensory perception is predetermined by our awareness of what it is used for; both the shape and incorporation into space of the perceived object often depend on this awareness." Thus if we understand the function of an object, we understand what it looks like. Mukařovský gives the example of a tool:

> If we are aware of . . . the purpose of the handle . . . , we shall interpret it during the process of perception—regardless of its actual position at a given moment—as that part of the object which is usually the closest to us and the one from which we begin to apprehend the shape. If we cannot, however, identify the handle in the process of perception, it will appear to us as an accidental protrusion illogically disturbing the unity of the shape, and the shape itself will be unsatisfactorily ambiguous for us.[27]

As members of a "given collective," we will understand the object's function and our perception of it will be arranged in space accordingly. If we are not in that collective, we may see an ordinary household object as incomprehensibly abstract. Mukařovský goes on to problematize this idea of function somewhat, acknowledging that objects are not "inevitably connected with a single function," that "it is possible to use a thing for another purpose and with another function than its usual one or even than the one for which its producer designed it" and that "an object can change its conventional function in the course of time."[28] We might use a hammer, in other words, to drive nails, but in a moment of rage we might use it to bludgeon our enemies; two hundred years hence the same hammer may be in a museum, functioning as an aesthetic or historical artifact. These variables depend on both collective agreement and individual use. "The awareness of the collective" "sets individual functions into complex interrelations, the regularity of which governs the collective's entire active attitude toward reality." The individual (always assumed to be a member of the collective) will have these accepted attitudes and functions at his disposal, but "in his actions he can deviate from this regularity by using things in functions that are not connected with them by common consensus, or by reversing—in the multiplicity of functions which have often accumulated around each of these things—their customary hierarchy and rendering a normally secondary function dominant." An individual can decide to "misuse" things, and this misuse may have a disruptive effect.

Functionality, then, emerges as having a hierarchical structure, since "in essence all the functions are potentially present in every human act insofar as they are at all compatible with the given act." Mukařovský identifies three categories that must be distinguished in understanding this process:

> a) the reality to which the functions are applied, b) the set of functions lodged in the awareness of the collective and bound by internal interrelations into a structure and c) the individual who introduces a constantly renewed accidentality into the functional process and thus sets the structure of functions in motion.[29]

He goes on to relate what he has said in general terms to the specific question of architecture, which he characterizes as a "typical example of polyfunctional production" and cites unnamed "modern theoreticians" who "rightly understand a building as a set of life processes for which it is the setting."[30] The key to Mukařovský's understanding of architecture is the complexity of its functions, the simultaneity with which architectural space must be able to accommodate diverse human acts. A building, then, which we might like to think of as static and predictable, is rather a dynamic "set of life processes"—it would be less surprising, we might imagine, if such a building were to seem to shift or change in formal character as its functions change. Such an understanding of architecture and perception, then, might help to account for the Castle's apparently bizarre and inconsistent configurations.

Architecture "organizes the space surrounding man" in relation to these functions and activities and must relate to "man in his entirety"—whatever, apparently, man might be thinking or doing. Thus, "the functionality of architecture is a very complex matter"—indeed. This structural dynamism also reflects developments in Prague structuralist thinking about language and literary studies, which increasingly split off from earlier formalist prescriptions of linguistic synchrony as the model for literary study, finding this model too rigid to accommodate the complexity of the literary text. Central to this complex functionality are "four functional horizons": immediate purpose, historical purpose, the organization of the collective (the social horizon), and the individual horizon.[31] These functions need not be parallel or in agreement, but all combine "in a state of constant hierarchical interrelation"; and to properly apprehend and judge an architectural space, it must be considered with relation to all of them.

At this point in the essay, the behavior of this individual begins to sound strikingly like the behavior of the poet or writer, if the objects in question were only linguistic, and the "given collective" the community of speakers—this essay dates from the time when Mukařovský was expanding his theories about poetics into the broader realm of aesthetics. In his poetics, the poet, in using linguistic "objects" in nontraditional ways, disrupts conventional linguistic functionality (communication) and thus enters the realm of the aesthetic. Mukařovský here transposes this linguistic theory into more general terms, with the idea that any individual using any object "against the grain" of habituated usage may disrupt hierarchy.

With regard to *The Castle*, however, it would seem that "the set of functions lodged in the awareness of the collective and bound by internal interrelations into a structure" is precisely what K. cannot perceive or penetrate; what K. adds as the individual, moreover, is precisely that condition of "accidentality" which Mukařovský mentions. In the Castle, however, it is a condition born of foreignness. The very structure of language in a structuralist system and, by extension, of architectural space, depends on a collective agreement among individuals. This may not necessarily be a language in the traditional sense, and it may be, as the Prague School theorized, a commonality of usage of any kind, including the kind of scientific rhetoric that members of the circle developed, employed, and, indeed, policed and enforced. Nonetheless, all accurate perception in a structuralist system—even, as here, spatial and formal perception—relies on the "magic of a common language."[32] Yet the notion of structures—actual, material structures—as intimately connected with the notion of a common language has far more tangible, historical precedent than the disembodied "architecture" of this theoretical essay.

In Prague in the nineteenth century, architecture became, in a very real and literal sense, linguistically motivated—polemical, even. Indeed, the history of the Czech National Theater serves as a profound reminder of the physical—particularly, architectural—ramifications of language politics as they played out in Prague. The theater funding project, begun in the mid-nineteenth century, not only pitted Czechs against German-speakers for the title of "National" (which nation? where?), but caused deep rifts among the leading Czech nationalist coalitions. The project was initially launched in the wake of the post-1848 crackdown on Czech nationalist political activity; the crackdown was a set of centralizing, Germanizing, and Catholicizing policies that further politicized all Czech literary and cultural activity by rendering it the only legal rallying point for nationalist ambitions and activities. Against this background, the Committee to Build a National Theater was established, essentially, as a radical nationalist project that quite openly used the building of a national theater as a proxy for the building of a linguistically defined nation-state.[33] Donations to the cause cut across class boundaries, with the Bohemian gentry, bourgeoisie, and even the peasants (only recently freed from requirements of forced labor) contributing most of the funds; indeed, fund-raising activities themselves became important events for cross-class cultural contact and Czech speaking; in a very real sense, then, the process of funding a building was also that of building a nation. Soon after its long-awaited completion, and ironically before the formal inauguration, set for September 1881, could take place, the massive building was set on fire by lightning and burned to the ground. Remarkably, the intensified, almost desperate campaign to fund rebuilding was even more successful than the first, and the participation of workers and peasants was much more extensive. As a result, the replacement building was funded and built within two years and was inaugurated by 1883. This history alone guaranteed the long-term association not only of the theater but of theater *buildings* with the fortunes of the Czech nation.[34] Indeed, nationalist divisions over architecture throughout the republic were maintained right down to the building materials that were used: in Moravia, for example, prewar buildings of red brick are almost invariably German-built and housed German churches or cultural institutions. Such interrelations of architectural, national, figural, and linguistic identities also informed the nineteenth-century history of Bohemian Jews with relation to the empire and to their fellow subjects. Emancipation began in 1842, and the ghetto had been razed by 1852. By law, then, Jewish equality and integration—physical and civic—went hand-in-hand with German language adoption. These changes had their visible architectural ramifications as well: the razed Jewish ghetto ultimately was replaced by the modern, cosmopolitan "Paris" street where Kafka's family lived, a broad boulevard evocative of Haussmann's renovations to Paris that connected Old Town Square (where Kafka's father's shop was) to the ring street along the river.[35] Thus, a long history had paved the way for thinking about language in relation to architecture, the institutions it housed, and their position with relation to power, all in very concrete, material terms.

"In the Castle and in the Village": Němcová's Architectural Grammar

The Prague School's stress on the importance of "a common language" for accurate spatial and architectural orientation also had a significant Czech literary precedent. Božena Němcová's architectural narrative "In the Castle and in the Village" takes great pains to render this social grammar clear and accessible.[36] Němcová's role as a codifying linguistic force, furthermore, had recently been featured in the philological journal *Naše řeč* (*Our Language*) that Kafka mentions early on in his correspondence with Jesenská. In its linguistics methodology, *Naše řeč* was far from even proto-Prague School theory, tending more to the historicism that structuralism would ultimately critique and focusing on individual word or usage analysis (and criticism) rather than structure. In keeping with the journal's general interests, its late 1920 discussion of *Babička* (translated as *The Grandmother* or *Granny*), Němcová's best-known work, focuses on the novel's contributions to the

Czech language and particularly on the way Němcová introduced spoken Czech to the written language. Excusing her occasional Germanisms as being period-typical and understandable given that she learned Czech only as an adult, the essay portrays Němcová as an invigorating, enriching, and ultimately unifying force, while stressing that she uses more colloquialisms than exclusively literary constructions. This discussion in particular highlights the spoken-written split that was so marked in Czech while praising Němcová's effective bridging of the two.[37] As a subscriber and regular *Naše řeč* reader, Kafka would have had these issues in mind with respect to Němcová as a result of this article that appeared not long before he began work on *The Castle*.

Babička is the Němcová novel most frequently mentioned in relation to *The Castle*, and the two works' structural similarities cannot be denied: a stranger (in Němcová's text, the Czech grandmother) enters the unfamiliar realm of the German landed gentry, and a girl is seduced by another outsider with unhappy consequences. Max Brod cited *Babička* early on as a source for *The Castle*, Czech critics followed up on this connection as soon as censorship conditions permitted, and a number of subsequent critics mentioned it in passing. Typical of such references, Ronald Gray suggests that "it may also be that Kafka was very slightly influenced by the realistic nineteenth-century Czech novel, *The Grandmother*, by Božena Němcová" and leaves it at that. More recently, Alfred Thomas has made a much stronger, more detailed case for *Babička*'s influence on *The Castle*, positioning Kafka's novel as a de-idealizing force vis-à-vis both Comenius's *Labyrinth of the World* and Němcová's nationalist classic: whereas Comenius's Pilgrim progresses "away from the city toward the gradual resolution of his predicament in the 'paradise of the heart,'" Kafka leaves "K. forever mired in the petty power relations of the castle."[38] Similarly, Thomas argues that while Němcová presents a bucolic idyll of a nostalgically constructed Czech village life, "Kafka's novel draws on certain structural parallels and so inverts—and subverts—the idealized relations between the village and the manor house that obtain in Němcová's novel." I am in agreement with this overall analysis, as well as with a number of Thomas's specific points, in particular about the way in which the juxtaposition highlights *The Castle*'s complex representation of gender and power relations (my topic in chapter 7). I would further argue that *The Castle* positions itself similarly with regard to Němcová's novella "In the Castle and in the Village," evoking the structures of an earlier fictional project and worldview to highlight the workings of the Castle, edifice and novel both. However, whereas Thomas argues that Kafka foregrounds social and gender divisions that *Babička* glosses over, I find that "In the Castle and in the Village" has an almost opposite relationship to Kafka's text: K.'s consternation in regarding the Castle has more to do with the clear distinctions he *would* have found in Němcová's novella, but which he cannot rely upon in the Castle world he confronts.

Němcová's Czech title "V zámku a v podzámčí" clearly distinguishes two realms, defining their spatial and social relationship. It is at once a territorial and an architectural title. The most precise workable English rendering of this title—"In the Castle and in the Village"—only partially retains the explicit description entailed in the Czech, which literally reads "In the Castle and in the collection of buildings in the area below the castle." The title thus makes an explicit and hierarchical distinction, but it articulates this difference as existing within an overall whole, as etymology emphasizes. "Podzámčí" is the area below, subordinate to, physically, socially, and etymologically dependent on the central term "zámek" (which Thomas translates as "manor house," in the tradition of the Bohemist Robert Pynsent). This articulation of differences within a whole multiplies throughout the narrative.

The story meticulously describes functional distinctions of the depicted world's social (dress, speech, language), spatial, and architectural arrangement:

> The castle stood on the hilltop and below it lay the town. The river running around the town along the base of the hill formed a boundary between the castle and town estates, while the town itself was enclosed by one of its tributaries. The town citizenry were divided into three ranks. The first rank was composed of well-to-do tradesmen and farmers who had their own houses, yards, and large fields and whose wives and children wore hats and held coffees in formal parlors. The town council and mayor were elected from the ranks of the wealthy in accordance with the advice of the old proverb, "*Where there's wealth, there's wisdom.*" The second class was formed of the poorer tradesmen, those who had only a piece of land and a small house. Their women wore caps and the first rank took it very badly if the second rank let their daughters wear hats, thereby setting them up as equals to their first-rank daughters. Finally, the third class was called the riff-raff, the subtenants who lived "from hand to mouth." Anyone wishing to associate themselves in any way with the first rank would take it as the greatest insult when a subtenant kissed the hand of a lady of the first rank. She would rush to wipe it so as not to be soiled by the dirty kiss, or she would extend her sleeve only.
>
> The courtyards of the rich and the houses of the poorer craftsmen were for the most part by the water, along the embankment. In each of these yards there were a number of small rooms installed specifically for the subtenants: these rooms were dark; in each there was a small window and no floor, stove, or fireplace. To heat themselves in the winter and to cook their provisions, the subtenants would go to the large outbuilding in the yard set aside for their use. For such a room, a subtenant had to pay twelve gold coins rent per year; for this rent, however, they were dependent on the master of the yard in which they lived.[39]

These passages and others like them act as a primer, delineating each aspect of the social and architectural structure and explaining its significance with reference to the other relational terms. Every detail of human life, from bonnet strings to cooking practices to coffee, is rendered legible in an overall grammar of social and financial status. The story's plot is driven by certain destabilizations which create tensions between and among the ranks of the rich and poor. These destabilizations for the most part originate outside the social collective, with an individual who, one might say, "sets the structure of [plot] in motion." For example, the castle family, the Skočdopoles, suffer for a time from the pretensions of the new mistress's faux-French maid. The narrative figures these imported pretensions in specifically linguistic terms, as the maid insists on being called "Mamsel" (and brings a lapdog named "Joli"), while her mistress refuses to be called anything so lowly as "Skočdopole," insisting instead on the more aristocratic "Springenfeld" (the Czech name's exact German calque).[40] These distinctions are the more clearly articulated through a transitional section in which a chorus of villagers comments and moralizes on village life in the rhythmic tones of a language closer to spoken Czech, a section which not only further defines the depicted community but bridges the gap between Czech as spoken and Czech as literary language, which was a key factor in the development of a Czech national identity, and precisely the feature *Naše řeč* had emphasized in its article. By such means, the lives of the rich and foolish are brought into sharp contrast with the extreme poverty and hunger of the latest exiles from the village—a family of three grown too poor and sick even for the poor and sick. Yet before this poor family actually leaves the environs described by the title of the story, the infant brother and mother die, providing an opening through which the young boy can be brought back into the fold of the village, into the arms of a poor but nurturing foster mother and father.

Despite the trials of a cholera epidemic and the insensitivity of the wealthy to it, the story is in effect an affirmation of community. The society of the castle and village remains a linguistic and social collective that understands and accepts its internal stratifications and divisions. The Skočdopoles, despite their Teutonic and Gallic airs, are marked by their name as good-hearted Czechs like their village counterparts, and the story's sometimes biting social commentary focuses most on those who forget or betray community. Shared cultural identity provides the common referent that allows for the supreme legibility of the depicted world. Each difference and distinction is articulated and explained by the omniscient narrator or the villagers with relation to the overall hierarchy defined in the title, and so the reader is on a par with the community in terms of information and understanding and does not long retain "stranger" status. Indeed, Němcová's tremendous cultural importance derives in large part from the fact that in the very act of writing she was also actively resurrecting a literary language and its speakers—especially peasants—as literary subjects. In writing literature in Czech for Czech readers she was, given the historical context of the National Revival, committing a political act—and, from the perspective of nationalist political ideology, she could, as a Czech, rely on a very specific kind of shared cultural context. In fact, Němcová was as much creating as affirming this shared cultural and linguistic life—hence the specificity of the grammar she provides.

All of Mukařovský's claims about the functionality of architecture as social space presume an individual who is conversant with the social grammar of the milieu in which the architecture functions. Němcová, writing in the mid-nineteenth century, seems to share this presupposition about the importance of a common language for accurate architectural orientation; a common language also articulates social function, community, even property relations. In Kafka's novel, the question of grammar as a social system necessary to the successful navigation of physical and civic structures becomes paramount—K. clearly fails to negotiate successfully the social grammar of the Castle realm. The natives' frequent emphasis on the inherent foreignness of his questions and comments makes explicit the link between social rules of conduct and linguistic grammar in the narrower sense in which it is traditionally understood. K., clearly conversant in the "language" of the Castle realm, nonetheless consistently makes mistakes that seem to mark him out as a non-native "speaker." While this is easy to accept on the level of analogy between social and linguistic grammar, it is important to understand that circumstances in Kafka's own life suggest that we take the linguistic element more literally.

Kafka's experience of Czech reminds us that it is possible to be idiomatically conversant, even fluent, in a language in which one would nonetheless miss nuances of meaning and association, a situation which can lead to misunderstandings graver than could arise in a language known less completely—since fluency would produce in both speaker and listener a false sense of security, of understanding everything very well, and thus failing to seek clarification. K.'s experience of the Castle realm replicates such a structure repeatedly in a variety of perceptual and social situations. Prague structuralists, however, base their arguments about norm, violation, and reception on the presupposition of a *community* of speakers. Kafka, on the other hand, had—since the end of the war at least—been dependent professionally and personally on his knowledge of Czech, which remained to him nonetheless a foreign language in the following sense. Despite having spoken it all his life, the intricacies of its *written* form (which can be quite different from the spoken language) continued to elude him, as is clear from extant professional documents and letters to Milena Jesenská and his brother-in-law. He also claimed, however, never to have felt entirely at home in German, and wrote to Jesenská that Czech (perhaps because he was raised by Czech nannies, perhaps because his sexual experiences had been with Czech shopgirls and prostitutes) seemed the more intimate of the two languages, a distinction also in keeping with his relation to Czech primarily in its simpler, less formal spoken form. This fragmentation of languages—the division of spoken and written, private and public, not just as different modes within language but as different languages altogether—challenges the legible, comprehensible linguistic system that structuralist models rely on as the ground against which violations may be recognized and judged. Such a fragmented linguistic state of affairs may be precisely the situation that Němcová, like other writers of the Czech National Revival, and even the linguists of the Czech philological journal to which Kafka subscribed, sought to remedy with their insistence on Czech linguistic and grammatical purity, a commitment in which even the Slavo-centric Prague School and its rigidly maintained, theoretically stringent "Circle"—from which theoretical detractors could be expelled—may be seen to participate.

"There Is No Difference between the Castle and the Village"

Němcová's story "In the Castle and in the Village" thus presents all the information that Kafka withholds, and Kafka's K. is the unknown variable that the Němcová story is entirely without. The primer offered by Němcová's narrator is nowhere to be found in Kafka's novel, where the detailed explanations offered by "native" characters often create confusion where K. believed himself to understand, rather than clarifying matters for him. K.'s difficulty in negotiating both the physical and social spaces of the Castle can be seen to stem from an inability to perceive certain lines or divisions within the Castle world, divisions such as those Němcová depicts with such clarity. This suggested relationship offers the possibility of reading Kafka's narrative world as one in which such lines have been withheld from view—a disorientation effected more by erasure than transgression. And yet erasure may not be just the correct model either. Something even less easily definable seems to be at work, for in Kafka's novel as in Němcová's story, detailed architectural descriptions interspersed with meticulously articulated social situations—especially with regard to the physical positioning of characters—establish within *The Castle*'s first pages a similar interdependence of physical and social structures. These scenes, however, are filtered through the questionable perceptions of K.—the perceptions of a stranger, as everyone including K. himself stresses throughout the novel. In the minds of the Castle natives, this status as stranger is equivalent to a kind of myopia, a perceptive dysfunction attendant on K.'s position, as if to see the Castle clearly one must be from the Castle.

The central indeterminate structure of Kafka's novel is certainly the Castle itself; all K.'s experiences in the Castle world appear in relation to the novel's dominant architectural trope, which functions on narrative, social, physical, and rhetorical levels. This architecture is very strange. Its central referent would seem to be an edifice, but this edifice seems radically indeterminate, subject to strange shifts in structure and orientation. Again, Kafka's narrative opens with the perspective of an unknown, all but unidentified party staring at that which already defies description:

> Es war spät abends als K. ankam. Das Dorf lag in tiefem Schnee. Vom Schloßberg war nichts zu sehn, Nebel und Finsternis umgaben ihn, auch nicht der schwächste Lichtschein deutete das große Schloß an. Lange stand K. auf der Holzbrücke die von der Landstraße zum Dorf führt und blickte in die scheinbare Leere empor.[41]

> It was late evening when K. arrived. The village lay under deep snow. There was no sign of the Castle hill, fog and darkness surrounded it, not even the faintest gleam of light suggested the large Castle. K. stood a long time on the wooden bridge that leads from the main road to the village, gazing upward into the seeming emptiness.[42]

In chapter 3, I read this scene as a landless landscape resistant to surveying, in which any geographical features are absent or invisibly architectonic and any meaningfully distinct architecture is obscured. When read against the first view and approach to the castle in Němcová's story, this passage seems almost to systematically erase the distinctions that Němcová's text so painstakingly maintains. K. may or may not be looking at a castle—he cannot tell, all lines being obscured by the mists and snow. But, in keeping with the socially distinct and distinguishing architecture of Němcová's novella and linguistic project, this initial lack of clarity gives way to greater definition as K. confronts the apparent rigidity of the Castle's governing rules. No sooner has K. arrived at the inn (where there is no room) and retired to his makeshift bed than he is awakened by the urgent proddings of the Castellan's son. As the social context becomes clearer, so too do spatial and architectural relations:

> A young man in city clothes, with an actor's face, narrow eyes, thick eyebrows, stood beside him with the landlord. The peasants, too, were still there, a few had turned their chairs around to see and hear better. The young man apologized very politely for having awakened K., introduced himself as the son of the Castle steward and said: "This village is Castle property, anybody residing or spending the night here is effectively residing or spending the night at the Castle. Nobody may do so without permission from the Count. But you have no such permission or at least you haven't shown it yet."[43]

The first words spoken in the novel thus invoke a rule—as clearly and starkly as any unfamiliar newcomer could require. These social rules provide structure for the amorphous realm of K.'s initial vision. In keeping with Němcová, the boundaries of the village and its ultimate authority are quickly defined, along with K.'s position as an unsanctioned outsider. K.'s seemingly ingenuous response—"Ist denn hier ein Schloß?" ("Is there a castle here?")—indicates an uncertainty of his whereabouts well within logical possibility, given the mistiness of his arrival, and receives a simple, direct answer: there is a castle, that of a certain Count Westwest. K. asks again whether one must have permission to stay in the town, and thus checks that fact for accuracy: "'Und man muß die Erlaubnis zum Übernachten haben?' fragte K. . . . 'Die Erlaubnis muß man haben.' . . . 'Oder muß man etwa die Erlaubnis nicht haben?' "[44] ("'One needs permission to spend the night here?' asked K. . . . 'Permission is needed. . . . Or is permission not needed?' ")[45] From all this K. deduces that he too must get permission. Indeed, the exchange displays a near-parodic concern for clarity.

No sooner is this structure mapped out, however, than its simple lines begin to waver. The indeterminacy of linguistic mode—whether the verbal exchange and clarification is purely communicative and referential or more rhetorical and ironic—lends an aura of uncertainty to the entire scene that presents clarification as its primary function. The questions about permission seem to turn ironic with the Castellan's rephrasing of K.'s question: "Or perhaps permission is not needed?" This uncertainty comes to a head as K. belies his former ingenuousness and identifies himself as the Land Surveyor ordered by the same Count of whom he had ostensibly only just heard. K., thus newly identified by function as a Land Surveyor, offers his own explanation of the present confusion: the snow obscured the path and led him astray. All the clarification has led us on a circuitous route back to the opening scene of the novel, supplying on its way the unknown quantity K. of the first sentence with an identity, purpose, and role, and the Castle with certain existence—both soon to be called into question. Speech, which seems initially to clarify as it does in Němcová's novella, has trouble sustaining such clarity. Speech plays a double role there as well; it is both communicative and indicative of rank and status, as in the Czech peasant woman's chorus or the maid's French pretensions, but the roles dovetail neatly, working toward the double goal of articulated unity. In Kafka's novel, by contrast, a confusion of linguistic modes—indicative, metaphoric, ironic, rhetorical—rob speech of its apparently clarifying function.

The first scenes of the novel establish a pattern that will recur throughout—boundaries are unclear or unknown, speech intervenes to clarify these boundaries, and this same clarification raises further questions about the validity and existence of the very lines it draws. Yet K.'s reactions to his perceptions single out clarity—of line, of rule, of structure, both physical and social—as the basis of both aesthetic and functional value for him. His purported (and much contested) position as Land Surveyor further accentuates the importance of lines, boundaries, and contours: discovering and describing invisible but intuitable lines forms the basis of his profession. Although the actual lines drawn by any surveyor would be a projection, a good surveyor would see to it that they reflected the geographical and socially recognized contours of the mapped region, so the nature of K.'s profession further stresses the interconnectedness of social and physical structures and depends upon their legibility.

"Ihr sehet das Schloß an?"

> Form exists for us only as long as it is difficult to perceive, as long as we sense the resistance of the material.
>
> —Roman Jakobson

> Look how the chimneys started reeling around drunk—there!
> The stuttering lips were pale with horror
> And his glance was riveted up high.
> What? Is the boy delirious in broad daylight? . . .
> Slowly I get out my glasses.
> And it's really as though the chimneys
> craned their necks.
>
> —Velimir Khlebnikov

When K. is confident in his understanding of the Castle's role in the strange town, an understanding he believes clarified in conversations since his arrival, he looks at the Castle and sees its shape accordingly: "Now he saw the Castle above, sharply outlined in the clear air and made even sharper by the snow, which traced each shape and lay everywhere in a thin layer"[46] ("Nun sah er oben das Schloß deutlich umrissen in der klaren Luft und noch verdeutlicht durch den alle Formen nachbildenden, in dünner Schicht überall liegenden Schnee"[47]). Now the snow, the very quality that obscured perception the night before, only accentuates the clarity of his vision, marking the distinction between the nearly buried houses of the village and the thinly snow-covered Castle: "on the hill everything soared up, free and light, or at least seemed to from here"[48] ("auf dem Berg ragte alles frei und leicht empor, wenigstens schien es so von hier aus"),[49] lines which through a subtle reversal of word and vowel order recall yet reverse the "scheinbare Leere empor" ("seeming emptiness") of the opening paragraph. These passages, like many in the initial scenes of the novel, markedly eschew copulative verbs for verbs of perception, thus always allowing for K.'s shifting perspective to change the novel's portrayal of spatial relations. On the strength of this apparent loftiness, we learn that "on the whole the Castle, as it appeared from this distance, corresponded to K.'s expectations"[50] ("Im Ganzen entsprach das Schloß, wie es sich hier von der Ferne zeigte, K.'s Erwartungen."[51] Following the paradigm laid out in the first pages (confusion—clarification—disruption), the next sentences immediately call this statement into question. The clarity of vision now afforded K. reveals that the Castle falls into neither of two architectural categories familiar to him: it is neither a "Ritterburg" (hearkening back to the novel's displaced romance structure) nor a "Prunkbau" (a modern and purely residential structure). Instead, it appears to be a mere collection of small buildings, and "had one not known that this was a castle, one could have taken it for a small town" ("hätte man nicht gewußt daß es ein Schloß ist, hätte man es für ein Städtchen halten können")—in short, but for his newly acquired knowledge, the scene might match the amorphousness of his initial impressions.

The Castle tower should (according to his expectations) constitute the organizing principle that determines the hierarchical structure of the Castle, but the only tower visible instead marks a lack of distinction between a church and a domestic dwelling. This lack of distinction apparently fixes K.'s attention as he continues in his approach. His expectations are soon even more firmly disappointed, as he sees that, after all, the Castle is only a little town, "pieced together from village houses" ("aus Dorfhäusern zusammengetragen") distinguished only by the material of their construction, "distinctive only because everything was perhaps built of stone." The firm, clear distinctions which for K. confer value can be found only in the stone masonry—yet even this potential clarity is corrupted by the effect of the crumbling plaster ("der Stein schien abzubröckeln"). The contrast between the expectations conjured by the word "Turm" and the tower he actually sees evokes the image of the absent tower of his past, his homeland, on which those expectations were based:

> The church tower, tapering decisively, without hesitation, straightaway toward the top, capped by a wide roof with red tiles, was an earthly building—what else can we build—but with a higher goal than the low jumble of houses and with a clearer expression than that of the dull workday.[52]

> Jener Turm, bestimmt, ohne Zögern, geradenwegs nach oben sich verjüngend, breitdachig abschließend mit roten Ziegeln, ein irdisches Gebäude—was können wir anderes bauen?—aber mit höherem Ziel als das niedrige Häusergemenge und mit klarerem Ausdruck als ihn der trübe Werktag hat."[53]

There was a comprehensible tower—earthy, but with clear lines reflecting its higher religious purpose, lines which separated this purpose from the confusion of everyday life. The sharpness with which this memory comes into focus in turn produces an even greater dissatisfaction with the castle tower:

> The tower up here—it was the only one in sight—the tower of a residence, as now became evident, possibly of the main Castle, was

> a monotonous round building, in part mercifully hidden by ivy, with little windows that glinted in the sun—there was something crazy about this—and ending in a kind of terrace, whose battlements, uncertain, irregular, brittle, as if drawn by the anxious or careless hand of a child, zigzagged into the blue sky. It was as if some melancholy resident, who by rights ought to have kept himself locked up in the most out-of-the-way room in the house, had broken through the roof and stood up in order to show himself to the world.[54]

> Der Turm hier oben—es war der einzige sichtbare—der Turm eines Wohnhauses, wie sich jetzt zeigte, vielleicht des Hauptschlosses, war ein einförmiger Rundbau, zum Teil gnädig von Epheu verdeckt, mit kleinen Fenstern, die jetzt in der Sonne aufstrahlten—etwas Irrsinniges hatte das—und einem söllerartigen Abschluß, dessen Mauerzinnen unsicher, unregelmäßig, brüchig wie von ängstlicher oder nachlässiger Kinderhand gezeichnet sich in den blauen Himmel zackten. Es war wie wenn irgendein trübseliger Hausbewohner, der gerechter Weise im entlegensten Zimmer des Hauses sich hätte engesperrt halten sollen, das Dach durchbrochen und sich erhoben hätte, um sich der Welt zu zeigen.[55]

Lines are jagged, irrational. Interior and exterior have become confused. The tower now indeed appears—and Mukařovský's rhetoric seems strangely apt—as an "accidental protrusion illogically disturbing the unity of the shape," with "the shape itself . . . unsatisfactorily ambiguous." The series describing K.'s impressions of the tower could serve as a custom-made example of Mukařovský's description of perceptual difficulties. Whatever the function of the Castle, it is clear that it does not match K.'s understanding of what it should be. Again borrowing Mukařovský's logic and rhetoric, if a building is "a set of life processes for which it is the setting,"[56] K.'s confused architectural perception arises from a misunderstanding of the "life processes" which constitute it. Following this logic—which also seems to be the logic of the Castle natives themselves—the functional models against which K. judges the Castle's structure are inappropriate to its actual social function. K. believes himself to understand the Castle's function and the "life processes for which it is the setting" following his encounters with "natives" at the inn, but this ill-founded belief only intensifies his feelings of disorientation and confusion. His attempts to align his perceptions of unfamiliar social and physical structures with his own prior knowledge and experience of the world outside likewise fail: in addition to the church tower of his youth, the fortifications of a "Ritterburg" or medieval castle also contribute to his expectations. Both church and castle represent varieties of male patriarchal rule. As Mukařovský discusses, in Gothic times, both "Burg" (castle) and, somewhat later, the Gothic cathedral were the dominant architectural forms that corresponded to the dominant social institutions that housed them. In fact, their presence—potentially independent of size, population, or geographical importance—conferred "city" status. They not only performed and signified their function, but also signified and produced a particular political status and organization. These earlier architectural forms, however, are historically and functionally out of step with the term "Schloß." In fact, as Mukařovský also notes, the "Schloß" did not emerge as a dominant architectural form until the Renaissance, when it was designed to perform the dual function of residence for the landed gentry and administrative seat for the surrounding estates and villages.[57] Despite this clear precedent, however, K. is particularly disturbed that this "Schloß's" tower emerges from a "Wohnhaus" (residence or dwelling) although such a relation is by no means at odds with the function of a "Schloß." In K.'s outmoded estimation, the political or religious significance that a tower ought to represent should be clearly separated from the "Wohnhaus." Thus K.'s perceptual dysfunction may also be seen in historico-linguistic terms: he is using the architectural terms and grammar of an inappropriate, bygone era—insisting on reading as Gothic a term (*Schloß*) that demands Baroque. His everyday language may simply be out of date—as might happen when, as in the case of the Czech National Revival, you decide to base your official language *not* on the "everyday speech" of the peasants still speaking it, but on texts that were several hundred years old—resulting in an enormous gap between written and spoken Czech usage and even grammar that persists to this day.

K. elsewhere looks back with nostalgia for his life outside the Castle. One attraction it seems to hold for him is the relative clarity with which social and architectural lines were drawn, as evident in his nostalgia for the cemetery wall that is likely associated with the same unambiguously upright tower he now recalls. The teacher, whose appearance on the scene intervenes in K.'s reverie, proceeds to describe K.'s situation: "Are you looking at the Castle?" ("Ihr sehet das Schloß an?"). K. answers in the affirmative, offering his habitual explanation, "I am a stranger here" ("ich bin hier fremd"). From this the teacher immediately deduces (correctly) that K. does not like the Castle—"Strangers never like it" ("Keinem Fremden gefällt es"). This comment similarly follows Mukařovský's phenomenological description, according to which K. could not possibly like the Castle because it will not display the compatibility of shape and purpose traditionally associated with aesthetic "liking," since as an outsider, he cannot understand what that purpose is. It would seem, then, that stranger status precludes, rather than inaugurates, aesthetic experience—which would seem to be in contradiction with the early Prague School alignment of defamiliarization, poesis, and aesthetic experience which Mukařovský later expands to apply to nonverbal media. On closer examination, however, Mukařovský's passage describing the "unsatisfactory" ambiguity of the "irrational protrusion" involves a viewer seeking not aesthetic experience, but functional comprehensibility.

Structuralist theory casts "aesthetic function" as the interruption or absence of utilitarian function via a disruption of expectations about the relationship of form to function. This disruption focuses the viewer's attention on form and materiality as such. K.'s view of the Castle might be construed, then, as aesthetic experience in this modern sense of disrupted functionality. K., however, does not merely want to *experience* such disruption, even if he were able to identify it with aesthetic experience; he wants himself to produce it. K. wants clear lines to violate—he wants to understand the terms of the violation and be in control of it—not just to stray in strangeness and be perpetually surprised by incomprehensibility.

Chapter 5

✦

Reading Klam(m)

Immer M. oder nicht M., aber ein Prinzip
—Kafka, *Tagebücher*, 1921

KHA is the barrier between killer and victim, wolf, downpour and man, between cold and body, frost and comfort. EM is the division of volume, by knife and aim, into a multitude of small parts. Khlam (junk)—the principle of comfort destroyed.
—Velimir Khlebnikov

"Note," as Jakobson reminds us in the 1921 essay published in *Kmen* (an essay on Velimir Khlebnikov, who also wrote about a character called K. and about the internal divisions of the word *khlam*), "that appellative words—and hence personal names in general—undergo a rich variety of phonetic and formative modifications." Although the Castle world seems to be a single-language population, the castle official Klamm (the official K. tries to meet and whose mistress he steals) is bilingual in the sense that his name operates, like the Kafka-Jesenská relationship, in two languages. That the presence or absence of a single letter changes the linguistic identification of a noun is a common feature of Czech/German philology, the legacy of long-term bilingual occupation of shared and mingled territory, testament to a reality that failed dramatically to fit into the boundaries of a nation-state. Semantically as well as morphologically, the linguistic duality of Klamm's name is particularly common to proper nouns: it echoes the ambiguous ethnic identity of the Skočdopoles/Springenfelds of the Němcová story (Němcová herself, the literary grandmother of the new Czech nation, has a name that means "Mrs. German") as well as of Jesenská's husband, Ernst Pollak (the German Jew whose name in Czech suggests "Polish man," or "polák"), who used both the Czech (Polak) and German spellings of this name until 1938, the distinction turning on the doubled consonant just like his structural descendant Klamm's. The doubled consonant in Klamm is "M."—the notation for Milena in Kafka's diaries. His 1921 entry "Immer M. oder nicht M., aber ein Prinzip" ("always M. or not M, but a principle") refers to Jesenská, but it might equally refer to the principle by which the proper name "Klamm" passes from German into Czech. Reading names interlinguistically was a normal part of Prague life: add a letter, change languages and therefore meanings. Or, just add "K" to turn Milena into an authentically Czech sweetheart. Kafka claimed that only by this insertion does the proper name/word "Milena" become authentically Czech, since "k" renders the diminutive but also sexualizes the name, further transforming the "full," "heavy" "Milena" into the Czech "sweetheart" or "lover" (*milenka*):

> And in regard to Milena, the name has nothing at all to do with Germanness or Jewishness. The people who understand Czech best (apart from Czech Jews, of course) are the gentlemen from *Naše Řeč*, second best the readers of that journal, and third best the subscribers, of which I am one. And as such I say to you that the only thing really Czech about the name Milena is the diminutive: milenka. Whether you like it or not, that is what philology says.[1]

The role of this single letter has powerful ramifications for *The Castle* as well, as "K." enters a new linguistic and cultural context, possibly with the aim of transforming it.

Adding the letter K. was a task actually (literally) performed on the manuscript of the novel; when Kafka decided to shift from first person to third, he crossed out "Ich" and wrote in "K." throughout the first thirty or so pages of the draft. (See figure 7.) The K.s, as a result, dance over the page with a flourish that sets them apart from the other letters; they are marked, separate—foreign, even, to the shapes and rhythms of the other letters. A rendering other—and also, a rendering—at the level of the letter—more personal. A signature, again and again.

The doubling of K. and Klamm is hard to miss: the two exist in a skewed structural mirror and cannot ever meet—Klamm waits for hours in the Herrenhof inn to avoid even being seen by K. Something separates them, though they share a woman and, of course, an initial. This relationship lends itself to a reading of K. as akin to "Klamm," albeit a version missing key parts. Complex visual, semantic, and etymological relations significantly complicate such a reading, however, particularly in terms of suggested gendered and sexual symbolism. The German noun *Klamm* means "ravine or gorge"; the adjectival meaning, "tight, close, narrow" or "numb or stiff with cold," renders an obvious female sexual image either frigid—perhaps virginal—or effects a bizarre blend with the "stiff" male erection. Charles Bernheimer cites the noun *Klammer*, "clamp, bracket, parenthesis," and the verb *klammern*, to "clasp, clinch, clamp."[2] The image of a "narrow, tight," "clasping" "gorge" concentrates physical fears and fantasies about the female sex organ; etymology thus casts doubt on Klamm's potential phallic status. Thus the word's implications are complicated enough in one language: in the split within

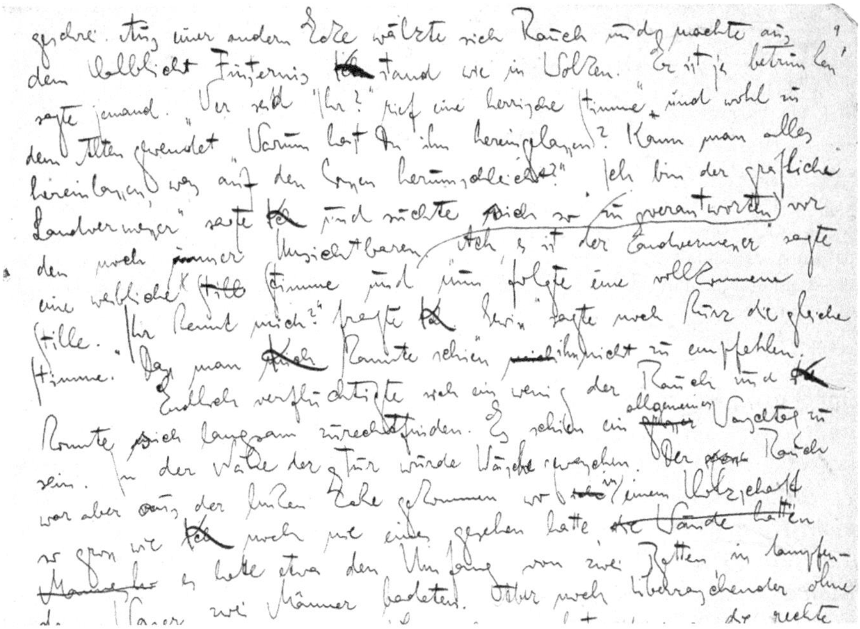

Figure 7. Detail from the Castle notebook showing the Ks written over the first-person pronoun "ich" to change the narrative perspective. MS. Kafka 34 fol. 9r. The Bodleian Library, University of Oxford.

language, that troubling homonymy that also haunts the novel's eponymous "Schloß." Pursuing this strange psychosexual division etymologically, Bernheimer also links the name with Freud's example of the Latin *clam* as a word which can have opposite meanings, the verb *clamare* meaning "to cry" and the adverbial *clam* signifying "softly, quietly, secretly." If a word has opposite meanings, could it be considered deceitful, as Jacques Derrida would later claim? Do such words betray us, revealing the poison in the gift? Certainly Kafka seems to imply something similar here, as in Czech, the near morphologically identical but etymologically unrelated noun *klam* means "illusion," "delusion," or "deceit." The difference is that of one letter, a visual difference only, accessible only through writing: "M. oder nicht M."

What separates K. from Klamm? Letters; writing; a woman: this much we know from the plot of the novel. Reading between languages but within a single word reveals another potential source of separation: an imperative from a foreign grammar. In one instance in the manuscript, the Czech form of the word appears—written by accident, apparently, not for Klamm but rather for K. The "lam" is struck through, leaving K. (See figure 8.)

In Czech, the verb *lámat* (to break) gives—archaically—the familiar imperative *lam!* (break!). If in the Czech word *klam* we perform this imperative on itself and break it off, we are left with K., alone. The Czech

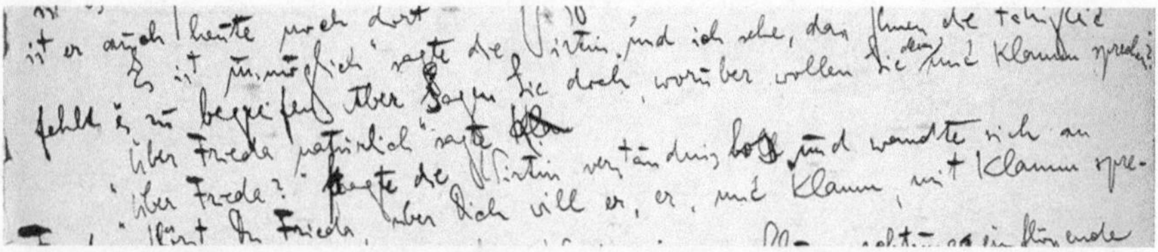

Figure 8. Detail from the Castle notebook. The Landlady has asked K. what he wants to speak to Klamm about and he responds: Über Frieda natürlich, sagte K~~lam~~ (About Frieda naturally, said K~~lam~~). The preceding and following lines of text include "Klamm" with the standard German spelling. MS.Kafka 34 fol 30r. The Bodleian Library, University of Oxford.

imperative, in other words, sunders K. from Klam. Is he thus castrated, or undeceived? Performing the simple imperative *lam!* on the German "Klamm," however, reveals that the Czech familiar, the intimate imperative, separates—"breaks"—the letters "K" and "M," while abstracting the deceitful Czech *klam* from the German "Klamm" leaves M.—alone. Or, if performing an imperative on itself would make a verb reflexive, *lámat se* would render Klamm "refracted"—a fine term to describe the influence of Milena Jesenská throughout *The Castle*, and indeed, to describe the entire novel's overall representational strategy. The languages interpenetrate, intermingle: they do not remain distinct. If "Klamm" is a name "violated by Czech," as Kafka asserts of the name "Milena," what of K.? The single letter "k," in German only a cipher, is a complete word in Czech. It is a preposition, a dative preposition of motion—specifically and exclusively, motion toward something into which one cannot enter.

In a further discussion of Kafka's attention to letters on the page and their potential for play—both visual and aural—Malte Kleinwort offers a meticulous reading of an instance of the phrase "bei K." (with K.). In the clause "schon hatte Frieda das elektrische Licht ausgedreht und war bei K. unter dem Pult" ("Frieda had turned off the electric light and was with K. under the bar"), "bei K." is split off from the rest of its sentence at the bottom recto of the page. Noting that, especially given the habitual period after K., the sentence might have ended with the phrase, Kleinwort argues persuasively that this combination of punctuation and page placement would necessarily have caused an interruption, however momentary, and caused the attention to hover on the phrase both in the course of writing and of revision. The context, furthermore, is K. and Frieda's initial sexual encounter on a tavern room floor—with Klamm (visible through the keyhole) in the next room. The "peculiar combination of intimacy and strangeness" that characterizes the encounter that follows is prefigured in this phrase, "bei K.," which is, as Kleinwort notes, the phonetic equivalent of *bajka* in Czech—the word for "fable." The "Pult" (counter) under which Frieda joins K. and that ends the clause is the identical word in Czech, further suggesting and even encouraging the interlinguistic, homonymic reading. Taking up the suggestion, Kleinwort turns his attention to the first draft of the novel and notes that there, Frieda cries out in response to Klamm's summons that she is "bei K.! bei K.," which is later changed to "Ich bin beim Landvermesser! Ich bin beim Landvermesser!" ("I am with the Land Surveyor! I'm with the Land Surveyor!") Thus originally, the text directed readers to imagine the phrase "bei K." as spoken aloud, suggesting its Czech homonym.[3] Kafka's revisions were often guided by "cutting away" elements he felt were too explicit or obvious; perhaps drawing attention to the interlinguistic aural pun fell into this category for him. Given that Czech had always been more a spoken than a written language for Kafka, it makes sense that much of the interlinguistic play would revolve around aural homonyms.

The exclusively *written* linguistic duality of Klam(m), however, makes it clear that Kafka is also thinking very much in terms of letters on the page and the shifts between languages they can indicate. With this in mind, one might notice that if the phrase "bei K." were read strictly phonetically, adhering to Czech rather than German orthographic rules, it would theoretically yield not *bajka* but *bejk*, a slang diminuitive of *býk* (bull)—or rather, following the punctuation's instruction to pronounce the name of the letter "K." rather than the sound it represents, it yields *bejka*, the word's accusative and genitive singular. *Bejk* might be a fallen sort of "fable"—without the mythic aura ("that's bull"). It is also a companion of the most common Czech slang epithet, *vole*, the vocative of *vůl* (ox—today, used similarly to "dude"). More frequently *bejk* refers to a womanizer (but with a positive connotation), a "horndog" or, as my dictionary gives it, "randy bastard." Unsurprisingly, given its slang prowess, *bejk* is further a specifically spoken form; in spoken Prague Czech (not in Moravia), the long "hard ý" becomes "ej"—departing from the strict phonetic orthography of the standard written language. When the spoken language is represented in writing, as in slang, the spelling must change. "Bei K." is thus a translinguistic homophone (sounds the same, means differently across languages) and a translinguistic homograph (spelled the same, sounds differently across languages)—and both meanings offer commentary on the scene, its characters, and the relationships it depicts. Kleinwort reads the "fable" in *bajka* to refer to fiction, amplifying K.'s status as a potential writer-figure; but on the other hand, he could just be a lying "randy bastard." Czech meanings seem to undercut the characters and their relationships: *klam* is deceit, and "bei K." arguably announces a fable, a horny liar, or his bullshit story.

Does Czech then expose the truth of the coercive male lie, a critique of a system that uses women for sex or as a means of approach to another man? Or is Czech simply over-cynical, putting the worst possible spin on these relationships? Alternatively, does this disruptive ghost of the Czech language in a German text align with the social system of the Castle world in which K. can only ever be foreign? Or does it represent the potential of that world's disruption, its lurking interlinguistic presence constituting the fissure in Klamm's name, exposing the delusional nature of the Castle system, a bilingual "minority literature" of the word? Or, finally, does Czech sunder K. irrevocably from M. by means of a hidden, formally intimate, but ultimately severing Czech imperative ("*lam!*"), the fissures of languages proving too much or too little for them? Just how different, how entirely grammatically and functionally distinct, "k" is from the Czech preposition "v" is appropriately illustrated by the title of an April 1918—pre-Czechoslovak statehood—essay by the graphic designer and architect Vlastislav Hofman (Czech: one "f"; one "n"). The essay is entitled "Země v klamu," "v" being the locative preposition that indicates the state of being within a place: here, the land, or world, or country in delusion, or illusion, or deceit. Exactly what land, and what deceit, is unclear from the title, but what is crystal-clear from the phrase is the spatial relation determined by the single prepositional letter—in isolation—and the grammatical case it governs.

This "double asymmetry" anticipates Sergei Karcevskij's later discussion of the doubly asymmetrical linguistic sign: every sign is potentially a homonym and a synonym, and "a single sign always has several functions, and a single signification is always expressed by several signs."[4] For Karcevskij, a student of Saussure, the meaning of a sign at any given time is constituted by these intersections. The differential (rather than fixed or unitary) nature of the linguistic sign is paramount and requires both resemblance and difference. Both homonymic and synonymic series are open, "for it is impossible to predict where a given sign will be carried in the play of associations." It is context, the concrete situation of individual use, that fixes meaning—complicated enough even if Karcevskij assumes, as all Prague School theory does, a single language that is equally and spontaneously comprehensible to a community of speakers, all of whom must constantly negotiate general communicable meaning and individual expression. But a bilingual situation brings the other language "series" also in play, particularly for the nonnative, conversant speaker (fully bilingual people experience less interaction between languages than highly conversant, even fluent speakers). The Czech meanings of these homophones/homographs, furthermore, are relevant to the Castle system (the general) and the individual situations in which they are used, but these meanings serve less as referent than as commentary.

This double asymmetry encapsulates and doubles the novel's title and central structure, its core problem, and that of languages. Stanley Corngold comments on homonymies as follows:

> For modern semanticists homonymies are "invalids" giving rise to "pathological conflicts"; Kafka gives gainful employment to these martyrs of reason. Thus "Das Schloss" (The Castle) also means "the lock" and is related to various verbs expressing the idea of closure, of walled-aroundness; its hero, the "Landvermesser," is a "country

> surveyor," furthermore, "a materialist mis-measurer," but also—by suggestion—"a hubristic lout."[5]

Thus language dictates that a surveyor be a mismeasurer and a lout—and both these secondary meanings are arguably quite true of K. as he spies, lurks, has sex with his employer's mistress on a barroom floor, and then dallies with her rivals. This sense of "Landvermesser" would be amplified by *bejka*, the interlinguistic pun it replaces in Frieda's announcement of their union, but "Landvermesser" gets there on its own secondary meaning. Yet if, as I have been reading him, K. is a "non-native" speaker of Castle language, such secondary meanings are precisely those he might well fail to understand and anticipate, although everyone around him seems to expect him to both mismeasure and act loutishly. Or to be constitutionally unable, as "k," to do more than approach the Castle. As Michelle Woods points out, this very topic of secondary meanings in second language comes up in Kafka's comments on Milena Jesenská's translations.[6] And the notion of foreign speakers is a part of the novel's conception from the very outset; a fragmentary sketch of the idea that will become *The Castle*, predating the 1922 draft by six years, makes this question of language explicit: "'He's a stranger,' says a native of the visiting narrator, 'he's hanging around for no reason, look at him.' He spoke of me as if I were deaf or did not understand his language."[7] Perhaps the man was right—or at least right in thinking the visitor does not understand his language *as a native*. "It is easy for things to seem queer when you are a stranger," explains this proto-K. Indeed—but in this world, that is our fixed perspective; there is "an infinite amount of native language—but not for us."

Negotiating linguistic difficulty of a different kind has, of course, long been the territory of Kafka scholarship. Analyses of the linguistic or rhetorical (as opposed to thematic or representational) generative origin of Kafka's fictions accounted for much of the critical literature of the 1970s and '80s. This primacy of language is also central to my argument, but I contend rather that this very primacy brings the text closer to, rather than further away from, events and relations in the extra-fictional biographical and historical "real world" of Kafka's Czechoslovak Prague. When Scott Spector writes of the overall experience of Brod's anachronistically defined circle of German Jewish writers, the floating structures he describes—located firmly in tangible politics, daily papers, elections, publications—seem at one with the precariousness Kafka identifies as the peculiar provenance of metaphor: both describe a structure that is itself stable, but whose orientation is subject to change at any minute and whose position is indeed unchartable—yet of the utmost importance to be navigated precisely.

Chapter 6

✦

F:M

(The Correspondence with Jesenská)

> M. means the disintegration of a certain quantity into infinitely small parts . . . equal as a whole to the original quantity.
>
> —Velimir Khlebnikov

> "Why do you torture me so?" he asked with difficulty.
> "We aren't torturing you," said the girl. "You want something from us and we don't know what it is. Speak openly with me and I will answer you openly."
>
> —*The Castle* manuscript, alternative beginning

On August 1, 1920, Milena Jesenská published an article on bathing suits. (See figure 9.) Franz Kafka was almost desperately delighted. A dedicated swimmer, he was sure to see himself in the piece:

> There are two kinds of people: those who go swimming to exercise, for the delight of cool waters, for whom the river is a great joy, for whom the clouds in the sky, the waves in the water and the warm air are worlds in and of themselves. They swim with long strokes, they swim on their backs, they swim under water, they jump in the water, they caress and flatter the waves and are happy in them. They would most like to swim naked, water is their element, sun is their element, nakedness is good, joyful. But, since it's not permitted and isn't possible, they'll need to put on clothes.

For these people, she recommends close-fitting, simple black swimwear that won't restrict movement and will cover the body only where absolutely necessary. But there are other people:

> The others: These are the ones who swim in the water without panting or sputtering. They don't even keep their chins underwater all the

> time—no, they swim in a well-mannered fashion, their bodies stand in the water like poles with weights at the bottom. Their shoulders are out of the water, not even a hair gets wet. This swimming has nothing to do with sport or exercise, but only by chance do such people manage to keep themselves above water and not sink.[1]

Kafka responds the same day. He's had a nightmare about Milena rejecting him, which was worse because she did it while wearing too much powder and sitting next to a Dostoevsky doppelgänger. It sounds awful. And then, the delight of the fashion column. Jesenská has apparently told him not to buy the newspaper, but Kafka pleads he's borrowed it from his (Czech) brother-in-law: "The *Tribuna* is lying in front of me. . . . Please grant me this pleasure." At first he says he doesn't even care what it says because he hears "the voice, my voice" ("ich höre die Stimme, meine Stimme!")—her voice that has become his own.[2] At this point, he has spent time with her in Vienna and knows what her actual voice sounds like, but he always writes of hearing her written Czech, and it has always been an embodied, sensual experience for him. Here he comments on this phenomenon: "I don't know how it happens, after all I only read it with my eyes, how did my blood find out so quickly," suddenly running hot.[3] All this from the experience of hearing, and then seeing (or so he sequences it), Jesenská's Czech prose. The prose is flanked by a lingerie ad and itself comments on bodies in various degrees of nakedness, but her writing is always bodily for him, it *is* the source of his excitement. As for this piece, he finds it "beautiful," even "funny" ("lustig"), a rare but sincere compliment from him. He may, in fact, recognize "his [own] voice," because he certainly recognizes himself in it:

> Naturally I belong to the second group; this weight on the feet is really my own property and I do not at all consent to the publication of matters of mine which are strictly private; someone once said I swim like a swan, although it is no compliment. But it is exciting. I feel like a giant who's keeping the public away from you with outstretched arms—it's difficult for him, he's supposed to hold the public back but, at the same time, doesn't want to miss a single word or a single second of seeing you.[4]

This representation of what for him is an intensely personal experience now appears under the title "Fashion" ("Móda") alongside advertisements for "fine ladies' underwear" and carpets and curtains.[5]

The frisson of public-private tension is a hallmark of his discussions of her journalistic writing. He imagines her audience (female, he specifies) complaining that it takes her too long to get to the fashion in this column, that it is all only Milena: "Only, and I am living off this Only" ("Es ist 'nur' Milena. Nur, und von diesem Nur lebe ich"). In another way it is our "Only" as

Moda.

Plavky.

Maximilian Weiner,
jemné dámské prádlo a výbavy.
Originální modely blůz.
Telefon 1906. Praha, Václavské nám. 19.

KOBERCE - ZÁCLONY
JAN STOUPA
PRAHA II., JINDŘISSKÁ ULICE ČÍS. 1.

Divadlo a hudba.

Cyklistika.

Figure 9. Milena Jesenská, "Plavky" (Bathing Suits), cropped with advertisements. *Tribuna*, August 1, 1920. Collection of the National Museum, Prague, Czech Republic.

well. For us, the uninvited readership of these intensely personal letters, these moments in which Jesenská includes or evokes Kafka in her public columns are the only remnants of Jesenská's side of the correspondence, the voice Kafka heard and found so moving. Kafka *does* clearly find the public-private breach exciting, even titillating, but he is at the same time bothered by it. He is used to reading women—his correspondence with Felice Bauer spanned years, and he had many other women correspondents—but he is less used to reading women *in print* or *in Czech*. That is, he has had many women write to him, but none of them were professional writers.

The correspondence constituted Kafka's most intimate encounter with Czech as a written language, as well as his most sustained engagement with a woman writer—and arguably his most intimate relationship with a woman, at least in terms of its intensity. When Kafka implied in an early letter that Czech was a language of greater warmth for him ("herzlich"), it suggests associations of spoken or physical intimacy—and any prior relationships he had with Czech women were domestic (servants) or sexual (casual liaisons). But Jesenská brought the Czech language, women, writing, and sexuality together, as well as bringing Kafka's own prose into Czech. Categories long separate were now "on the same page" for him, both figuratively and literally. An epistolary courtship was hardly new territory for Kafka, given his long and agonizing correspondence with his former fiancée Felice Bauer, but Jesenská's sustained interest in Kafka's writing, her intimate involvement with it as translator, and Kafka's genuine respect for her own professional writing distinguishes this relationship from all previous affairs. Certainly he finds their textual intimacy erotic, an effect heightened by fantasies of power exchange:

> What is particularly beautiful about your translation, that it is faithful (scold me on account of this "faithful"—I know you can do everything, but maybe you scold best of all, I'd like to be your pupil and constantly make mistakes so you would constantly scold me; I'm sitting at my desk, scarcely daring to look up, you are bent over me and your index finger is always glittering over me, finding fault, isn't it so?).[6]

Drawn from a letter dated May 30, 1920, this extraordinary passage nests an eager fantasy of teacher-student discipline between references to fidelity—in translation. This confusion of textual and physical bodies, however, belies the almost exclusively textual nature of their affair—an affair possibly never fully consummated sexually, and indeed only rarely interspersed with face-to-face meetings. And yet they saw each other as lovers—the textual and the sexual thereby becoming all the more entangled. This entanglement intensifies Kafka's discomfort when occasionally, in Jesenská's print writings, the language of intimacy that Kafka recognizes from their correspondence turns out to be the language she is speaking, or rather, writing, to the world at large. Akin to K.'s interpreting the "Schloß" in terms of an inappropriate architectural grammar, both correspondents struggle with signification and interpretation when it seems unclear exactly which language, that is, which register and frame of reference, they are conversing in: The intimate? The public? The letter? The newspaper?

The life circumstances of both correspondents could not have been better calibrated to heighten such linguistic sensitivity, or to render each more fascinating to the other. Kafka was a German-speaker based in the dominantly Czech-speaking capital of a newly established Czech-speaking republic (although during the first months of the correspondence, he was convalescing in a sanatorium in Meran, Italy). Jesenská was a Czech-speaker married to a German-speaker and living in the German-speaking capital of a newly crumbled empire, from which she was writing articles for a Czech-language Prague newspaper. Independently of their bilingual relationship, both Kafka and Jesenská had ample reason to be actively aware of the problems posed by the question of languages, of the problems of relying professionally and personally on one's ability as a non-native speaker. The circumstances of the correspondence could only amplify such awareness; although both wrote in their native tongues, they were not reading in them, and the letters are replete with misunderstandings arising from this particular problem of languages, compounding difficulties inherent in the communicative potential of language in general terms.

Because we have only one half of this correspondence, and because only one of the correspondents went on to become a globally influential cultural force, most readers experience the letters as a single-authored text. Kafka's responses and quotations, along with Jesenská's journalism from the period—as well as her translations, as Michelle Woods has demonstrated—constitute the only traces of her side of the correspondence, but they are eloquent traces, enough to make it clear that her letters were extensive and obsessive as well. And Jesenská had every reason to be hungry for exactly the kind of intellectual and emotional intensity that Kafka could offer her. Her personal life prior to her involvement with Kafka left her well-versed in various problems of intimacy and estrangement, including their uneasy cohabitation in similar linguistic forms, a concern she takes up in her own writing. Her family situation, education, upbringing, and early adult life left her painfully aware of the role language plays in demarcating inclusion in or exclusion from a given community. Jesenská's heritage and upbringing would also have given her an intimate familiarity with national political history and contemporary Czech nationalism—as well as with the antisemitism that sometimes accompanied it, which she actively rebelled against.

Jesenský Family Politics: Intended and Unintended Consequences of Women's Education

Jesenská's (purported) martyred ancestor Jan Jesenský (Jesenius) is an icon of Czech intellectual history and of the Hussite wars, but his life prior to his death on Old Town Square in 1621 (in front of Kafka's future home) also exemplifies the difficulty of tracing a consistent national identity in terms of map, language, or affiliation—even in the case of a famous Czech patriot.[7] Certainly Milena Jesenská's father claimed this ancestry, although it is not clear on what grounds, as Jesenius does not seem to have had a son, and of his adoptive daughter, little is known after her father's death. Even should this claimed lineage prove accurate—and it certainly seems to have been widely accepted during Milena's father's lifetime—Jesenius himself had a typically central European, that is to say multinational and multiethnic, intellectual and ethnic history. Jesenius was of Slovak and/or Hungarian (Magyar) heritage, was born in Wroclaw (then Breslau) in what is now Poland, referred to himself as a "Hungarian knight," and died a Czech martyr. During his lifetime he was physician to a Saxon prince, medical consultant to Emperor Rudolf II, a good friend of the Danish astronomer Tycho Brahe (about whom Max Brod would write an important historical novel), rector of Prague's Charles University, diplomat for the Bohemian Estates (the Bohemian Protestant nobles who briefly succeeded in rebelling against the Habsburgs), and finally, one of twenty-six rebels executed after the Battle of White Mountain—the watershed from which nineteenth- and twentieth-century Czech revivalists and nationalists dated the beginning of their nation's linguistic, cultural, and political subjugation. So it is rather by his later life and particularly the manner of his death that Jesenský became Czech—neither mode being a means by which any Austrian imperial or Czechoslovak census would ask after such identification.

Nonetheless, this Czech lineage—whatever its accuracy or its national origins—was embraced by Jesenská's father and by her aunt, the writer Růžena Jesenská, who was also intensely and actively nationalist. Known in the 1890s for her Decadent poems and plays, in the early years of the twentieth century Růžena Jesenská edited a magazine for Czech women and also frequently contributed to journals and newspapers, among them *Venkov*, the venomously anti-German and antisemitic organ of the ultra-nationalist Czech Agrarian Party. Women were in fact consistently prominent figures in the nationalist movement, and Milena Jesenská's education itself was arguably a product of Czech nationalism.

The progressive education Jan Jesenský provided his daughter was rare for women in central Europe. Founded in 1890, Milena's school, Minerva, was the first Gymnasium in the Austro-Hungarian Empire devoted to the project of women's education, and it was founded with a nationalist project in mind. (In a prominent example of the symbolic importance of women to the Czech nationalist, progressivist cause, Tomáš Garrigue Masaryk took his middle name from his wife's family name.) It was widely understood that women were to play a crucial role in strengthening the Czech nation and language, and so Czech daughters must have a modern Czech education which they might pass on as mothers to the children of a modern Czech state.[8] If "Minervistky," as the Gymnasium graduates were called, were to raise the nation's children, they were also meant to live in the world and have an impact on it. In their modern education as in their language, girls from Minerva were to exemplify the contrast between the active women of a progressive Czech nation and what were considered to be the backward-thinking, strictly traditional gender roles adhered to in the Bohemian German and German Jewish communities.

Lived reality, of course, provided exceptions to such nationalist generalizations. German-speaking girls could sometimes attend Gymnasium with the boys as "private students"; the German medical school in Prague admitted women before the Czech school, and Kafka himself attended a prominent Prague philosophical salon hosted by the German-speaking Berta Franta. Nonetheless, it is incontestable that women writers occupied a more central and prominent position in nineteenth- and early twentieth-century Czech letters than in German literature of the same period.[9] Not only was the most celebrated nineteenth-century novelist Božena Němcová a woman, but writers such as Karolina Svetlá (who, like Němcová, was raised bilingually and educated in German) and Eliška Krásnohorská were also central figures in the women's movement and instrumental in improving educational and economic opportunities for Czech women—including, in Krásnohorská's case, the founding of the Minerva school. Krásnohorská wrote popular books for girls, translated literary works from Polish, Russian, and English, and wrote a number of critical essays, thus serving as an immediate model of intellectual activity for her pupils. Jesenská herself would have had to look no further than her own family to find such a model, or a model of a more flamboyant kind, for that matter—although her aunt Růžena was by the end of her life a prominent nationalist, her youthful Decadent writings were still notorious for their violent sexuality and lesbianism.

Some of these women writers—the aunt, Němcová, and the dramatist and Janáček librettist Gabriela Preissová—were certainly familiar to Kafka, because he mentions them in his journals or correspondence. However, it is also true that throughout most of his life and in most of his fiction, Kafka associated women with the domestic and the sexual, which occupy an opposite, even antagonistic, space that is distinct from the life of writing. It is not that he hadn't tried to include Felice Bauer in this world—not as writer, but as reader and responder to *his* writing—but she did not respond to his early gift of "The Judgment." Devastated by her silence on the matter, Kafka grew intensely jealous of her other reading material. Indeed, his letters to Felice are full of these anxieties about what their marriage might mean for his writing, as are his related journal entries: taken together these form a fantastic narrative of courtship incompatibility, with Felice apparently worrying over upholstery swatches as Kafka writes her of his plans to live in a cellar and have his meals left at the door. These letters place Kafka's conflict with the female and domestic in a stark light, and Felice, with her typically bourgeois interests and concerns over apartments, furniture, finance, and family, appears irreconcilably at odds with Kafka's inner world. Furthermore, for most of his life, there was little to suggest that Kafka did much to counteract this paradigm in which women occupied the domestic and bodily in opposition to the writing life by, for example, seeking out and reading women writers. In the extensive journals he kept until giving them to Jesenská, women do not figure as intellectual or writerly influences. Almost the only women writers Kafka mentions with anything but horror were Czech, and this only after 1918—his loathing for Else Lasker-Schüler (the woman, her poetry, and her prose) is profound and unusual enough for Reiner Stach to include an entry in his volume of "finds" entitled "Kafka Doesn't Like Else Lasker-Schüler."[10] Jesenská, as Kafka early acknowledged, challenged the accumulated assumptions of a lifetime.

This intertwining of gender and national roles and identities in the figure of the Czech woman writer not only had broad cultural currency, but had demonstrable effects on Kafka's thinking as well as on Jesenská's. Both correspondents, however, also resisted complete identification with their inherited ethnic groups and families. Kafka's attitude toward his Jewish identity was often ambivalent, while his difficult relationship with his own overbearing father is legend (and chronicled in excruciating detail in his famous intercepted letter to his father). Yet of the two correspondents, Jesenská was by far the more outwardly defiant and rebellious. Whatever the nationalist aims of her school at its founding, by the time Jesenská attended it, her biographer Alena Wagnerová claims, most Minerva students saw school as more a space of increased freedom *from* rather than increased duty *to* home or nation. These students were drawn from notable professional families and in their own right came to constitute a specifically female Czech intellectual elite, although their prominence and comparative wildness also earned them their own street rhyme (the untranslatable punning "Dívky z Minervy, nervi mi nervy," literally "Minerva girls, don't get on my nerves").[11] "Minervistky" studied ancient and modern languages and philosophy, and many of them did not want to forgo these topics of discussion or the freedom they'd found in their teens upon graduation. Jesenská and her friends, for example, frequented the Arco—a café-home to the German Jewish intelligentsia—in Milena's case because her education had given her a taste for discussing Dostoevsky and Kierkegaard, and that was where she found others who shared this taste. She then openly slept with the German Jewish lover, Ernst Pollak, whom she met there—much to her father's dismay. She was also known for petty thievery, running up debts, and giving her friends drugs from her father's medical supplies, but it was the Jewish lover that precipitated her father's committing her to a mental institution, very much against her will. Yet such relationships were hardly the oddities that Jesenská's father's extreme reaction might seem to suggest. It apparently became so common in Prague for educated Czech women to date German Jewish intellectuals that Pavel Eisner could write *Milenky* (*Sweethearts*), a study devoted to the phenomenon, a few years later.[12] In part such relationships can be explained by the titillation of sexual dalliance across an ethnic and religious divide, but the "Minervistky," whatever their deserved reputation for wildness, had serious intellectual interests and were drawn by the possibility of intellectual discussion, and this was certainly true of Jesenská.

Upon coming of age, and thus being able to release herself from the mental institution where her father had put her, Jesenská eloped with her lover and moved to Vienna, with the result that her father largely disowned her and cut her off economically. Postwar Vienna was beset by high inflation, food shortages, and tremendous poverty. Jesenská's journalism from this period reflects some of these conditions, but it took a while for her to begin writing it. Her life in Vienna was very far from what she was used to. Pollak, despite sharing his wife's interests in writing and the life of the mind, did little to include her after marriage in his Viennese intellectual (or sexual) life, and although he may have felt threatened by it since his own output was minimal, he never took her writing seriously. Having been a bright young thing in Prague, prominent if somewhat infamous, Jesenská was now known only as Ernst Pollak's young Czech wife. She was lonely, desperately poor, and personally had little option but to watch her husband's open affairs and field the blatant advances of his friends. Wagnerová connects this promiscuous atmosphere with the opinions of the Freud pupil Otto Gross, who saw sexual relations as a form of communication between the sexes, advocated the radical revision of what he saw as obsolete and oppressive moral and familial norms in favor of a new matriarchal order—and was himself institutionalized by his own father, Hans Gross, a noted criminologist and also Kafka's former professor. The case was much publicized and elicited support, and so Jesenská would have had even more reason to be sympathetic to Otto's theories, given their biographical parallels. Gross also suffered from mental illness and severe morphine addiction and died in early 1920, not long before Kafka and Jesenská began writing each other. Kafka had known him slightly, and so he came up in the correspondence, Kafka describing a night train journey during which Gross analyzed a Bible passage at great length, interrupting his disquisition occasionally by shooting up and nodding.[13] Malte Kleinwort even connects *The Castle* child Hans and his father Otto Brunswick with Hans and Otto Gross—a refracted reversal in keeping with the novel's representational relationship to Jesenská and her world.[14] Certainly Gross's theories were much discussed and practiced among the Vienna café denizens, including those at the Herrenhof, where Pollak and his circle were most often to be found.[15] Jesenská herself subscribed to Gross's ideas about sexual morality, but she found the selective adoption of them by her husband's friends to be coercive and oppressive, and soon came to view the café scene that espoused them with cynicism. This cynicism comes through in her depiction of that world.

Disowned by her father and marginalized by her husband and her less-than-fluent German, Jesenská nonetheless soon began to carve out a new identity for herself as a journalist, contributing fashion columns and feuilletons about life in Vienna to the Czech dailies. Scenes from everyday life had been a popular Czech genre since at least the nineteenth century—much of Božena Němcová's oeuvre falls into this category—and while nineteenth-century vignettes had tended to focus on rural and village life, the feuilleton spaces focused on life in the city, following the French tradition from which the feuilleton took its name. Jesenská's columns from Vienna—no longer the capital of any state her Prague readers were citizens of—give the sense of shedding light on a city that is at once old and familiar as well as new and quite fallen. Yet the urban imagery and characters suggest a common postwar, urban culture, a shared experience of poverty, shortages, profiteering, and cynicism. Bridging the cultural and linguistic (and no doubt financial) gaps from another angle, Jesenská also began to try her hand at translation—in fact, this project provided her entry to *Tribuna* at her friend Staša Jílovská's suggestion. As Michelle Woods explains in her excellent *Kafka Translated*, women were at the forefront of what was understood as the new Czech nation's "duty" to translate; Jílovská herself had been encouraged to translate by the publisher Josef Florian, who would later go on to publish translations of Kafka in book form.[16] Jesenská's output at this time was considerable; in addition to her columns, she translated not only from German, but also from English, French, and Russian (some of these last, perhaps, from German translation; the record is not entirely clear). Jesenská's career benefited from the wave of internationalism that characterized left-leaning Prague journals and newspapers at that time, and which offered some respite from the various strains of national and linguistic chauvinism that otherwise were causing such trouble in her life. As part of this project, she approached Kafka about translating several of his stories, and so began their mutual textual fascination.

In "The Coffeehouse"

Although Kafka and Jesenská had earlier met in the Arco, this physical meeting made little impression on either one. Their real relationship began and ended in writing, a key difference distinguishing it both from their own prior involvements and from the Prague trend of interethnic dalliance they might seem to be part of. Even Kafka's tortured, tortuous correspondence with Felice Bauer had been inspired by his initial impression of her personally, and women for him generally were strongly associated with domesticity and the life of the body, both aspects of life he felt his writing life constrained him to sacrifice. Jesenská, however, initiated the correspondence with Kafka by expressing an interest in his writing—significant for Kafka, who had been so stung by Bauer's lack of response to "The Judgment"—and specifically an interest in translating his German writing into Czech: for Kafka, unprecedented. The ensuing progression toward intimacy was compulsively textual. They wrote each other in every conceivable meaning this could have. She wrote his writing, in a sense, into Czech with "a fidelity," he says, he "had not believed possible."

This interlinguistic literary relation inaugurated their intensive, obsessive, at times more than daily exchange of letters, with each letter also serving as a reading of the other's writing, and then a reading of the reading, and so on. The rapport was not restricted to their intimate correspondence. In a little-noted fact of literary history, Franz Kafka became a compulsive reader of Czech fashion columns. Jesenská wrote him in her feuilletons, incorporated and revised his images, and transformed Kafka himself into image and meditated on aspects of his personality, either as private jokes or as more serious critique. Kafka read and understood these allusions, as the commentary from his letters makes clear.

One such allusion derives from Jesenská's August 1920 feuilleton "Kavárna" ("The Coffeehouse").[17] Like her nineteenth-century predecessor Němcová and Kafka's later novel, Jesenská portrays social relations in terms of architectural space, but she also contextualizes this space in terms of shifts in the dominance and social function of buildings, thus offering a mediating term between the poles of Němcová's clarity and *The Castle*'s disorientation:

> People used to mingle at the forum, mingle at the monastery, mingle in salons. Today there are no forums, no monasteries in this sense, nor even salons that serve this purpose. Today there are coffeehouses. I don't mean those genteel coffeehouses where mothers take their little girls on Sunday afternoons or people go to drink hot chocolate or eat a few *kolatches*. I don't even mean the ones that during the day are tired, grey, drowsy, and come alive at night with a band, a few girls wearing makeup, some "soldiers of fortune," and a red lantern hung from the gable.
>
> I mean these so-called "literary" coffeehouses, the famous coffeehouses known throughout the city as gathering places for the intellectual and bohemian worlds, like the Prague "Union," the Vienna "Central," the Berlin "Westens," the Paris "Montmartre." Coffeehouses with quite a singular existence that no one understands until they have penetrated it to the bottom, until they have breathed a good lungful of its air.[18]

Jesenská begins by describing a shift away from social spaces that themselves signified a social, political, or religious unity of purpose: the same shift (from *Burg* or cathedral to *Schloß*) that would so confuse K. on viewing the Castle. A central concern of that novel is thus immediately manifest in this earlier feuilleton with which Kafka was so taken. Jesenská's stress on the social nature of architectural types also recalls Němcová, whom Kafka had already suggested as Jesenská's precedent early on in the correspondence. What defines these coffeehouses is the people that frequent them and what they do there. Here, much like Němcová, Jesenská provides a primer for the uninitiated, articulating the various social strata of café society and identifying its inhabitants by category:

> The first among the guests are the "great ones." Those who already have a name for themselves in the official world, those who are the glory of the coffeehouse, whose pictures and caricatures hang on the walls of the place and who, when they come, sit around the table like capitalists of the spirit and only a precious few are allowed to sit with them.[19]

Somewhat below these café "officials" in rank come what Jesenská calls the "real basis of café life—even "café air"—the journalists and aspiring literati, and below these, "mainly, mainly the crowd of 'castaways,' . . . people who will never get anywhere and will never be good for anything, heroes of resignation and quiet melancholy of whom the world knows nothing and will never learn" ("hlavně, hlavně zástup trosečníku, . . . lidé, kteří nikdy nikam nedojdou a kteří nikdy ničeho nezmohou, hrdinných resignovaných a tichých melancholiků, o nichž svět neví a nikdy se nedozví"). Without directly naming it, Jesenská equally describes Vienna's Herrenhof, the coffeehouse frequented by Jesenská's husband and the namesake of the *Castle* inn where K. first seduces Frieda away from Klamm. Jesenská's coffeehouses share more than a name with Kafka's Castle world: the officials, their hierarchies of influence, their exchanges of documents and women, and even their portraits seem of a piece.

For Jesenská, "the most remarkable thing is the collective life. . . . The whole community, its laws, its jargon. That is what is so closed off and separate from the entire rest of the world." This social grammar—explicitly the "laws" and "jargon"—fascinates Jesenská as it did Němcová before and Kafka after her. But unlike Němcová, Jesenská speaks of irreducible strangeness and exclusivity; the feuilleton's reader is not embraced into the collective but given a guided tour, and in this Jesenská comes closer to Castle logic. The atmosphere will retain its strangeness, cafés will keep their "singular existence that no one understands until they have penetrated it to the bottom"—as if to really see it, you must be of it. In this way, too, the coffeehouse resembles the Castle. "Kavárna" gets at the crux of the matrices of gender, sexuality, language, and identity that Jesenská seems to have so destabilized for Kafka and that he, in turn, destabilized in the Castle world. Like Castle women—literally, like the village girl whom Olga passed among the Herrenhof grooms, like Frieda moving from Klamm to K. to K.'s assistants—the women of the café circulate, "move slowly from table to table, whether single, unfaithful in marriage or divorced. In the end they belong to the coffeehouse, lose their surnames and are called only nicknames of their Christian nicknames." Their linguistic aspect is in decline, and the articulated differences and specificity entailed in the Christian-surname combination are reduced to mere ciphers, abbreviated signs of familiarity, abstracted from any familial or religious resonance.

Like the intensely linguistically attuned relationship in which it arose, Jesenská's text engages closely but problematically with the notion of a common language so central to *The Castle*. The Kafka-Jesenská correspondence itself is not conducted in a common language: the correspondents make forays into the language of the other but by and large remain in their own. Yet Jesenská and Kafka seem, for a time, to create a private realm, a linguistic space in which—in two languages—Kafka literally begins to see letters fall from his name, signs fall away, having become superfluous through the wonders of an intimate and hence common language: common only to them. In the course of the early stages of the correspondence, Kafka's signature similarly drops letters, devolving from "Ihr F Kafka" to "Kafka" to "Ihr FranzK" (from which Jesenská derives the nickname "Frank") to "Ihr F" to "F" to simply "Dein" ("Yours"), at which point he remarks "(now I'm even losing my name—it was getting shorter and shorter all the time and is now: Yours.)"[20] In Kafka's logic, the dropping of letters—the decrease in the presence of actual linguistic material—signifies increasing intimacy; the increasing particularization of context renders possible a reduction of verbal matter. Furthermore, the more private the context, the more universal (potentially) the signs become, a reduction in particularity rendered possible by and also indicating the diminished potential frame of reference; we are left ultimately without even initials, without even the vestiges of personal names, but only with a grammatical sign ("Dein") to indicate the intimacy of the context.

Yet Jesenská takes up this notion and transposes it in her feuilleton "Kavárna," writing to Kafka (as several private jokes make clear) in the *newspapers*, as she occasionally did. One such joke—Jesenská's phrase "capitalist of the spirit" ("kapitalista ducha"), plays on Kafka's earlier characterization of Franz Werfel as a "capitalist of the airspace" ("Kapitalist Luftraums," which would translate into Czech as "kapitalista vzduchu"). Even without Jesenská's half of the correspondence, it is clear that she was critical of Werfel and furthermore called him fat, and that Kafka is defending his friend. Jesenská goes on to link "Kapitalist Luftraums" to a more tangible form of capitalism—these "fat cats" of the coffeehouse world may formerly have been revolutionaries and bohemians, but they become bourgeois with their success, distance themselves from their former environs, concentrate only on perfecting the form of the one good original idea they ever had, and invariably have a villa outside of the city center: "Od té doby není průkopníkem, ale majetníkem, který spoří a střádá a který tloustne. V duchovním slova smyslu možno totiž také tloustnout" ("From then on, he's not a pioneer, but an owner who saves, puts by, and grows fat—fat in the spiritual sense of the word, as well"). Kafka would have recognized the reference to their letters, though whether or not he knew that Werfel was also trying to capitalize on Jesenská is an open question. But through such allusions, Jesenská could render the most public of all written spaces into a realm of secret communication. She could also do the opposite, laying before the public the private nuances of their lovers' discourse and incorporating this discourse into her own writing, writing on which Kafka placed a high value. Jesenská's "Kavárna" recalls Kafka's comment on intimacy to accentuate the diminished potency of such intimate signs in the world she depicts, a world in which such forms no longer are restricted to particular relationships between individuals, indicative of private grammars, but have, like sexual intimacy, gone public, become standard currency in circulation like the women themselves. In response to the "Kavárna" feuilleton in which women and texts circulate among the same men and with the same ease, Kafka expresses jealousy over the easy availability of her *text* in the newspapers—must she really show it to everyone who buys the *Tribuna*?[21] The text in question describes the easy exchange of female bodies among male writers, and is written as an insider by the woman he is in love with, but in Kafka's case, this might not be a case of displaced anxieties—the text might well be of the first importance. Kafka and Jesenská first met in a coffeehouse, but he wasn't swept away until the letters.

Jesenská's "Kavárna" feuilleton looks forward to *The Castle*—both in terms of broader issues such as spaces and their social function or the odd hierarchies of a closed society, and in terms of atmospheric details and imagery—the problem of air, the emphasis on stasis, the lack of progress. The pictures and caricatures on the coffeehouse walls of those "who have a name . . . in the official world" resonate with the portraits of Castle officials that K. sees throughout his journey; the circulating coffeehouse women who are known only by nicknames might easily go by Frieda or Pepi, the sexually available women of the Herrenhof in *The Castle*. Another affinity that identifies the text as taking place in dialogue with Kafka is the triple repetition of "stýkali" (translated here as "used to mingle"), the verb derived from *styk*, the exact equivalent of the German word *Verkehr*—"traffic," but also communication as well as intercourse in all its meanings. This term and concept holds a privileged position in the later *Castle*, but also in earlier stories such as "The Judgment," which famously ends with it ("In diesem Augenblick ging über die Brücke ein geradezu unendlicher Verkehr" ["In this moment an endless stream of traffic was going over the bridge"])—lines which, according to Max Brod, Kafka associated with intense ejaculation.[22] This story was among those Jesenská translated, although just when is unclear, as the translation was never published, but Jesenská's correspondence with Kafka (*Briefsverkehr*) is itself—at the level of the word and concept—wholly implicated in the complex interchange of sex and text (*Briefsverkehr* v. *Geschlechtsverkehr*). I return to this concept of *Verkehr* in relation to *The Castle* in the next chapter, but it has its own centrality in this exchange of letters. Interlinguistic wordplay, part of a program of near-fanatical close reading, was also central to the correspondence—perhaps most particularly on the topic of personal names. Jesenská's "Kavárna" should be understood as taking its place in that exchange as well.

One key passage from the correspondence underscores the tremendous importance with which Kafka invested personal names and confirms his interest—with regard to proper names, at least—in reading interlinguistically. This instance surrounds Kafka's reading of Milena's Czech name:

> (what a rich, heavy name, almost too full to lift and which I didn't like very much at first, it seemed to me a Greek or Roman name gone astray in Bohemia, violated by Czech, the accent has been betrayed and yet it is wonderful in color and form—a woman to be carried in one's arms out of the world, out of the fire—I don't know which—and she presses herself willing and trusting in your arms, only the strong accent on the "i" is bad, doesn't the name jump away from you? Or is that perhaps just a leap of happiness, which you yourself make with your burden?)[23]

> (was für ein reicher schwerer Name vor Fülle kaum zu heben und gefiel mir anfangs nicht sehr, schien mir ein Grieche oder Römer nach Böhmen verirrt, tschechisch vergewaltigt, in der Betonung betrogen und ist doch wunderbar in Farbe und Gestalt eine Frau, die man auf den Armen trägt aus der Welt, aus dem Feuer ich weiß nicht und sie drückt sich willig und vertrauend dir in die Arme, nur der starke Ton auf dem i ist arg, springt dir der Name nicht wieder fort? Oder ist das vielleicht nur der Glücksprung, den du selbst machst mit deiner Last?)[24]

This letter further reminds us that such interlinguistic reading—*particularly* of names—was a widespread cultural habit in linguistically, ethnically, and politically charged Prague. The passage resonates with Prague's linguistically ironic or shifting names and recasts the "question of language" that so occupied the census takers, the government, the philologists, and the newspapers, rendering it more intimate, minute, and local. The question here is not "Which language *should* I be using?" but "Which language *am* I using?" or "Aren't *you* in the wrong language?" The passage collapses even the distinction of bilingualism as Kafka reads in two languages at once, or one language through the other, getting a little lost in the process. Throughout the correspondence, the interaction between their two languages and the particular problems of the non-native speaker continue to occupy Kafka. Here he complains of Czech's strong initial syllabic stress, which remains foreign to him despite his long exposure to the language, and elsewhere he hears the same phenomenon as an assault, an assault clearly related to the ethnic slurs pronounced in Czech on the streets of Prague against the Jews. Perhaps for this reason, Kafka insists on reading Jesenská's name as belonging to another language, a language not its own. Kafka's intransigence on the subject of Jesenská's Czech name betrays a difficulty or reluctance on his part to accept Jesenská as genuinely Czech, perhaps because she is less his physical lover or caregiver (like other Czech women of his experience) than his colleague in writing. She confuses categories he has long kept segregated, and in "Kavárna" this confusion comes to a head as the "traffic" in women is also *by* a woman: Jesenská writes, performs, and translates "verkehren" as "stýkat se" and emphasizes through repetition that she has done so. These concerns with naming, language, and exchange travel and traffic from correspondence to feuilleton to fiction: the trajectory of a foreign proper noun derived from defunct grammatical systems straying in the Czech lands leads directly to the Castle.

The next chapter argues in detail how the destabilizations wrought by Kafka's relationship with Jesenská in turn produce a profoundly disruptive system of gender, sexuality, and power in the world of the novel. But it would be wrong to understand Jesenská's influence as active *only* with regard to gender and sexual relations. The relationship shook Kafka to his core, which was (by his own account) where he was a writer. Thus the influence of this correspondence is deeply, profoundly lexical and linguistic as well as thematic and representational—one grows out of the other—and the dynamics are replicated again (always with a shift, a difference) at the level of structure. Physical wandering, an uncompleted journey, tiredness, lack of progress in the written task: all appear in Kafka's account of reading Jesenská's Czech prose, which places us deep in the rhetorical and narrative territory of K.'s approach to the Castle:

> I took a small outing (not the long one I mentioned that never materialized) and for nearly three days I was unable to do a thing, not even write, due to (a not unpleasant) weariness. I just read, the letter, your essays, again and again, convinced that such prose does not exist only for its own sake, but serves as a signpost on the way to a human being, a road one keeps following, happier and happier, until arriving at the realization some bright moment that one is not progressing, simply running around in one's own labyrinth, only more nervously, more confused than before.[25]

> Einen kleinen Ausflug habe ich gemacht (nicht jenen großen, den ich erwähnt habe und der nicht zustandekam) und war fast drei Tage fast unfähig vor (einer nicht unangenehmen) Müdigkeit etwas zu tun, selbst zu schreiben, nur gelesen habe ich, den Brief, die Aufsätze, öfters, in der Meinung, das solche Prosa natürlich nicht um ihrer selbst willen da ist, sondern eine Art Wegzeiger auf dem Weg zu einem Menschen, auf einem Weg, auf dem man immer glücklicher weitergeht, bis man in einem hellen Augenblick erkennt, daß man ja gar nicht weiter kommt, sondern nur in seinem eigenen Labyrinth noch umherläuft, nur aufgeregter, verwirrter als sonst.[26]

This letter to Jesenská introduces *avant la lettre* the crucial Castle characteristic of weariness (*Müdigkeit*), which characterizes Klamm, other Castle officials with their heavy heads, a woman K. meets in a cottage who is associated with the Castle, and so on. The letter also introduces the figure of the labyrinth that governs K.'s hapless wanderings through Castle streets and even prefigures the rhetoric of the journal passage I've read in conjunction with Kafka's start on *The Castle* (discussed in chapter 4), but with a crucial difference. In that journal passage, "this literature" might lead away from mankind altogether, while here, "such prose" leads to an individual and potential for happiness that turns out to be only an illusion (or delusion [*klam*]). The emotional and visual tone of the letter is far brighter than the passage that echoes it in the novel, but the letter does prefigure the structural, rhetorical, and figural logic of *The Castle*:

For the first time since coming here, he felt truly tired. At first, the long journey hadn't seemed like much of a strain to him—how he had kept wandering through the days, steadily, one step at a time!—but the consequences of those exertions had to go and make themselves felt now, at the worst possible time, of course. He felt an irresistible urge to seek out new acquaintances, but each new acquaintance had only increased his weariness. In his present state, if he could force himself to prolong this walk to the Castle entrance, that would be more than enough.

So he set off again, but it was a long way. The street he had taken, the main street in the village, did not lead to the Castle hill, it only went close by, then veered off as if on purpose, and though it didn't lead any farther from the Castle, it didn't get any closer either. K. kept expecting the street to turn at last toward the Castle and it was only in this expectation that he kept going; no doubt out of weariness he was reluctant to leave this street, what amazed him, too, was the length of this village, which wouldn't end, again and again those tiny little houses and the frost-covered windowpanes and the snow and not a living soul—[27]

Zum erstenmal seit seinem Kommen fühlte er wirkliche Müdigkeit. Der weite Weg hierher schien ihn ursprünglich gar nicht angegriffen zu haben—wie war er durch die Tage gewandert, ruhig Schritt für Schritt—jetzt aber zeigten sich doch die Folgen der übergroßen Anstrengung, zur Unzeit freilich. Es zog ihn unwiderstehlich hin, neue Bekanntschaften zu suchen, aber jede neue Bekanntschaft verstärkte die Müdigkeit. Wenn er sich in seinem heutigen Zustand zwang, seinen Spaziergang wenigstens bis zum Eingang des Schlosses auszudehnen, war übergenug getan. So ging er wieder vorwärts, aber es war ein langer Weg. Die Straße nämlich, diese Hauptstraße des Dorfes führte nicht zum Schloßberg, sie führte nur nahe heran, dann aber wie absichtlich bog sie ab und wenn sie sich auch vom Schloß nicht entfernte, so kam sie ihm doch auch nicht näher. Immer erwartete K., daß nun endlich die Straße zum Schloß einlenken müsse, und nur weil er es ewartete ging er weiter; offenbar infolge seiner Müdigkeit zögerte er die Straße zu verlassen, auch staunte er über die Länge des Dorfes, das kein Ende nahm, immerwieder die kleinen Häuschen und vereiste Fensterscheiben und Schnee und Menschenleere—[28]

This passage draws on rhetorical and thematic elements in the letter and distorts them, torques them. The terms twist and recombine in new configurations, much like the represented geography of the Castle realm. Reading and rereading prose that seemed to point in a new direction may only lead back to Kafka's own labyrinth—but with a difference, subject to an even greater confusion. K.'s professional, architectural, and spatial confusion throughout the novel finds some of its roots in this reaction. The difference resulting in Kafka's confusion is both writerly and gendered: a crucial intersection in a changing labyrinth.

Chapter 7

✦

"Official Decisions Are as Shy as Young Girls"

Gender in *The Castle*

The Castle emerges from the aftermath of Kafka's correspondence with Milena Jesenská, of which only one half is extant—but the transformative power of Jesenská's missing texts reverberates throughout. The effect of this relationship on Kafka was systemic, structural—as was its influence on Kafka's last novel, where the effect is perhaps most far-reaching on issues of gender, precisely in this multiply resonating, systemic way. The disruption of what the novel itself construes as traditional assumptions about gender and power starts at the beginning, or even before then. First, the title and central image (the "Schloß" or "castle" that also signifies a lock) suggests from the outset that the apparently dominant, masculine structure is alternately or perhaps simultaneously symbolically feminine, a possibility that K. finds disorienting. Before the text begins, either meaning might hold sway; the noun's grammatical gender is neuter. Like any homonym, the "Schloß" of the novel's title requires context and contiguity to establish its significance and symbolic value—and hence stabilize its gendered symbolism. If the novel teaches anything, however, it is that such values in language are never fixed or absolute, and gender and power interact unstably, though consistently coercively, throughout.

Further evidence of Jesenská's centrality to the novel's conception—and, by extension, of her disruption of Kafka's understanding of gender and sexuality—comes in the very literal form of a doodle: a female figure on the first page of the manuscript. The first Castle notebook was assembled from pages of earlier notebooks; its early pages are nested among projects and entries. The first scene written (not the first scene of the novel's most finished form) appears under this sketch of a female figure accompanied by the word "Mädchen" and "Elisabeth." A line is drawn across the page indicating a fresh start, and the novel begins with the simple sentence "Der Wirt begrüsste den Gast" ("The host [or landlord] welcomed the guest"). The initial encounter transpires between these two men, but the maid Elisabeth immediately attracts the nameless guest, who soon demands that the landlord "leave them alone."

The ensuing short conversation proceeds to introduce much of the novel's guiding structural principles, thematic territory, and even lexicon: the lack of direct communication (*Verkehr*) between the Castle and the village folk ("die Herren vom Schloss verkehren nicht mit uns" [literally, "the gentlemen from the castle don't traffic with us"]), the guest's status as stranger or foreigner (*der Fremde*), and the attention this status is already attracting in a place where so few strangers visit. This paucity of strangers is emphasized when the Guest repeats the question ("wenig Fremde?"), which is answered in the affirmative, laughingly, apparently at once "trusting and foreign" ("gleichzeitig zutraulich und fremd"), implying a tension or contradiction between the two. Despite promising, even tender beginnings, the Guest quickly accuses Elisabeth of ulterior motives, insisting that although the natives (apparently) are "all a pack of rabble," she's even more dangerous than the others and has likely been sent from the Castle to spy on him—an accusation the maid suggests only demonstrates his lack of understanding, the first iteration of the most oft-repeated conversational exchange in the novel. Malte Kleinwort draws attention to this version's marked distance from its main character, especially when compared to the close perspective of the later novel draft.[1] The characters appear in a stark, nearly empty room—"bald," it is specified; there is little in the way of context besides their gender, their status as foreign or not foreign, and their stated roles—but of these, the Guest has *only* his stranger status, whereas the girl is referred to by employment and class (chambermaid) and by a given name, as well as (most frequently) by her gender ("Mädchen"). She thus has more potential dimensions than either male character; for all that the Guest insists on a task, a struggle, and the likelihood of his being attacked, these are his claims only, whereas the third-person narrator (absent in the later draft) authoritatively assigns the girl more possible roles, cultural knowledge, and belonging. She also seems physically stronger than her interlocutor, for as soon as the Guest exhausts himself with what Kleinwort calls the "unrestricted logic of mistrust," he collapses—swoons, even—at which point she takes on yet another role, that of nursemaid and comforter. This fragment was discarded in favor of a later opening, and the Guest shifted to the first person before going back to the much closer third-person narrative perspective of the final draft. But the centrality and complexity of the female character and the comparative incapability and paranoia of the guest remain, similarly reflecting dynamics that Kafka himself diagnosed (and excoriated in himself) in the contours of his correspondence with Jesenská. With only increasing nuance and complexity, Jesenská's palpable if refracted influence continues to shape *The Castle*'s representation of elements likewise central to the correspondence: difference in sex and gender, in origin, and the possibility (or impossibility) of communication across such apparent linguistic or experiential divides. It even makes itself felt in matters of style.

Although I see a divide between Kafka's representations pre- and post-Jesenská in both his fiction and confessional writings, critiques of Kafka concerned with gender first tended to find its depiction fairly consistent throughout his work. Evelyn Tornton Beck argued in an early and influential feminist critique that "nowhere in Kafka does woman speak for herself"; as all Kafka's narrators are male, "the angle of vision in Kafka's texts is andro-centric necessarily."[2] Deleuze and Guattari saw Kafka's female characters largely as "connectors" and liaisons, falling into a category they refer to as sister-maid-whore.[3] As if following the Guest's assumptions about Elisabeth's likely role, some of these critics have seen women in *The Castle* as a site or source of traffic "between men" in keeping with the rest of Kafka's oeuvre, where female characters are more absent, grotesque, or merely instrumental. Though arguably appropriate to earlier female characters—Fräulein Bürstner or Pepi in *The Trial*, for example, or the monstrous Brunelda of *Der Verschollene*—such arguments apply less to *The Castle*, as subsequent commentators on gender have noticed and explored. Whereas Larysa Mykyta stresses that the novel's female characters act alternately as "obstacles" to writing and "paths" to salvation, she also notices that the women themselves consistently correct K. in his misapprehension that sexual liaison with them can confer power and access—though she finds they can act as a disruptive force in such processes.[4] What these readings have in common is a sense that Kafka's female characters in *The Castle* as much as anywhere else are primarily oriented toward the male subject; they may be maids, whores, conduits, or obstacles, but all with relation to men. Such dynamics are certainly in play in the novel, but we would have no reason to believe that our perspective on the women K. meets is less distorted by his anachronistic or otherwise inappropriate assumptions than our perspective on any other structure or system he regards. Indeed, these readings seem rather to parallel the misunderstandings K. himself suffers from in his dealings with both women and the Castle. Despite protests from the women themselves that they are not conduits to the Castle, not a means of traffic between K. and the official world, and that they should not be judged or used as such, K. ignores these warnings and persists in acting as though that is exactly what they are—to his own perpetual frustration and failure. To the extent that women *are* presented in terms of these dynamics, they are portrayed as unjustly trapped and used—that is, the Castle system is hardly an egalitarian and mutually respectful one, but it does not break down along gender lines in the way that K. seems to assume it should. To complicate matters further, gendered characteristics do not align with male and female characters. Even the starkest implied binaries, those that seem hard-wired in the depicted world—Castle to Village; man to woman—do not play out in the ways that K.'s prior life experiences seem to have led him to assume. In this way, I argue, K.'s experience of the Castle world resembles Kafka's experience of reading Jesenská in personal letters and in print.

The Castle is the most autobiographically allusive text of Kafka's maturity, and most of these allusions lead back to Jesenská, from direct reference and representation to shared thematic concerns and patterns of imagery and rhetoric. Frieda, like Milena, is a denizen of an establishment called the Herrenhof, and the social dynamics of the novel recall the coffeehouse culture depicted in the "Kavárna" feuilleton as well as the more obvious parallel to Milena's situation with Kafka and her husband. Klamm's structural position in the Herrenhof mirrors the position that Jesenská's husband occupied in the Vienna coffeehouse of the same name, where Ernst Pollak was one of the diminished "great ones" she refers to with such irony. Such parallels have been recognized since Kafka's letters to Jesenská were first published in 1953, but the scope of Jesenská's refracted image in *The Castle* does not stop with them. Gisa, the assistant schoolteacher, no sooner looks at K. than starts scolding him, destroying his belongings and ultimately scratching his wrist with the claw of her cat. The schoolroom switch that Kafka evokes in his letter fantasizing about teacher-Milena's scolding becomes in the novel the more salacious cat-o'-nine tails, effaced and literalized into an abused cat who is nonetheless used as schoolroom discipline and leaves tracks on skin. Jesenská's influence also plays out in Amalia's situation and characterization in ways complex enough to merit their own section here, and even Jesenská's Vienna landlady (referred to in the correspondence as Frau K., for that matter) seems a probable reference point for *The Castle*'s Landlady. The "real-life" Frau K. played no small part in the Jesenská-Kafka relationship, at least as it is represented (directly) in the correspondence or (obliquely) in Jesenská's journalism. Nor does character alone exhaust the ways in which Jesenská's image and influence play out in the novel. Klamm's henchmen, for example, pass Amalia's sister Olga among each other in her whirling dance—a literalized, compressed version of the circulating women in "Kavárna," while the correspondence's scrutiny of names—as nationality, identity, orthography—is revisited via Klamm's multilingually referential name. This refracted representation demonstrates the extent to which the relationship with Jesenská remained active in Kafka's thought, although character remains just one of the ways in which this influence makes itself known. In the previous chapter, I juxtaposed a passage from a letter in which Kafka reads Jesenská's Czech name with a passage from Kafka's diary that itself rhetorically and thematically anticipates a passage describing one of K.'s early wandering journeys. While there was nothing particularly gendered about *that* passage in the novel, the journey it describes—which K. believes will take him to the Castle—instead lands him in a village cottage. This cottage is precisely the kind of "Wohnhaus" K. wishes to be clearly distinct from the Castle (and for gendered reasons, as discussed in chapter 7), and thus the wandering that echoes Kafka's early letter to Jesenská lands K. in the midst of a scene dominated by women, to which I return in detail in the next section. Another passage describing a different failed approach to the Castle follows a parallel structure and further recalls the kind of nostalgia for lost clarity in the face of confusion that besets K. in his wanderings:

> They went on, where to K. had no idea, he couldn't recognize anything, didn't even know whether they had passed the church. Due to the sheer effort of walking he could no longer control his thoughts. Rather than remaining fixed on the goal, they became confused. His homeland kept surfacing, filling him with memories.[5]

> Sie gingen, aber K. wußte nicht wohin, nichts konnte er erkennen, nicht einmal ob sie schon an der Kirche vorübergekommen waren, wußte er. Durch die Mühe, welche ihm das bloße Gehn verursachte, geschah es, daß er seine Gedanken nicht beherrschen konnte. Statt auf das Ziel gerichtet zu bleiben, verwirrten sie sich. Immer wieder tauchte die Heimat auf und Erinnerungen an sie erfüllten ihn.[6]

Again, K.'s spatial, quasi-architectural confusion evokes images of his native land that in turn supply a set of expectations that hearken back to a time of straight lines and clear boundaries—when the young K. was able to scale the churchyard wall, when he could gain mastery, when a knowing transgression of known rules might be apprehended (the teacher catches him at it), but where being caught meant recognition, thus compounding the sense of victory attained. Expectations based on such experiences, however, though conjured as an antidote to the disorientation he feels, only heighten K.'s confusion about his current journey, which he misunderstands as a transgressive night visit to the Castle. Instead, the journey lands him in *another* "Wohnhaus"—another space and scene dominated by women, this time by Olga and her sister Amalia, who herself has a strong and disturbing association with the Castle. The confusing path leads to a confusing domestic configuration—not to the male-dominated Castle he was expecting. This nostalgia for clarity—discussed in my introduction with relation to "The City Coat of Arms" and in chapter 4 with relation to the Castle—here consistently coincides with a particularly gendered confusion about the present scene. In *The Castle*, however, it is K.'s dated and inappropriate expectations that help *produce* the confusion, as much with respect to gender and sexuality as it was with respect to architecture. This pattern functions not only at the level of individual scene, but at the novel's most basic structural level.

Marthe Robert writes of K. as "the inverse of the traditional quest hero," having no Grail, no object endowed with symbolic significance or fixed meaning to guide him through his travails.[7] The romance structure that readily suggests itself throughout the novel is thus divested of the very terms that rendered the quest comprehensible and meaningful. The defining characteristics of medieval romance have been identified as "the perpetual search for noble deeds, a highly civilized code of behavior, and a great stress on the influence of ladies."[8] These elements are all early identified in Kafka's narrative, but in divested form. The "search for noble deeds," for example, appears in greatly reduced circumstances, since even K.'s highest aspirations—to enter a building, to survey a town—could hardly be categorized as noble, much less anything he actually achieves.[9] As for the second category, this Castle operates—in the view of an outsider—under a highly *uncivilized* code of behavior: its women are at the mercy of the whims of unsightly officials whose unruly servants must be whipped into their stalls at night. And thirdly, while there is a "great stress" on the importance of women, the word "lady" (serving to distinguish women perceived to be chaste, refined, and of noble birth) would ill describe the novel's central women characters. But the elements are all there, "divested of their traditional supports": in the Castle we have "the perpetual search for . . . deeds, a . . . code of behavior, and great stress on the influence of [women]."

Other important displacements in the novel also conform to such a pattern—or rather, to K.'s desire for such a pattern—and shed light on the nature of K.'s failures in negotiating the Castle world, which are directly related to rules governing gender and sexual relations. K. assumes that the Castle world's social structure will provide both legitimate and transgressive yet tacitly acknowledged and effective means of approach, just as the courtly societies of romance did. By day the hero might gain access to the court and courtly privilege by performing services and currying favor with his liege, while by night, he might bed the lord's wife or mistress, thereby securing her help for reasons of love or fear. Either of these methods might prove highly effective, but it would be important to be able to tell them apart, since the knight would get nowhere trying to sleep with the queen in broad daylight in front of the king or secretly fighting battles for him, furtively covering up his involvement in important victories. Yet the villagers' and officials' reactions to K. frequently give the impression that he has been committing precisely these kinds of faux pas. His worst mistakes result from his mistaken belief that he does know the rules, and he himself recognizes this danger: "he always told himself quickly after such fits of satisfaction that this is precisely where the danger lay." This is precisely the logic Kafka associates with getting lost in Jesenská's essays, believing himself to be following a road only to realize he has made no progress and is only more confused.

For Kafka, the experience of reading Jesenská also recalls Božena Němcová—who is, as we have already seen (chapter 4), an important referent for *The Castle*. Thus in Kafka's encounter with Jesenská as well, an unfamiliar stylistic and functional landscape evokes an earlier remembered clarity, one that provides context but also, by contrast, may accentuate the strangeness of new surroundings. Němcová and Jesenská share language and gender, but whether they share a style or project is less certain. Němcová's role in the reestablishment, reinvention, and even invention of Czech as a literary language led her to create for her readers a sense of "insider status," of being "native speakers" of the language she herself had had to learn. Such linguistic-national boundaries were renegotiated and reiterated on the pages of *Naše řeč*—which Kafka *also* mentions in conjunction with reading

"Milena," name and writer both. Yet Jesenská is writing (in the feuilletons, at least) from Vienna to her homeland and in her native language—to a linguistic community she is physically distant from, but on whose native knowledge of her written language she could rely. She is distanced from her native language, but she can assume that her readership shares it. Kafka would not have been the imagined audience for the feuilletons referred to here, at least—although he is incorporated as a reader in "Kavárna." Yet Kafka *has* been studying the language, its foundational texts and grammar. He is conversant. Could studying give someone a "native" or insider command? Němcová's experience and fiction might suggest that it could and seems to offer such a path, while Kafka's novel suggests that non-native status could never confer comfort, that one would only always be strange—stuck in one's own labyrinth.

Kafka further claims that Jesenská's style is marked by "Entschlossenheit" ("resolution").[10] The term is semantically aligned with K.'s *remembered* tower that tapered "bestimmt, ohne Zögern" ("decisively, without hesitation"), although it is also morphologically suggestive of the Castle and its more wavering architecture; similarly, the "hellsichtige Klugheit" ("clear-sighted intelligence") that Kafka claims characterizes the writing of the Czech women also contrasts with what K. will experience as "etwas Irrsinniges" ("something crazy") in the glittering of the Castle realm's tower and its battlements: "unsicher, unregelmäßig" ("uncertain, irregular") and "wie von ängstlicher oder nachlässiger Kinderhand gezeichnet" ("as if drawn by the anxious or careless hand of a child").[11] Thus Kafka's rhetoric in the letter—to which I return at greater length in discussing "Josefine the Singer" in the following chapter—here associates both Němcová and Jesenská with the stylistic and functional qualities K. values in the *remembered* tower—clarity of line, purpose, and potent symbolism—and *not* with the strange hybrid *Schloß*-structure of tower encroached upon by the domestic sphere of the Wohnhaus, the traditional domain of women and children and the quotidian "Werktag." Yet Jesenská's journalism, with its household concerns, reports of daily life, fashion columns, and publication in newspaper dailies, is both domestic and quotidian in more than one sense. With regard to gender, then, as well as architectural function, K.'s perception of the Castle's structural irrationality derives from K.'s inappropriately rigid distinctions between form and function: domestic concerns bound up in the stylistic clarity he expects to transcend the domestic and feminine (the existential problem of Czech women writers with good style). Read in this light, K.'s bitter disappointment at entering the Barnabas household instead of the Castle—"so it was a misunderstanding, a vulgar, low misunderstanding and K. had completely abandoned himself to it"[12] ("ein Mißverständnis war es also gewesen, ein gemeines, niedriges Mißverständnis und K. hatte sich ihm ganz hingegeben")[13]—constitutes yet another misreading of linguistic, architectural, and gendered signs and structures. Such experiences had become intensely bound up with Jesenská. Her combination of gendered, sexual, and writerly roles causes consternation, categorical confusion. K. is reading by the wrong rules.

Gender as Structure

Similar categorical confusions reverberate in the structure of gender and power relations in *The Castle*. The "structurality" of gender in the novel is hard to miss, and one line of criticism argued that both Castle-Village relations and the community's sexual relations adhere to near-perfect Lévi-Straussian structural paradigms—the exchange in women that actually facilitates relations between men rather than between members of the opposite sex. Sexual intercourse with Klamm, for example, has conferred value on both Frieda (until she abandons him for K.) and on Gardena, the landlady, who becomes a valuable village bride as a result—or at least so K. reasons, although the Landlady disputes this conclusion. Yet scrutinizing the particular constituents occupying these structural positions yields a much more complex and contradictory picture of the relationship of gender and power.

Klamm himself, for example, displays traits that are hardly consistent with the strength, action, and dominance associated with period notions of masculinity. We only ever see Klamm sleeping and witness even this much through a small hole—the vaginally suggestive keyhole—to which access is possible only via a woman gatekeeper. The landlord at the Herrenhof inn refers to Klamm's delicacy, an attribute already identified as maidenly with regard to Olga. When, while waiting for Klamm, K. climbs into his fur-lined coach and dribbles on himself, Klamm apparently will wait endlessly for him to leave; when K. is finally called inside, the coachman erases even his footprints from the snow, lest they should affront Klamm's sensibilities. Klamm's refusal to see or be seen suggests that like their decisions, officials themselves are "as shy as young girls."

Aside from his delicacy and somnolence, furthermore, what we know in greatest detail about Klamm is how difficult it is to know anything about him. Klamm's messenger Barnabas (although this relationship too remains in some doubt) has assiduously collected different accounts of Klamm's appearance. He believes he has seen him once, but this sighting did little to fix his image in Barnabas's mind; the messenger could neither recognize Klamm from his assiduously collected accounts nor even explain how the man he saw differed from his expectations. Klamm appears as a changing series of impressions and characteristics, his only consistency of appearance provided by his clothes.[14] Klamm's nebulous, shape-shifting physicality and the mystery that enshrouds him suggest parallels with the gender schema of Kafka's contemporary Otto Weininger—but not with his portrayal of masculinity:

> Women can appear everything and deny everything, but in reality they are never anything. Women have neither this nor that characteristic; their peculiarity consists in having no characteristics at all; the complexity and terrible mystery about women come to this; it is this which makes them above and beyond man's understanding—man, who always wants to get at the heart of things.[15]

Reiner Stach employs this passage and others like it in reading Kafka's *female* characters as a series of embodiments of the Weiningerian "W" principle, starkly identifying Kafka's "aesthetic projection of women" with Weininger's theory: "perhaps as a result of the passive core of their constructions, Kafka's female characters act entirely as variations on Weininger's feminine type."[16] While *The Castle* does play with Weiningerian and other stereotypes about men and women, it does so in no such straightforward manner. Just substitute, for example, "Klamm" or even "officials" for "women" in Weininger's account, and it might describe K.'s epistemological experience not only of Klamm but of the whole Castle world. If K. represents a Weiningerian man who "wants to get at the heart of things," to penetrate and know the core, to enter the Castle, to scale the churchyard wall, then the Castle world figures schematically as nebulous, being-less Woman. Thus the structure of the patriarchal culture that the novel portrays—with its institutionalized rape, all-male leadership, and circulation of female bodies—is subject to a dramatic and surprising inversion.

No such simple inversion, however, can sustain the Castle world's many complications of gender identity and social function, which are as unchartable as its physical topography and architecture. The conflation of phallic tower with female-dominated "Wohnhaus" in K.'s initial morning approach to the Castle presents gender and power in an architecturally structured relation that is sustained throughout the novel but is not stable. Again, it is the "Schloss" as the *integration* in a single structure of domestic dwelling and seat of religious and political power that so disturbs K., a duality also inherent in the term itself (is it a phallic castle or vaginal lock?). That public and private, symbolic and quotidian, and, similarly, masculine and feminine can be fused architecturally in this way profoundly disorients K., and this architectural disruption prefigures the further confusion of traditional male and female roles and spheres that helps to render the Castle world so spatially and socially incomprehensible for him.

The novel everywhere evokes gender difference only to destabilize it on the structural level. It arranges masculine and feminine characteristics not solely along the axis of Male to Female, but rather in relation to two axes: Male-Female and Castle-Village. These axes together make up the nexus of gender and power relations, but as axes they are not strictly perpendicular and at times seem even parallel; their key terms, much like other elements in the novel, seem to shift along these axes that in turn shift in relation to each other. Nor are the effects of such shifting limited to Castle officials or the central edifice itself. Gendered attributes figure prominently in descriptions of villagers, but the distribution of these attributes adheres not to any single stereotypical pattern, but rather to several such patterns at once. The early pages of the novel again set the scene. The first conversations between the Landlord, Schwarzer, K., and the peasants, for example, create a homosocial atmosphere: men do all the talking, all the arranging and jockeying for position with regard to the Castle, but their roles and identities are presented as either performed or produced. The Landlord is "extremely surprised and confused by the late arrival" ("von dem späten Gast äußerst überrascht und verwirrt")—a "Wirt"(landlord) "verwirrt"(confused) by a guest—and his status seems linguistically produced: his reaction appears in ironic relation to his vocation or calling, his behavior structured by a perverse linguistic performativity. A more traditional sense of performance, on the other hand, characterizes Schwarzer. Schwarzer is costumed ("dressed in city clothes"["städtisch angezogen"]), and seems even to bear the suggestion of stage paint: his physical attributes ("narrow eyes, thick eyebrows" ["die Augen Schmal, die Augenbrauen stark"]) are exaggerated and described only after we are told he has the face of an actor. The peasants, previously seated and quiet (as befits an audience awaiting a performance), turn their chairs to see and hear better ("besser zu sehn und zu hören").[17] Thus the entire negotiation of role, property, and position takes place under the rubric of performance, with each characteristic either linguistically produced or attendant on costume or social position—at least so far as the interrelations among the men are concerned. Village masculinity here is not essential but theatrical.

The Landlady's "mächtige Gestalt" ("mighty figure") waiting in the wings first breaks this theatrically homosocial atmosphere—she is the first woman to appear in the novel. Her lead-in consists of K.'s perceptions of the peasants and his interpretation of their behavior: "He watched the peasants gathering timidly and conferring, the arrival of a land surveyor was no trifling matter"[18] ("Er sah die Bauern scheu zusammenrücken und sich besprechen, die Ankunft eines Landvermessers war nichts Geringes").[19] Far from the burly peasants we might expect, these men have been only passive observers throughout, and even as they gather (hardly in itself a decisive action, but nonetheless their first) they do so shyly. Against this backdrop of shy manhood, K. seems invested in asserting that his arrival is no small or trifling matter, such that "nicht Geringes" appears in opposition to the "entrance" of the Landlady: "The door to the kitchen had opened; filling the doorway was the mighty figure of the landlady, the landlord approached her on tiptoes in order to report to her."[20] ("Die Tür der Küche hatte sich geöffnet, türfüllend stand dort die mächtige Gestalt der Wirtin, auf den Fußspitzen näherte sich ihr der Wirt, um ihr zu berichten."[21]) Of the characters described in the first scene, only one seems to possess any stable, inherent quality independent of affect, costume, or station, and only one, for that matter, seems associated with any traditionally masculine attributes: in both cases the Landlady, whose "mighty form" ("mächtige Gestalt") appears flanked by "shy" ("scheu") peasants for whom a Land Surveyor is "not trifling" ("nichts Geringes"), and by her husband who must stand on tiptoes to report to her on the other. The next reference to a woman, to K.'s absent—perhaps imaginary—wife, contrasts with the power suggested by the Landlady's imposing body. K. speaks of having a "Frau und Kind" (wife and child) at home to feed. This set phrase pairs women with children as per tradition and relegates them to a passive, marginal role, waiting offstage for the man to bring home sustenance. The wife and child are never mentioned again, however, and apparently K. sees them as no impediment to his engagement to Frieda, calling their very existence into question. Why did K. mention them at all? Another assertion of his masculinity, a (false?) proof that he is not "trifling"? With this single allusion, K. relegates the equivalence suggested by the set phrase to the mythological realm of his inaccessible and only dimly recollected former life—to the realm of churchyards clearly marked out for the storming and towers that gesture unflinchingly toward symbolic significance. "Frau und Kind" implies an identity and role for women that is all but irrelevant to the world K. now inhabits. Henceforth, women and children are rarely associated in the novel at all, and never in a positive light. When strong women like Frieda, the Landlady, and Amalia are seen in caretaking, nurturing roles, they are occupied more often with childlike adults.

Men, however, are several times seen occupied in child-rearing—the teacher and his "child-pile" enter the narrative early on, and a father sings songs with his children in the Bridge Inn. Men are also, on the other hand, often indistinguishable from children, the assistants proving only the most obvious example of a pattern established in these early descriptions of the Landlord and his wife. As K. patronizingly pats the cheek of his youthful, "soft, almost beardless" ("weichen fast bartlosen") host, his massive, elderly wife looms in the background "with her elbows sticking out" ("weit die Elbogen vom Leib," her elbows stick out far from her body, also flesh or even womb). A weak and henpecked husband under the thumb of a strong, overbearing wife is unusual neither as misogynist imagery nor as gender role reversal, but the potential for a pun on "Leib" as womb complicates the image, prefiguring the phallic tower jutting out of the "Wohnhaus" that K. encounters a few pages hence. And in the actual "Wohnhaus" scene depicted shortly after K.'s first glimpse of the Castle, women appear in positions of power—a woman's hand steadies K. when he stumbles going into the cottage, a woman's voice recognizes him, while the two men present float passively in a gigantic, womblike washtub, and are later replaced by—or transformed into—children.

Yet if the early pages of the novel seem to establish a pattern that simply reverses common gender stereotypes, no such pattern can be followed with any absolute consistency. Brunswick's cottage also houses, for example, a traditional "Frau und Kind" image—the only such image depicted in the novel, but one that makes a strong impression on K. and is revisited in his later conversation with the woman's son, Hans. Her appearance comes as a surprise to K., despite her seeming congruence with the impression he has given of his own former life:

> But even more surprising, though one still couldn't make out the exact nature of the surprise, was the right-hand corner. Through a large garret window, the only one in the back wall, came a pale snow-light, surely from the court-yard, which lent a luster as of silk to the dress of a woman who almost lay wearily in a tall armchair set deep in the corner. She held an infant at her breast. A few children were playing around her, peasant children by the looks of them, but she seemed out of place among them, though illness and weariness can make even peasants seem refined.[22]

> Aber noch überraschender, ohne daß man genau wußte worin das Überraschende bestand, war die rechte Ecke. Aus einer großen Luke, der einzigen in der Stubenrückwand, kam dort, wohl vom Hof her, bleiches Schneelicht und gab dem Kleid einer Frau, die tief in der Ecke in einem hohen Lehnstuhl müde fast lag, einen Schein wie von Seide. Sie trug einen Säugling an der Brust. Um sie herum spielten paar Kinder, Bauernkinder wie zu sehen war, sie aber schien nicht zu ihnen zu gehören, freilich, Krankheit und Müdigkeit macht auch Bauern fein.[23]

We might deduce—although the text tells us, in fact, that we cannot be sure—that the woman's aspect is surprising precisely because it is so stereotypically soft and feminine in comparison with the "mighty form" of the Landlady. Her weariness, detachment, and the comparative finery of her costume all correspond to stock fin-de-siècle and Art Nouveau images of womanhood. The overlay of this "declining" womanhood with the image of breast-feeding, however, specifically recalls the Hus monument near Kafka's childhood home on the Old Town Square in Prague (discussed previously in chapter 2).[24] Cynthia Paces describes in detail the politics of this monument's figure and how it came to be figured in this way: in earlier designs, the woman had been a soldier, then a mother in a more active stance (these designs were covered in the press, with images), whereas in the final version—unveiled in 1915—she is separate from other figures on the monument and is depicted as motionless and passive: "this figure of the nursing mother, this ahistorical symbolic woman transformed the Hus Memorial from historical monument to Art Nouveau allegory."[25] (See figure 10.)

Kafka's novel, by contrast, aligns these passive characteristics with affect, costume, and position, giving little information about the woman's actual physicality, only about her attitude and framing with relation to house, light, and window. Like the specific nature of the surprise she occasions, it is

Figure 10. Woman nursing, Jan Hus Monument. Photograph by Alex Zucker.

unclear whether her apparent detachment and otherworldliness derive from her gender, her class, or simply her illness. At last we are told she is from the Castle, and indeed her sleepy, detached quality and aesthetic framing coincide more with the images of Castle officials, such as the picture of the Castellan that K. discusses with the Landlord, than of other village women such as the Landlady.

In lexical and even sub-lexical terms as well, this passage recalls descriptions of the Castle: the "bleiches Schneelicht" ("pale snow-light") that illuminates her dress and gives it a "Schein" ("shine") recalls the "alle Formen nachbildenden . . . Schnee" (shape-tracing . . . snow) that earlier gave the Castle such definition in K.'s eyes, making it seem to soar above the village houses "frei und leicht empor, wenigstens schein es so von hier aus" (upwards, free and light, or at least so it seemed from here).[26] Similarly, the woman is surrounded by "Bauernkinder . . . aber schien nicht zu ihnen zu gehören, freilich . . ." (peasant children . . . but she seemed out of place among them, though . . .)—the "freilich" ("admittedly," "of course") interrupting and serving *semantically* as an almost throwaway rhetorical qualifier to the assertion that "Krankheit und Müdigkeit macht auch Bauern fein" ("illness and weariness can make even peasants seem refined"), but also lexically and phonemically further echoing the earlier descriptive passage's "frei und leicht." The passage also participates in the schein/schien alternation that characterizes the first two Castle descriptions, and even multiplies or disperses it, "Schneelicht" picking up not only the ubiquitous "Schnee" but echoing with a similar vowel shift the "leicht" of the earlier passage—all of which refers back to the "Schnee" (snow), "Lichtschein" (gleam of leight), and "scheinbare Leere" (seeming emptiness) of the novel's opening lines. While Kafka is hardly well known for his poetic manipulation of phonemes, in a novel so concerned in its first pages with establishing and deforming patterns, such marked verbal, vocalic, and phonetic patterning seems likely to be purposeful, and other elements of the novel also suggest such patterning.[27] The Castle woman suckling the baby even recalls lexically (though not in terms of the image it conjures) the framed portrait of the Castellan, the "Brustbild" ("half-length portrait"; literally "breast-image") of a fifty-year-old man: the image of the nursing woman is a "Brustbild" in a very literal but defamiliarized, non-colloquial sense. These images have more in common than that, however. In keeping with the interchangeability of the men and children in the enormous washtub, the Castellan's head that droops on his own chest ("den Kopf hielt er so tief auf die Brust gesenkt"[28]) has here been replaced by the head of the nursing infant. The Castellan can no longer support his head with his hand, while the woman "lag wie leblos"[29] ("lay as if lifeless"). Thus images of femininity and of the Castle are constructed at the level of image *and* language in markedly similar ways. Furthermore, since characteristics are plotted along two axes (Castle-Village, Male-Female), it is difficult to determine which attributes are associated with which axis and pole: is the woman passive because she is from the Castle? Or are Castle officials passive because they have feminine characteristics? The physical description of the Teacher—young, slight, and narrow-shouldered—does not suggest masculine prowess but rather is strongly reminiscent of Schopenhauer's description of women: "Das niedrig gewachsene, schmalschultrige, breithüftige und kurzbeinige Geschlecht" ("That low-grown, narrow-shouldered, wide-hipped and short-legged sex").[30] Yet the teacher's forceful presence has an immediate impact on K. In a manner usually reserved for people associated with the Castle, the Landlady appears framed twice, first by the kitchen door, then by the kitchen window. And, while her "mighty form" ("mächtige Gestalt") serves immediately to distinguish her from every man depicted thus far—her confused husband, the shy peasants, and Schwarzer's actor's face—the word "mächtig" also appears five times on the next page, three times to characterize Castle power, and twice to mark K.'s lack of it. Is the Landlady strong because she is a woman in contrast to the weak men around her? Or because she is masculinized while the men are infantilized and feminized? Or has she derived Castle-like power from the liaison we later learn she has had with Klamm? That attributes appear in a structured relation to both gender and Castle (power) seems clear, but the direction of influence and causality within that structure is as unstable as Kafka's experience of pursuit and assault in metaphor or K.'s experience of village streets and Castle architecture.

The nature of this relationship between gender and Castle attributes and their functions is all the more complex in the depiction of Barnabas the messenger. Barnabas's clothing and general appearance recall the image of the Castle woman with the child, while his white attire suggests a purity appropriate to his namesake, the saint and apostle, or even the bridal costume. His lips, described as "männlich und doch sanft" ("manly yet soft"), blend feminine and masculine characteristics after the fashion of Klamm, the Castle structure, and the Landlady. Barnabas's lips draw K.'s attention when they open and close as he speaks, an added emphasis on speech gesture that reminds us of Barnabas's status as Castle messenger—an association that might also explain his allure. Due to or despite his feminine attributes, Barnabas also has capability and (K. thinks) power through his relation to the Castle. Influenced by this perception, K. willingly relinquishes control of his body to Barnabas, hanging on him as they make their way through the snowdrifted streets, a journey K. believes will lead him to the Castle. But it seems K. has misunderstood Barnabas: the gleaming of his coat has led K. astray. Rather than guiding him to the mysterious, inscrutable realm of the Castle, he leads K. back to the domestic sphere. Once there, he removes the coat that K. believes to be the official costume linking Barnabas with the Castle and reveals his coarse peasant clothes and huge, muscular chest. The disillusionment K. feels at this overt display of masculinity coincides with his disappointment over Barnabas's destination. And yet, as it later emerges, the source of Barnabas's coat was not the Castle, but rather the hands of a Village woman, his sister.

Clearly, the distribution of gendered characteristics in Kafka's *Castle* corresponds to no single, clear dividing line between male and female characters. Rather, the novel abstracts gendered characteristics from the sex of characters, portraying gender as a structured social entity intersected by power (Castle-Village) relations. And just as it is unclear which traits are most associated with which axis, and in what direction that causality would flow, it is unclear how a reader—or surveyor—would draw the line that distinguishes either "Castle" from "Village" or "Male" from "Female." Some such line seems to be drawn, however, at least in the minds of the Castle natives. Evidence to this effect lies in the sex-specific system of exchange between Castle and Village, which in comparison to other elements in the novel seems to function in keeping with a rigorous and rigid, lucid, and spontaneously comprehensible (to everyone but K.) social grammar—as if *they* had all read a version of Němcová 's "In the Castle and in the Village," that is, a primer of Castle life, while K. knew nothing about it. As unchartable as they seem, the divisions between Castle and Village and men and women are nonetheless absolute and govern what appears to be an entirely hierarchical and exploitative system. Whatever the difference in *nature* between the Castle and Village may be, in practice, they need messengers and letters to traffic between them. And however incoherently gendered attributes may be distributed among them, only women are sexually commandeered by officials, who are only men.

Hier Ist Kein Verkehr(?)

In his study on Kafka and his fin-de-siècle context, Mark Anderson traces the concept of *Verkehr*—"the movement of people, goods, money, or information" with primary meanings of "traffic, trade, commerce, exchange, social and sexual intercourse"—throughout much of Kafka's oeuvre, but not in relation to *The Castle*.[31] He certainly could have: the concept is central to this novel as well. The following discussion relies heavily on Morrison's understanding of the *Verkehr*, but in the Castle world, its polyvalence has been considerably trimmed down. The primary modes of *Verkehr* are either writing or sex, associations that supply the compounds *Geschlechtsverkehr* (sexual intercourse), *Brief-* or *Schriftsverkehr* (written correspondence), and *Aktenverkehr* (the circulation of bureaucratic documents). K. does not grasp his limited options, resorting repeatedly to those meanings of *Verkehr* apparently bracketed off from Castle exchange. He asks the landlord about monetary compensation from the Castle (a request rendered doubly out of step by the reference to his wife and child), to which the landlord gives the cryptic reply that no one complains about that here, a reply K. might well interpret to mean that everyone is satisfied with their wages, but a reply that might as easily indicate simply that questions of the exchange of money for services do not come up, that they are not appropriate to the system. Similarly, Olga is surprised that K. believes that Barnabas works for the Castle for financial consideration, while the sledge-driver Gestacker will take no payment for transporting K. through the village. His conversation with Gestacker reveals another way in which K. misunderstands how *Verkehr* can function in this world: he assumes that the street is an appropriate venue for "traffic" and misguidedly asks to be driven to the Castle along this route, twice receiving the reply "hier ist kein Verkehr"[32] ("there is no traffic here"), and indeed, K. never manages to reach the Castle by any street on foot, either. Apparently, the Castle system allows for neither financial nor vehicular, nor even pedestrian, traffic. K.'s expectation that people might work in exchange for money or that he might find traffic on a street seems abundantly rational both to K. and to his readers, but outlandish to natives of the Castle world.

Indeed, despite the unstable structural relations between gender and power, the system of exchange with the Castle is extremely limited and binary. Men and women occupy different, rigidly defined roles with respect to the system of *Verkehr*, roles by all appearances determined by sex. Women's *Verkehr* with the Castle is strictly physical: it is sexual intercourse. Frieda's own story most clearly illustrates the female side of this equation. Her station in life is entirely determined by her relation to men. By becoming Klamm's mistress, Frieda has worked her way up by the means available to her. Although she depicts herself as the helpless victim of Klamm's vulgar servants, Frieda nonetheless picks up a whip and drives them into a stall. Similarly, the Landlady's youthful liaison with Klamm increased her value as a potential wife and villager afterwards. But if women are limited to sex, sex as a mode of *Verkehr* with the Castle is limited to them. When K. tries to use his relationship with

Frieda as an approach to the Castle, he makes no more progress than he does with the streets. In fact, his relationship with Frieda only lowers her status, rather than elevating his as he had hoped. For men, there may be no physical contact: the *Verkehr* is verbal. For K., as a man, only words—and never direct speech, but words mediated by ancient (messengers, letters) or modern means of conveyance (telephones)—will do. Conversely, for women, sexual relations take the place of verbal contact. That is, while sexual contact may be initiated verbally, the messages themselves decrease in verbal importance and even resemble sexual acts themselves, while once sexual contact begins, it entirely replaces even this limited verbal contact. Thus the messenger whose picture the Landlady retains initially called her to the Castle by "Schriftsverkehr" (correspondence); the message's unambiguous function and the short shrift given its verbal construction distinguishes it from other messages depicted. Even more markedly, Amalia's letter from Sortini is so vulgar as to seem entirely sexual in nature, and we know only this sexual nature and none of its words, unlike the verbatim reporting of Klamm's letter to K. And as for Frieda, her position as Klamm's mistress involved spoken words, but this speech produced no verbal *exchange*: he would call her name (perhaps summoning her, perhaps only saying it) and she could speak to him, but he would not speak to her in any other way.

The rigidly maintained exclusion of male physical contact with Castle officials apparently breaks down once, when K. lands in bed with Bürgel, but as Bürgel himself makes clear, this is a slippage of the rules—and K. sleeps through it in any case. Since the narrative continues while K. is asleep, the incident also affords one of the novel's few breaks from K.'s narrow perspective. Eric Miller describes what goes on while K. is asleep as "a detailed description of the positions of K.'s body as he sleeps. Nothing more."[33] Certainly, there is no reason to assume that the positions of bodies are unimportant—especially when two men are in bed together and one of them has been dreaming of wrestling and vanquishing Greek gods. Indeed, all of the narrative breaks that Miller treats deal with bodies and sexual relations, with the notable exception of the opening paragraph about the Castle. If we see these breaks as a group—*including* the nonsexual opening paragraph—united by an organizing principle, the association of the Castle with these other scenes further confirms its status as a sexualized entity. Yet the Bürgel encounter holds out no possibility of *heterosexual* contact leading K. closer to the Castle—that possibility, if it exists at all, is strictly homoerotic, outside the norm, and furthermore remains unconsummated. Under ordinary circumstances, "official decisions are as shy as young girls," and K.'s body must be mediated by the word. K. may speak to officials on the phone, write and receive letters, or relay spoken messages. Barnabas and the Village secretaries traffic in words, shuttling them back and forth from their sources to their addressees. They cannot sleep their way to the top.

Women and Writing in *The Castle*: Frieda and Amalia

Thus sex (as opposed to gendered attributes) emerges as the single unalterable difference in the Castle world, one that becomes fully legible specifically with relation to the Castle and its system of *Verkehr*. The other major distinction, that between Castle and Village, is functional and, apparently, spatial. While K. is told that "there is no difference between the Castle and the Village," however, he is never told anything of the kind about men and women. That is, the world operates *as if* there is an absolute difference between Castle and Village whether there is one or not, and the text suggests there may not be, but there *does* seem to be some absolute, irreducible difference between male and female characters. Sex, it seems, is a more stable difference than class in the Castle world—and so it would be understood in postwar Czechoslovakia, where the hereditary empire had just been done away with and where by the early 1920s, some "foreign" nobles were being stripped of their lands and titles on the grounds of harm done to the Czech nation. Class divisions were still practiced and performed; classes were still architecturally, economically, and spatially separated, but with fewer assumptions (theoretically, at least) about their *inherent* difference in kind or, as English used to put it, "quality." By contrast, both in the novel and in 1920s Prague, sexual difference is accorded ontological status independent of what that difference *means*, which was changing rapidly in Prague, as I discuss at greater length in the ensuing chapter.

Given the incoherence of the distribution of gendered attributes among *The Castle*'s male and female characters, however, it is worth interrogating *how* sex can be clearly differentiated enough for the system to function so absolutely. While in the world outside the novel this distinction would have been fixed by assumptions about the binary nature of sexed bodies, in the novel itself, physical, bodily descriptions are quite limited and are far from reliably sex-specific—and there is no description at all of the protagonist. Extra-textual assumptions about unrepresented bodies do not govern this fictional world: the sex of the characters is fixed by language alone. Naturally such a thing is true at some level about any novel written, but here sex is accorded ontological status not by descriptions of sexed bodies or fixed patterns of gendered behavior, but by grammar. In other words, grammar supplants the body as the irreducible marker of sexual legibility. Proper nouns—names and titles—also serve an identifying function, but grammar is the more reliable indicator: the single letter "K." is not a gendered name, yet the Land Surveyor's sex is never in question. No individual words—not proper nouns, and not even individual pronouns or articles—are sufficient in and of themselves to reliably distinguish gender in all cases: German is an inflected language, but inflected pronouns and articles of different grammatical genders can be morphologically identical to one another. Grammatical gender thus remains consistently legible at the level of system, but *only* at this level: it is not always legible at the level of the individual sign, and this holds true even of those signs (pronouns and articles) for which indicating grammatical gender is a primary function. As the Prague School member Karcevskij would argue a few years later with regard to the problem of homonymy—a problem of insufficient morphological difference—"grammatical values are more stable" than individual signs; furthermore, "in the domain of grammar . . . the subdivisions always occur in pairs," arguably reinforcing the binary structure that language seems at once to rely on (as when the presence or absence of "s" determines a plural in English) and yet fails to consistently maintain. If all this seems unrealistically technical to have been actively present in Kafka's thinking, it is worth remembering that he subscribed to a philological journal at the time and had been actively engaged in improving his writing in a language far more heavily inflected than German. The different ways in which languages deal with grammatical gender would have been, to borrow again from the Prague School, "actualized" or foregrounded for him.

So, from among *The Castle*'s various social, architectural, sexual, and linguistic instabilities one clear and stable boundary emerges: sexual difference. The entire segregated system of textual and sexual exchange is ordered around this essentially grammatical difference—a difference sometimes indicated, like national identity in Prague surnames, by the presence or absence of a single letter. But if language orders sex—both in the sense of commanding sexual performance, as in Sortini's letter to Amalia, and in the sense of maintaining a legible system of sexual difference—sex several times *dis*-orders language, producing attendant ruptures in the smooth functioning of the sex-specific system of *Verkehr*. Like the Castle itself, language functions as a social structure with tangible, physical implications—a structure that can be misconstrued and misapprehended if interpreted in terms of expectations and experiences external to it (such as a foreign language), as K. learns when he first apprehends the Castle in daylight. This misconstrual disrupts K., however, rather than the system he regards. Nonetheless, sexual and social, linguistic and formal ruptures *do* coincide in several instances in precisely the way that K. himself—read as a writer figure—seems at once eager and powerless to effect on his own.

In one such instance, the passage describing K.'s initial encounter with Frieda—the most sexually explicit scene in the novel, and arguably in all of Kafka's fiction—constitutes an equally rare poetic moment: poetic not only in the Prague School sense that it foregrounds language as medium by violating established textual norms (and it does), but even in the more traditional sense of heightened sonority and verbal patterning. An intensity of rhythm, consonance, and repetition marks the beginning passage off stylistically from the vast majority of the novel:

> Three hours went past, hours in which they had one breath, in which they had one heartbeat, hours in which K. always felt that he was

> losing himself or wandering far into a strange country, as no man had yet gone before him, a strange country in which the very air had no trace of his native air, where one might die of strangeness, and yet whose enchantment was such that one could only go on and lose oneself further.[34]

> Dort vergiengen Stunden, Stunden gemeinsamen Atems, gemeinsamen Herzschlags, Stunden, in denen K. immerfort das Gefühl hatte, er verirre sich oder er sei soweit in der Fremde, wie vor ihm noch kein Mensch, eine Fremde, in der selbst die Luft keinen Bestandteil der Heimatluft habe, in der man vor Fremdheit ersticken müsse und in deren unsinnigen Verlockungen man doch nichts tun könne als weiter gehn, weiter sich verirren.[35]

This passage plays on expectations of poetry and prose, both in general terms and with specfic regard to Kafka. The introduction of more traditionally poetic devices violates the norm, in Prague School parlance, set by Kafka's famously terse prose style, but the passage raises these more traditional poetic expectations only to disappoint them. The repetition of "Stunden" and of "gemeinsamen" immediately thereafter, along with the rhythmic prominence of the words "Atems" and "Herzschlags," quickly suggest a pattern that is amplified by the material, bodily rhythms that breath and heartbeat evoke but disrupted the phrase that follows. Formally, then, the passage reproduces the novel's favorite structural and thematic trick: markedly setting up clear expectations only to undercut them. While the prose here "violates" the norms set by the novel's stylistic terseness and even approaches the lyrical by comparison, the broken rhythms and uneven, dispersed repetition in turn disrupt the comparative ease and familiarity that any sustained rhythmic regularity might produce. The overall linguistic effect is one of strangeness, since the formal arrangement produces a heightened awareness of language as material that coincides with the heightened bodily experience it describes—except for the fact that this passage (as opposed to the one preceding, which describes the lovers' physical location among the strewn garbage) is marked by mental abstraction and a near *loss* of consciousness, veering off from the shared awareness of breath and heartbeats. Thus rather than dovetailing nicely, signifiers and signified twist off from each other, recapitulating at the level of word and line the novel's broadest narrative-structural effects.

At the narrative level, K.'s experience of his union with Frieda reads like a parable for K.'s experience of the Castle world, a *mise en abyme* of the novel's narrative, one in which sexual intercourse with a woman stands in for K.'s initial entry into the Castle realm, reinforcing the aspect of the Castle as a sexualized, feminized entity. The *mise en abyme* functions structurally as well, replicating almost to the letter the open structure of the novel in its final and unfinished form. The passage hints—in keeping with Brod's memory of Kafka's stated intentions for the novel's end—that K. will die a stranger, perhaps of his very status as a stranger who is unable, ultimately, to be suitably nourished by Castle air. Again, however, the nested rhetorical and figural continuity of part to whole is apparent but also skewed: the terms of "stranger" status have shifted. Strangeness for once is identified with foreign territory rather than with the intruder K.; remarkably, this reversal occurs in tandem with a reversal in the key term's grammatical gender. Everywhere else in the novel, K. is referred to as "der Fremde" ("the stranger"), both by himself and by the natives. Only here is there any reference to "eine Fremde" ("a strange land"). The grammatical gender distinction parallels the relation of the scene's male and female bodies: the text presents K. as being in a strange land rather than as a stranger himself at precisely the moment that it also strongly suggests he is literally in Frieda. Phonemic parallels between the two feminine nouns in question—"Fr(ie)d(a)" and "Fr(em)d(e)"—further support the association, As Stanley Corngold and Benno Wagner remark: "the uncanny strangeness that K. registers is his swoon into the spaces of the woman's body."[36] So K. the would-be usurper succeeds in seducing the mistress of his (apparent or potential) master, but he finds the space this opens terrifying, linked with death. Frieda in the Herrenhof inn also phonemically fuses K.'s bodily occupation there with his boyhood invasion of the *Friedhof* (cemetery), an oblique reference which nonetheless casts a pall over K.'s transgressive accomplishment while drawing on an age-old convention linking sex with death. "Luft" similarly acts as a keynote, resonating with the pattern initiated by K.'s first daylight impression of the Castle when it appears "umrissen in der klaren Luft" ("outlined in the clear air") and playing off the tendency of this clarity to falter in K.'s mind, to disappoint expectations raised in the "Heimat" ("homeland") (or here, by the very "Heimatluft" ["native air"]).[37] Yet as established by his interest in the known but proscribed cemetery, K. does not want "a strange land," only a known quantity (like the boyhood cemetery) that he can enter transgressively. Thus, despite his stated interest in disrupting the system and creating something new that emerges in discussion with the Village Chairman, K.'s interest in transgression remains a function of his interest in the rule of law, in the system the rule establishes, and improving his own status with regard to it.

In this passage, strangeness further intensifies and collects around its own verbal signifier as grammar itself now exposes a destabilization of the morphology of the grammatical gender on which the novel's entire segregated system seems to hang: the grammatically feminine noun "Fremde" first appears in conjunction with an inflected article that replicates the masculine nominative—"die Fremde" nonetheless appears as "der Fremde." The sex act thus collapses and reverses distinctions maintained throughout the novel, but without generating a form in which these changes would be legible in isolation. Grammatical gender is distinguishable only within a system, and this system, here, has exposed its fissures, producing effects so strange they threaten to annihilate consciousness—effects which are also the very hallmarks of K.'s overall Castle experience of wandering, of erring without agency or self-control. Ironically, it is Klamm's voice that rescues K. from this land, pulling him back into his struggle and away from Frieda (doubly ironic because it is Frieda he summons), an effect that was for K. "kein Schrecken, sondern ein tröstliches Aufdämmern, als aus Klamms Zimmer mit tiefer befehlend-gleichgültiger Stimme nach Frieda gerufen wurde"[38] ("it came not as a shock but as a consoling glimmer when from Klamm's room a deep, commanding, yet also indifferent voice called out for Frieda").[39] K. experiences considerable relief at being summoned back from disjunction and freedom to his (he thinks) well-defined, homosocial, and comprehensible struggle with Klamm.

The coincidence of this unusually marked verbal material with an unusually marked (even graphic, for Kafka) depiction of sexual relations might suggest that this passage be read hermetically only, as an anomalous, isolated instance indicating potentials for physicality that are usually proscribed by the novel and its world. This other kind of being (for K.) and of writing (for the novel) seems to indicate a territory external to the struggle that K. views as central to his experience: a road to a strange land not taken, a structure which, if we read K. as writer figure, replicates Kafka's own sense of the incompatibility of sex and writing. Yet the passage is among the novel's most self-reflexive moments in terms of overall narrative structure and lexicon, an effect that calls the centrality of the homosocial struggle into question while indicating an equal importance for the bodily relations the passage represents. These relations, too, recall Kafka's experience with Jesenská—as does the simultaneous pull of sex and the fear of new possibilities—one of which, for Kafka, is certainly death.

Frieda's situation parallels Jesenská's in a number of basic ways—the triangulated structure of her relationships with K. and Klamm and her connection with an inn called the "Herrenhof" being the most obvious—but several important differences impose a limit on how literally we should read Frieda as a direct representation of Jesenská. Frieda's domesticity, her tendency to cling physically and emotionally, and her readiness to leave Klamm and marry K. all mark sharp departures from Jesenská's life and personality. Particularly missing from Frieda's character is any apparent corollary to the most important aspect of Jesenská's relationship to Kafka: writing. Such departures serve as stark reminders not to view the relationship that Kafka's text bears to elements outside it in terms of traditional representation. His characters are not fictionalized portrayals of real people. Rather, his skewed and often abstracted or refracted structural transpositions almost necessitate that the corollary to Jesenská's *writing* and its varied implications for Kafka could not be found within the limits of a single character. Linguistic interest and intensity do accrue *around* Frieda, however, much as they do around the early images of the Castle. And in this instance, the textual embodiment of coupling and its effects on consciousness itself incorporates the rhetoric and structure of the passage previously discussed in which Kafka first reacts to Jesenská's writing. The letter passage, so suggestive of the overall narrative structure and rhetorical environment of the novel as a whole, likewise prefigures the Frieda passage, but the shifts and substitutions between letter and novel are even more significant than the parallels. Jesenská's texts, which Kafka then refers to as written by "keine gewöhnliche Schreiberin" ("no ordinary writer"), correspond structurally to "die Fremde" through which K. wanders while apparently also sexually joined with Frieda, accentuating the confusion and tension surrounding textual and sexual relations that resurfaces throughout the correspondence. But in the novel at the level of representation rather than performativity, the boundary between sexual and textual *Verkehr* is precisely what is so strictly regulated and segregated in the Castle world. This segregation broadly reflects Kafka's own sense of mutual exclusion of the sexual and textual that his relationship to Jesenská challenged in new ways.

If Jesenská's writerly Czech prose becomes "die Fremde" in which "der Fremde" Kafka can get lost, it is still unclear precisely what attributes are responsible for its strangeness. As with the Castle's confusing system of gender and power matrices, Jesenská's prose may be so strange because a woman wrote it, or because a Czech wrote it, or because it is literary *written* Czech in an intimate setting. But the juxtaposition between the fictional and epistolary passages stresses the uneasy association of the bodily and the textual found in the letters themselves. For Kafka, the female is construed as the bodily—in the carnal sense, at least—an association related to Kafka's rejection of marriage, his construction of himself as writer *rather than* body, as writer *rather than* husband to a wife, and thus the category "woman writer" poses a challenge to Kafka's own segregated system. Another parallel between the Frieda/"Fremde" passage and Jesenská's writing comes even more directly—a phrase of her own that made such an impression on Kafka that he quotes it back to her in Czech: "Nejraději bych utekla třetí cestou která nevede ani k tobě ani s ním, někam do samoty" ("Most of all, I'd like to follow a third path leading neither to you nor with him, but somewhere into solitude").[40] Here, the path leads not into the female body but rather leads the female body away from men (from Kafka and Pollak both) and into solitude, which Kafka himself construes as the necessary condition for writing.

Echoes of Kafka's reaction to Jesenská's texts and K.'s reaction to the Castle buildings similarly intersect in the language that surrounds not bodily coupling, but Amalia's disturbing gaze:

> Her gaze was cold, clear, as immobile as ever, it wasn't directly fixed on what she was observing, but instead—and this was unsettling—went past it, only slightly, ever so imperceptibly, but undeniably so it didn't seem to be weakness, embarrassment, or dishonesty that

> caused this but rather a constant desire for solitude that dominated all other feelings.[41]

> Ihr Blick war kalt, klar, unbeweglich wie immer; er was nicht geradezu auf das gerichtet, was sie beobachtete, sondern ging—das war störend—ein wenig, kaum merklich, aber zweifellos daran vorbei, es schien nicht Schwäche zu sein, nicht Verlegenheit, nicht Unehrlichkeit, die das verursachte, sondern ein forwährendes, jedem anderen Gefühl überlegenes Verlangen nach Einsamkeit.[42]

This gaze, "kalt, klar, unbeweglich wie immer," combines qualities of clarity, constancy, and immutability that K. had hoped to find in the Castle tower, qualities consistent with his memory of the church tower of his childhood that tapered "ohne Zögern" ("without hesitation") and with the "Entschlossenheit" ("resolution") and "hellsichtigen Klugheit" ("clear-sighted intelligence") of Jesenská's prose. The disturbing quality of Amalia's gaze stems, however, from its *indirectness*, which distances it from the remembered Castle tower that seems to thrust purposively towards some higher goal. The three qualities that do *not* motivate this indirection—"nicht Schwäche" (weakness); "nicht Verlegenheit" (embarrassment); "nicht Unehrlichkeit" (dishonesty) die das verursachte"—are stereotypically feminine, but in this novel, all have been associated with Castle officials—"Unehrlichkeit" in particular being a fine translation of the Czech noun *klam*. We have already heard of Klamm's delicacy, while a few pages after this conversation, we hear of the proverb "amtliche Entscheidungen sind scheu wie junge Mädchen" ("official decisions are as shy as young girls"), to which K. replies without explaining further: "die Entscheidungen mögen noch ander Eigenschaften mit Mädchen gemeinsam haben" ("official decisions may share other characteristics with girls, as well").[43] The verb "scheinen," furthermore, while common enough in general, nonetheless occupies a privileged position in this novel. It initiates K. into the Castle world in the first lines and returns in his second view as well, forging a strong association with the frustrating indistinctness that characterizes K.'s experience of the realm. Amalia's gaze is thus distanced rhetorically from Castle officials but aligned with some of the Castle architecture's most disruptive effects. Similarly, the cold of Amalia's gaze precludes any possibility of "Leidenschaft" (passion) and "Lieblichkeit" (charm), the more stereotypically feminine characteristics that Kafka identifies as stylistic markers of Jesenská's and Němcová's prose (as discussed more extensively in chapter 8).

Yet despite K.'s critique, Amalia's gaze is not without direction—it is simply not directed toward him. It is motivated, rather, by "ein fortwährendes, jedem andern Gefühl überlegenes Verlangen nach Einsamkeit" ("a constant desire for solitude that dominated all other feelings"). This characteristic again recalls Kafka's quoted sentence of Jesenská's prose, the yearning for "a third path" that leads away from male lovers and toward solitude, and underscores the disturbing quality of female desire directed not at men but toward the isolated state he most associates with writing. Amalia's smile, however, mediates this discomfort, and makes, remarkably, "die Stummheit sprechend" ("her silence eloquent") and "die Fremdheit vertraut" ("her strangeness familiar"). This smile focuses attention back from the cold eyes to the warm mouth, the site Kafka associates with the pleasure of Jesenská's Czech prose. This speech is also revelatory; K. feels suddenly party to "die Preisgabe eines Geheimnisses, die Preisgabe eines bisher behüteten Besitzes" ("the discloser of a secret, of a formerly closely guarded possession").[44] This phrase associates the silent, eloquent language evocative of Kafka's experience of Jesenská's prose with a rhetoric suggestive of the "secrets" of virgin female sexuality *and* the traditional link between sexual possession and property relations. The rhetoric of property echoes the first *spoken* words of the novel: "Dieses Dorf ist Besitz des Schlosses" ("This Village is the property of the Castle") and Kafka's own dictum that in the world of the senses, language deals only with property relations—language in the realm of the senses, then, returning us to the task of the surveyor. *This* property, however—unlike the rest of the territory K. fails to survey—is a secret purposefully kept, rather than knowledge he simply does not have and fails to learn. Or so, at least, K. thinks. We have little reason, after all, to trust the surveyor's judgment in such matters. He is perceptive in that he is observant, but his interpretations of what he sees are often mistaken. He is an exemplary reader, but he is not necessarily the best example we are offered.

The Castle system requires the participation of its inhabitants; it requires that they read according to its rules. Amalia's refusal to participate and obey the command of the letter exposes the insult inherent in all such letters that otherwise rely on a particular kind of blindness among the villagers, a tacit community agreement that they will interpret signs in one particular way and not in others. Elizabeth Boa shows how the critical reception of this character makes for a telling barometer of sexual politics: Richard Sheppard, for example, writing before the influence of feminism became widely felt in literary studies, saw Amalia's act in a negative light, ruining the local fete and undermining the society's kinship structure by refusing marriage. Reiner Stach in his then-pioneering work on Weiningerian influences failed to take Amalia's full complexity into account, according to Boa, because such complexity would undermine the Weiningerian systematicity of his reading. Amalia remains a confounding figure, and critics are divided about whether she is successful in her defiance or merely marginalized by it, and about what, if anything, she is opting for. Boa sees her as an "agent of an act of revolt directed against a power system and its juridical superstructure" and interprets her silence as a sign that she has removed herself from the marriage market.[45] But Boa sees the Castle as a legible system of clear patriarchal structure, founded on a stable division of gender roles which parallels the hierarchical power structure of Castle and Village. In support of this view, she notes that there are no women among the Castle officials, and while the dominant powers of the Village are women, these strong women nonetheless actively participate in their own subjugation and thus support the system. Yet the Castle world does not seem to view sexual intercourse with Castle officials as degrading. Village women seem to be in a position that is if anything superior to their male Village counterparts, even to messengers and the Mayor. This sense of Castle sex *elevating* village women would explain why Amalia's refusal, which suggests that the attentions of the Castle official *are* degrading in some way, particularly explains the scornful reaction of the village women. That K., a foreigner, can interpret signs differently has far less effect, since such misunderstandings are expected of foreigners—but that a member of the linguistic community would read "against the grain" in this way has an effect so threatening that the misreader must immediately be ostracized from that community, and become a foreigner within it, lest she disrupt its functioning.

In this way, Amalia's literalizing gesture exposes the workings of texts that function smoothly in accordance with an accepted set of rules, rendering invisible the violence entailed in bringing about that smoothness. The difference in this world, of course, is that the smoothly functioning system is *overtly* violent and abusive, so a violent or abusive action would follow and uphold rather than violate the norm. Amalia's act, then, an act of apparent chastity, may be the only willed transgression possible in a system that is itself overtly transgressive. It is as if, like Bartleby the Scrivener, she "would prefer not to"—but unlike Bartleby, she seems to actually long for what she nonetheless refuses. If rather than interpreting the Castle and its system narrowly as an oppressive political regime, we instead read it as an analogue for the functioning of language as a social system, Amalia's act can be read as a rejection of the literary process—at least as it is represented by the segregated *Brief/Geschlechstverkehr* system (written correspondence v. sexual intercourse). The linguistic functioning of her gaze and smile, however, suggest some possibility of a "third path." Such a path would be possible, her situation suggests, only in isolation from the Castle's "community of native speakers," who would constitute the Prague School's necessary condition for literature but who seem capable of understanding Amalia's act in only one way, as conditioned by her sexed, gendered position. It further leaves open the possibility that such a third path does not necessarily oppose sexuality per se, although it is born of a refusal to act sexually, but rather opposes its function in the coercive and segregated grammar of the system. She might want sex (or letters), but not on these terms.

The political and ethical implications of Kafka's novel emerge more consistently on this formal, rhetorical, and even sub-lexical level than by any means that could be called narrative, anything that resembles the relation of events. In its structure as well as in its represented world, the novel most resembles the kind of cubic puzzle that can recombine along its many axes, suggesting an almost infinite array of patterns, all potential and active within the same recognizable structure, with each internal cube replicating the structure of the whole. Each of these parts, in the case of the novel, is likewise mobile, likewise shifts along its own smaller axes. Does this apparently self-transgressing structure (of the Castle or *The Castle*) itself ensure the constant potential for change, exceeding the power of the individual actors within it? Or does the potential for structural change come as the result of the actions of individual constituents, putting the individual parts, and thus the whole, in motion? Or, does the flexibility rather imply that all potential disruption is "always already" a feature of the structure, reinforcing its own nature and leading nowhere outside of it, so that transgression and rupture are thus *included in* rather than disruptive of the system? Of course, the cube toys have one solution, one way in which all sides will match smoothly. The solution used to be for sale (puzzlers could skirt the system while maintaining the structure's workings), or the cube could be carefully taken apart and realigned by color (frustrated users could dismantle the system, and then rebuild it). *The Castle*, however, as we should have learned early from Walter Benjamin, offers no such "solution"—no means, whether violent or sneaky or dutifully diligent, resolves it to a whole and stable state. Dissonance (apparently) *is* its natural state.

I have argued that common elements among Jesenská's and Němcová's texts and Kafka's reactions to them in his letters come together in this novel. These elements do not consistently align but rather behave much like gendered or classed characteristics in the Castle world, remaining constant as constituents, but shifting in relation to one another and to the whole—much like what Kafka says happens in metaphors. The relation of women to language and particularly to writing, to continue with the above example, is an active concern in *The Castle* at a structural and a rhetorical or stylistic level. The relationship to women's writing is also not a constant. At the level of imagery and representation, the novel most resembles Němcová's tale of a castle and a village. These traces of Němcová, however, seem aligned with K.'s old remembered order of architectural legibility and symbolic potency, while the world depicted in Jesenská's "Kavárna" seems more of a piece with the disturbing, hybrid structure of the Castle world. Stylistically, what Kafka values in the women's styles shares elements both with what K. longs for and is discomfited by, while Kafka's epistolary *reactions* to reading Jesenská anticipate the novel's narrative and rhetorical trajectories. Similarly, and clearly related for Kafka to women's writing at this point, the role of the Czech language likewise lines up with Castle elements in several different ways at once: with the social system of the Castle world in which K. (like Kafka in Czech Prague, or Kafka in Czech writing) can only ever be foreign; or as the only hope (illegible, of course, to K.) of that world's disruption through its lurking interlinguistic presence, with the fissure in Klamm's name exposing the delusional nature of the Castle system. But this same lurking linguistic presence may rather expose the delusional nature of any such hope—who is to say to what *klam* refers? An individual word is indeterminate without the system, and *klam*, like Kafka's reading of Milena's Czech name, is a foreign word gone astray. Or, finally, Czech separates K. irrevocably from M. with its Czech imperative: K(lam!)m: Czech is the interloping problem, not the means to a solution.

In the earliest draft fragment, a quickly established atmosphere of absolute difference and mistrust leads the Guest (the proto-K.) to construe as torture what the maid (proto-Frieda or proto-Pepi) quickly explains is only a lack of mutual knowledge and understanding. But the maid's simple, clear, direct, and logical request—highly reminiscent of the stylistic and personal qualities Kafka values in both Jesenská and her prose—that the Guest simply ask what he wants to know and she will answer honestly already seems to name an absurd impossibility, given their differences in background and, in this draft at least, the Guest's apparently pathological distrust. Direct, honest communication across difference would solve this problem. It is what is most needed and what seems furthest out of reach in the world of the novel, even as it would seem logically to be a simple, attainable solution. Language may structure and name such difference, but direct, straightforward communication across it seems to be precisely what language prevents.

Chapter 8

✦

Of Mice and Music

Viel Zeit, viel Zeit, die besser verwendet werden könnte, kostet mich das kleine Volk.

—Kafka, "Der Bau"

"There is a possibility that I could go on living in this fashion, only guard such a way of life against women." Guard it against women—why, they are already lurking in the "in-this-fashion."

—Kafka, journal entry, January 23, 1922

"My health is quite good, assuming that mouse phobia does not carry me off before tuberculosis does," wrote Kafka to his friend Felix Weltsch in November 1917, some three months after the hemorrhage that led to his tuberculosis diagnosis. Despite the flippant tone, Kafka's health was only rarely close to "quite good" from this point onward, throughout the nearly seven years until his death. Perhaps in this way mice and their squeaking became indelibly associated with Kafka's first months of grappling with his diagnosis, and perhaps this association was in part what led Kafka to return to the topic during his last months of rapidly declining health: he completed his final story, "Josefine the Singer or the Mouse Folk," about three months before he died in June 1924. Written during his final stay in Prague, this story focuses in great part on the squeaking, or piping, of the Mouse folk, about which—with reference to literal mice—he had had much to say. It is common—and important—to consider this story with regard to the way it figures more abstract concerns of artistic, gender, and cultural identity, but it is perilous to bracket off the literal too quickly in Kafka. Fear is so common a theme in his fiction and personal writings, and it so often concerns large existential matters such as sex, marriage, fathers (large enough in Kafka's mind to span continents), and his own body's failings that it would be easy to overlook his terror of anything so small as mice. Yet the terror seems genuine enough when he suffered a plague of mice while living with his sister in Zürau (Siřem), in western Bohemia, in the fall of 1917. The most harrowing night he recounts to Weltsch:

> The first fatal flaw of Zürau, a night of mice, a fearful experience . . . here and there in the night I had heard a delicate nibbling . . . but this time it was an uproar. What a frightful mute and noisy race this is! Around two A.M. I was wakened by a rustling around my bed, and from then on the rustling did not stop until morning. Up the coal box, down the coal box, across the room they ran, describing circles, nibbling at wood, peeping softly while resting, and all along there was the sense of silence, of the secret labor of an oppressed proletarian race to whom the night belongs. To preserve my sanity, I decided that the noise was concentrated around the stove, which stands at the other end of the room. But it was everywhere, and reached its peak when a whole swarm of them leaped down together somewhere. I was completely helpless, could find nothing in my whole being to cling to.[1]

"Josefine" with its sense of mice as a people united in a piping song can surely trace its origins to this letter, but the sense of terror expressed here is not present in the "Josefine" story. Terror of a different kind, however, was hardly absent from Kafka's life when writing "Josefine." Kafka was dying. In an irony he likely began to recognize even as he wrote, the completion of this story about vocal piping immediately preceded the spread of his disease to his larynx, which largely silenced him. On the day he wrote the last page of "Josefine," Kafka seems to suggest to his friend and doctor Robert Klopstock that he had made the connection: "I think I began to investigate that animal squeaking at the right time. I have just finished a story about it," and later that evening, he complained of burning in his throat when drinking and "said he was worried that his larynx might also be affected."[2] It was: decline was rapid and relentless from that point onward, and so this story on mice and their music would be his last word—in fiction, at least. If fictionalizing and allegorizing mice constituted in some way his creative recuperation of or triumph over an earlier domestic terror, there was no such recuperation from tuberculosis, which won the sad race Kafka had dourly identified so many years before.

The composition of "Josefine" not only marked a return to and creative recuperation of Kafka's "mouse phobia," but also coincided with Kafka's return to Prague from Berlin. "Josefine," then, is the fictional companion of this return, his last stay in his home city after months of a long dreamed-of life in Germany, a life that had been devoted to the study of Hebrew, to coping during postwar inflation, and no doubt to negotiating domesticity in the course of living with a woman (Dora Diamant) other than his mother or sister for the first time. Increasingly, it was also a life devoted to his illness. Remarkably, after a lifetime of dreaming of an escape from his home city, Kafka referred to what fiction writing he did in Berlin as "Prague work," excusing his relative reticence in his correspondence with Max Brod by means of the following: "I am writing so little [to Brod] because, as is only natural, I am continuing my Prague life, my Prague work, of which there was also very little to say."[3] Kafka was writing "The Burrow" during his stay in Berlin, and continuing to explore—again through an animal protagonist—the relationship between community and creative identity, as he had in "Investigations of a Dog," completed earlier that year. The other story that occupied him during this continuation of his "Prague life" and "Prague work" was "A Little Woman," which similarly built on his increased interest in women and female identity that had been so prominent in *The Castle*. Thus "Josefine" has much in common with these late stories and seems, by virtue of its sudden explosive creation on return to Prague, to share their status as belonging to his "Prague life" and "Prague work." The meaning of this "Prague life" *for* the work is, of course, the focus of this book—particularly with regard to the "other" Prague life, the Czech part.

But what connection might that "other" Prague life have with the mouse phobia of his Zürau life—his country life? Associations with Czech on the one hand and animals on the other had surely been complicated in the ensuing years since his pre-Czechoslovak-era stay in Zürau, and I have argued in the previous chapter that Kafka's understanding of the way Czech and female identity intersect had profoundly changed, in turn altering the configuration of the identity closest to Kafka's own heart: his identity as a writer. Though certainly brought to a head by Kafka's relationship to Jesenská, this reassessment of Czech as a literary or writerly language seems to have first begun during the Zürau period—a period also, coincidentally, intensely focused on the animal world. Indeed, judging from his letters, much of Kafka's life in Zürau was devoted to observing (or doing battle with) animals and connecting them to his life in various ways—in addition to his travails with mice, he gleefully likened the face of a pig to that of Franz Werfel and saw different varieties of Jewish doctors among the goats: "I am thriving among the animals," he claims triumphantly; he often refers to his "friends" the geese. Otherwise, he spent his time helping his sister (he called their domesticity a "minor marriage") and reading: "I limit my reading here to Czech and French, and nothing but autobiography or correspondence," although his request to Felix Weltsch for such material stipulated that it should not be "too narrowly military, political, or diplomatic."[4] This period that so closely coincided with his increased proximity to both animal and female companionship also marked his first protracted interest in Czech writings since his secondary school studies—and the Czech work he singles out for special praise is the correspondence of Božena Němcová, which he found "unsurpassed" in its "psychological acumen."[5] Furthermore, Brod sent him Gabriela Preissová's *Její Pastokyňa*, the play that would become the basis for Janáček's opera of that name, and Kafka read that as well as *Jenůfa*, Brod's influential translation of the opera: "reading it is music," Kafka claimed. During this time he also speaks of the "bright, singing dialect and the barking of dogs" as the constant sound of the village.[6] Zürau, then, set in motion the turning wheels of association among the concepts of animals, women, Czech, writing, and music that find their culmination in "Josefine" (a near-sonic anagram of Jenůfa, a kind of play on names that Kafka loved), but which also resurface in various configurations throughout his last stories. Yet Kafka's animal stories are far from agrarian, and he refers to them not as his "Zürau" work but as his Prague work: these texts are social, about encountering, representing, or performing otherness. They seem to have little to do with animals *as such* except as exemplars of alterity, but the alterity of animals is something Kafka recognizes and respects. Although he may find parallels to humans in their faces, in material terms, he does not expect them to conform to his way of life. Who would imagine that cats would use a litterbox, as Kafka was to discover to his enormous relief? And yet it would seem clear enough to the cats; it would not need explaining, and would be something cats would hold, unexamined, in common. Yet Kafka might well have gone on forever cleaning cat feces from his bed, so relieved was he at the feline-aided respite from the terrors of mice. The conflict between human and cat culture had such a simple solution, but one that required an interpreter, an intermediary, to discover (someone had to tell him of the miracle of the sandbox). These late animal stories have something of the missing sandbox about them—and thus address inter- and intra-species relations in a way that connects them with animal-themed texts by other Prague writers of his day.

Animals: "A Matter of the Age"

Kafka was of a piece with many Czechoslovak writers in writing animal stories at this time, and it seems he was quite aware of his company. In *Conversations with Kafka*, Gustav Janouch recounts Kafka's reaction to the young Janouch's "news" that his friend's international fame had spread enough for *The Metamorphosis* to be imitated—by the English writer David Garnett in *Lady into Fox*, published in 1922. Kafka responded with "a faint dissenting movement of his head," saying "he didn't get that from me. It's a matter of the age. We both copied from that." Janouch's Kafka continues with the apparently endless supply of philosophical wisdom he provides to his young friend on cue: "Animals are closer to us than human beings. That's where our prison bars lie. We find relations with animals easier than with men."[7] Janouch and Kafka are here interrupted, but in a subsequent conversation, Kafka offers further thoughts on why "people write so much about animals now," reflecting that they feel trapped and wish to return to nature. Kafka may well have said such a thing, but it is hard to ascribe to him the "return to nature" as a motivation in writing about animals. Kafka indeed loved walking in the forests and mountains, loved gardening and country living, but Gregor Samsa's transformation and exile in a single room does not offer *freedom* from a trapped existence in the way this offhand comment suggests. Similarly, the mole-creature in "The Burrow," with his constant worries about the state of his food stores and the risk of possible incursions from outsiders, seems no more liberated than the average citizen of postwar central Europe. For all that Kafka rejoiced in his domestic life with pigs and goats in Zürau in 1917, it is with no bucolic nostalgia that he returns to the topic of mice in his last months of illness, nor to the topic of animals more broadly in his last great period of productivity. As for Kafka's purported claim that "we find relations with animals easier than with men," his relations with actual "mouse folk" illustrate that this ease was not the universal rule. It seems unlikely that we can take Janouch's report as a reliable guide to Kafka's motives for writing these stories, however much he genuinely felt the pull of "longing for the land."[8]

A caveat: the reliability of these reported conversations with Janouch is always open to question. That some such conversations indeed took place when Janouch was a young man, the son of a colleague of Kafka's at the Workmen's Accident Insurance Institute, is certain. However, as the Czech Kafka scholar Eduard Goldstücker most thoroughly documented, the dates Janouch gives fail to correspond with established biographical fact (Janouch mentions meeting Kafka in March 1920, when Kafka was in Merano, for example).[9] It furthermore seems unlikely, as Hugh Haughton also observes, that Kafka would have spent all his free time with this young man, however admirable, or that he would have continually dispensed such pithy information about the meaning of life, truth, and issues, such as politics and the Czech language, about which he was otherwise often reticent.[10] Not only are Janouch's dates unreliable and the conversations unverifiable, but the Kafka who does little but expound truths and make prophetic pronouncements seems impoverished compared with the Kafka whose minute observations of the mundane are the hallmark of his writings about animals whether fictional (Gregor's wounded mandibles) or real (the distribution of cat excrement). So why, then, mention Janouch at all? In part because Kafka does mention him several times in letters—sometimes with some exasperation—and because two of the people who knew Kafka best, Max Brod and Dora Diamant, his last companion, recognized Kafka in the voice Janouch re-creates in his accounts. Then, too, Janouch's accounts do offer information, some of which can be corroborated or supported independently, about Kafka's life, thoughts, and habits during a period (roughly 1920–1922) during which Kafka kept no detailed journal. Thus it is neither wise nor necessary to jettison all insights the *Conversations* might afford, any more than it is to accept them at face value. As to the conversation above, according to Janouch, this exchange about animals marked the first and only time he visited Kafka at his home, Kafka then being on sick leave. The dates Janouch gives are imprecise, but the discussion took place on the walk home from the Workmen's Accident Insurance Institute, and since Kafka would leave work permanently in July 1922, these exchanges are effectively dated to the spring of that year, a period of intense productivity for Kafka. Since indications of how he thought about his own writings in relation to contemporary culture are scant in these years, the awareness expressed here of tapping into a kind of zeitgeist is of great interest, particularly as it might bear on this period of renewed creativity in 1922. Although Janouch refers only to the earlier *Metamorphosis*, Kafka might by then have been working on "Investigations of a Dog" and "A Hunger Artist"—in which the "fasting artist" becomes the sideshow to a menagerie and is replaced after his death by a panther—as well as on *The Castle*. Animals and their cultural currency would likely have been on his mind, which lends at least partial credibility to Janouch's story.

As to Kafka's sense of his participating in a zeitgeist, it is true that writings prominently featuring animals were extremely common in the early years of the Czechoslovak Republic, particularly in 1920–23. It would have been odd for Kafka *not* to notice that the world of Czech letters was practically crawling with animals at this time. Max Brod had long been advising and translating Leoš Janáček, who was then (1921–23) at work on *The Cunning Little Vixen*, based on stories that initially ran in the Brno paper *Lidové noviny*, which Kafka mentions reading during its run. The same composer's opera about a "Mr. Bug," *The Excursions of Mr Brouček to the Moon and to the Fifteenth Century*, offers a rhetorical connection only, as the "bug" is not in fact an insect but rather a bourgeois landlord; nonetheless, a bourgeois-beetle comparison of any kind would surely be noted by the *Metamorphosis* author, especially since his best friend, Brod, had actively advised on the composer's writing and revision process.[11] This opera premiered in Prague in 1920, and its evolution enlisted a large and eclectic array of prominent Czech writers as librettists, including the nationalist writer Viktor Dyk (known to Kafka via the Great Wall controversy involving Franz Werfel), the Czech Jewish anarchist poet František Gellner, and the poet and director František Serafinský Procházka: all were involved in writing the adventures of a then-famous Mr. Brouček. The original satirical novels were by this time the best-known works of the nineteenth-century Czech writer Svatopluk Čech, who had died in 1908 and in whose honor Čechův Most (Čech Bridge) was then built and named. Kafka was highly familiar, as it happens, with Čechův Most: the apartment on Pařiška Street in which Kafka wrote "The Judgment" and began *The Metamorphosis* overlooked this bridge. Thus the tale of the bourgeois Samsa family, their boarders, and their beetle son was composed within view of a prominent Prague monument to the writer best known for lampooning a bourgeois "Mr. Bug"—likely a case of proximity rather than influence, but tantalizing nonetheless. The Czech literary legacy of the bourgeois insect did not stop with this 1920 operatic revision of these beloved old novels. The year 1922 saw the first production of Karel Čapek's *Ze života hmyzu* (*From the Life of Insects*), usually translated as *The Insect Play*. (See figure 11.)

Figure 11. Cover of *Ze života hmyzu* (*The Insect Play*) by Karel and Josef Čapek. Prague: Aventinum, 1921. Accessed via Hathi Trust.

First published in 1921, this play premiered in Brno in early 1922 and in Prague in April of that year—around the time of Kafka's conversation with Janouch about animals—with stage designs and costume concepts (including bug-men hybrids of all sorts) by Josef Čapek, the playwright's artist brother. It is inconceivable that Kafka would have escaped knowledge of this play. Brod was then active as a critic of Czech theater, and while Kafka was in residence in Prague during much of this time—thus we do not have letters to Brod as documentation—their vast correspondence attests to the extent to which they entered into one another's intellectual concerns. Even had Brod failed to mention it, this play about insects as people was created by the leading creative collaborators of the Czechoslovak Republic. The Čapeks were ubiquitous—inescapable even—at this time: Josef Čapek's illustrations and graphics as well as Karel's feuilletons regularly appeared in the same publications as Kafka, those which we know him to have read regularly (*Kmen, Tribuna, Die Prager Presse*), and the play was soon in production as far afield as London and New York: the Čapeks were an international Czech export, emblematic of the new era in which Czech culture would take its place on the world stage.

In some respects, *The Insect Play* follows at least initially on the logic by which Janouch's Kafka explains the trend in animal fiction: a Tramp, disgusted by city life, absconds to the countryside and begins lamenting postwar civilization—to a flower. He is disillusioned, and wishes to become a part of Nature. He meets a Pedant, whose ambitions toward Nature are rather different: the Pedant's aim is to capture, mount, analyze, and categorize insects, by which means he will understand them, and therefore life, better. As the two fight over capturing a butterfly, the Tramp's dream—which makes up the bulk of the play and consists of overheard conversations among butterflies, dung beetles, crickets, flies, larvae, parasites, and ants, all highly allegorized and broadly recognizable as different "kinds" of people—makes up the rest of the play. In tone, form, and general outlook, the work could not differ more broadly from Kafka's late fiction, but in addition to the thematic concern with animals, these different works equally reflect and critique postwar Prague's concern with sorting people into "kinds"—explicitly, with the Čapek brothers, in a way that mimics entomological or animal classification. Like the Janáček opera, the play mocks both bourgeois and artistic or bohemian conventionalism.

A slightly earlier work by the Moravian Czech writer Rudolf Těsnohlídek would also have been known to Kafka (if not to the English author who wrote nearly simultaneously about a fox-woman). *Liška Bystrouška* (*Vixen Sharp-Ears*), a largely light-hearted series of tales with a folkloric, pastoral flavor, was serialized and illustrated in the widely read daily *Lidové noviny* in 1920 and was published as a prize-winning book in 1921. In 1922 the book was already on its way to becoming a libretto for Janáček's opera of the same name (also known in English as *The Cunning Little Vixen*). Max Brod was intimately involved in translating and promoting the German-language versions of Janáček's oeuvre, and so would have known of Janáček's studies of animal life and behavior undertaken in preparation for writing the opera. (He certainly knew of Janáček's musical fascination with what he called speech melodies (nápěvky mluvy), or the melodic imprints of everyday speech.)[12] Even more than the Čapeks, however, this collection of stories associates the natural with the Czech pastoral, although the two do not necessarily live in harmony. A forester forcibly adopts the vixen, who escapes. Ultimately the forester's affections are transferred to a gypsy girl—as are everyone else's. Gypsy, nature, and fox seem indistinguishable to the humans, and ultimately the fox is killed as a present for the gypsy girl, leaving the forester sad until a frog jumps on his lap, leading him to peaceful reflections about the circle of life. Again, we are far from Kafka's universe, but the opera's sense of a winning, cunning female sexuality tied both to nature and to the tonalities of Czech folklore and music tends toward the cluster of ideas "woman, body, music" that Kafka elsewhere claims are inimical to him.

This trend of animal-pastorals with folkloric overtones was hardly limited to Czech writers; in 1921 Franz Werfel published "The Goat Song," which likely plays on the false etymology of the word "tragedy" and retains a certain faux folk-Slavic flavor. Set in a nonexistent, orientalized Slavic country and detailing a goat-creature's escape from a murderous father and his subsequent role in inspiring a peasant rebellion (he also goes on to father a peasant child), "The Goat Song" reflects the peasant-animal association from which the Čapeks' work—the Tramp's romanticization of nature notwithstanding—departs. In *The Insect Play*, the different insects represent different kinds of people, including city dwellers—most memorably, perhaps, the petty-bourgeois dung beetles. Thus, of two local animal traditions with which Kafka's late animal fiction does not quite align, the animal-as-allegory by his Czech colleagues has more in common with him than the animal-as-pastoral by his friend, particularly in terms of a critical, satirical flavor.

The most urban and satirical animal stories by any of Kafka's contemporaries, however, have a somewhat more renegade history, and date from a decade previously, though they will be recycled for their author's better-known work, *The Good Soldier Švejk*, which was appearing at precisely this time. Indeed, like much of Jaroslav Hašek's life, this "animal work" reads more as performance art than text. Prior to his career as a novelist, in a bid to become more respectable and therefore more marriageable, Hašek got himself a job as editor for the animal magazine *Svět zvířat* (*The Animal World*). Hašek apparently understood promoting the magazine to be part of his job, and so "for publicity he would take a mastiff from the magazine's kennel on walks around Prague" with a sign advertising the magazine. The magazine kept quite a kennel, the "queen" of which, Ripellino recounts, "was a trained but rather unruly ape named Miss Julie" that Hašek had gotten from a Hamburg circus.[13] Given Kafka's 1917 "Report to an Academy" about the becoming-human of a captured, now-educated ape, this account of Hašek's local "Miss Julie" is tantalizing, although Kafka never mentions either his contemporary or his trained ape. It is Hašek's activity as a writer of what we might call covert fiction for this magazine, however, that makes its way into *Švejk* in the 1920s—the very height of the "age" of animal stories in Prague.[14] A decade previously, Hašek had developed a practice of making up animals for *Svět zvířat*, and describing them straight, in house style and its scientific-sounding rhetoric—including, for example, a whale with a belly full of formic acid, an alcoholic hedgehog, and a "Paleozoic flea." Hašek's later character Marek gives a further catalog: "a mammal of a kangaroo family; the Edible Ox, the ancient prototype of the cow; the Sepica Infusorian," ultimately wondering, "did Brehm and all those who followed him know of my bat from Iceland, the Faraway Bat?"[15] Although the scientific community, as it happens, did notice Hašek's curious bestiary and was apparently unimpressed, he was able to continue publishing these covert fictions for some time before being fired. Again, we see the satirical look at the scientific means of classifying fellow creatures, as well as a taunt at a reading public happy to accept such divisions and classifications if they appeared in print and appeared to be authored by an "expert." Of even more immediate interest for Kafka's own late work, however, are two feuilletons published in *Tribuna* in 1921, one on sharks, the other on a "real life" Prague character who ran a flea circus. The flea circus—given Kafka's last story about a "small people" and their artist—is the most startlingly pertinent. The narrator recounts meeting Mestek, the proprietor of the flea circus, in a terrible state of depression—a drunk has killed his fleas. Despondent, he holds a box containing "the scattered corpse of a male flea, a first-class artist who had been the soul of the circus. Mestek called him fondly, 'František.' The artist's corpse had been identified under the magnifying glass, recognizable because he was missing a leg."[16] For Kafka, who had the habit of imagining himself as a corpse, to encounter his flea-artist namesake identifiable by a bodily deficit would have been arresting, all the more so because this "missing leg" (a symbolic castration, if in context a light-hearted one) was explained as self-inflicted as a sacrifice to his art: "such artists break their own legs so they do not jump too much and disturb the graceful procession of the circus." Rather than a lone sacrifice to a solitary art, however, this sacrifice was to the greater artistry of the collective, and "František" was mourned by his flea lover, also an artist dedicated enough to break her own legs. Mestek mourns their great love and artistry, turning to the problem of the new generation of fleas who have nothing of their ambition, artistry, or glory in a way that—without the ironic, ridiculous turn the story takes—even looks forward to Kafka's "Hunger Artist." At this point, Hašek's text does turn towards a grander scheme of charlatanry as the two reminisce about being kicked out of Hungary for the "panslavism" of the flea circus, being scolded by priests, and ultimately hatching a plan to defraud the whole city. Any commonality with Kafka's themes or interests recedes and leads to a series of entirely Hašekian picaresque shenanigans.

Hašek's hijinks did not stop at fiction, or even fictional political parties, nor was his tenure as an animal-writer the only element of Hašek's life with animals to enter into his major novel: fraud, fiction, and animal come together in *Švejk* more tangibly, and illegally. When we first meet Švejk, he's no longer in the military, having been officially declared an imbecile—instead, he makes his living selling fraudulently pedigreed dogs, as Hašek himself had done some years previously. And while he certainly made money doing this, the element of life-performance as satire is unavoidable: written papers transform mongrels into pedigreed purebreds, but the dogs look the same. The fraudulent pedigrees and covert fictions place Hašek's animal "stories" in a zone far from the folkloric pastoral or the Čapeks' *fabula*-satire—but also quite far from Kafka's dog, mole-creature, or mice. What Hašek's life-work and Kafka's late fiction somewhat surprisingly share, however, is a concern (in Hašek, it might be more a celebration than a concern) for how language—and only language—categorizes living creatures. The categories these animals occupy are political, and social.

The Czech political contexts for Kafka's animal stories are not only animal-related. It would be difficult to overstate the historical and cultural importance of the Czechoslovak president Tomáš Masaryk's essays on the peculiar situation of the "small nation"—"malý národ," "kleine Nation," with "národ" also encompassing the sense of "Volk." It is crucial to consider how this prevalent rhetoric of "smallness" informs both the Burrow's "Kleinzeug" and "Josefine's" minute mouse people. In his widely published and reprinted inaugural address to the London School of Slavonic and East European Studies, Masaryk construes smallness as a cultural identity: regional, territorial, but always relational. And always linguistic, having to do with speech, explicitly, in his address: "We are always speaking of smaller and greater, of small and great nations. What, then, is the proper definition of a small and great nation? . . . What is the problem of a small nation, and how does such a problem come to exist?" Masaryk answers, first, that these terms rely on one another, that a "small" nation cannot exist without its corollary in terms of greatness: "the very notion of smallness and greatness is relative and correlative" however it is measured, even if only by counting, by territory or population—as we've seen, both near obsessions in Prague in this era. But such measures, he also points out, are in flux; if "smallness" and "greatness" are relational identities, it also follows that they are essentially and necessarily subject to change, and indeed historical and social mutability is a cornerstone of this apparently non-essentialist essay. Although unsurprisingly, it does turn out that small nations have many a virtue, their flaws ("timidity" and "cringing lack of frankness" among them) tend to come largely from histories of oppression, while great nations are probably decadent and like to make war and, for most of the essay, are Germans. The essay indeed performs its own relational and situationist logic. Masaryk favored historically contingent explanations for what he saw as national or ethnic characteristics, and his government sought to protect vulnerable groups from chauvinist slurs and worst. He included many Czech Jews among his closest circle of friends and was sympathetic to the Zionist cause as well. Yet in this same well-known essay, Masaryk also takes up precisely what he calls the "zoological" turn in classifying humans. He stresses that although his name is associated with realism in politics, "we never can approve of the Realpolitik of Treitschke, Mommsen . . . and the rest who have converted anthropology into zoology. I say that, though I am speaking in the country of Darwin and his theory of the survival of the so-called fittest." Although publications as far afield as the *New York Times* credited Mommsen in his day with resisting the overwhelming antisemitism of some of his colleagues, that historian had another outlet for his vitriol, writing famously in the *Vienna Neue Freie Presse* of the Czechs as "apostles of barbarism" who would swamp German cultural achievements in "the abyss of their Unkultur." The German response, he noted, had to be tough, because "the Czech skull is impervious to reason, but it is susceptible to blows."[17] Anthropology as zoology had its street analogue, as well, and whether one was called "Tschechischer Hund" or "Judischer Hund" or, not to split hairs, the ubiquitous "Schweinhund," the categorization of people into animal categories, and, indeed, the blending of categories to create a worse category yet, the hybrid pig-dog, was a familiar part of everyday speech. One possible reading of Kafka's "Josefine" is that it literalizes Masaryk's relational understanding of a "small nation," converting "anthropology into zoology" as street rhetoric suggests: mousefolk.

These political associations cannot be ignored, but for Kafka, such relational, correlative perceptions and identifications are not solely the province of politics, and social or ethnic identity is never the only kind of identity at stake when the stakes are high. As was evident in K.'s struggles with the Castle, aesthetic "identity" also has to do with its relation to use, to the quotidian, to the ground of the perceiver. In addition to thinking of Kafka's late work in terms of animals, we can also consider that in his last years Kafka wrote a number of stories that represent the relationship of artist to audience, or community, and the animal and artist stories greatly overlap. In the artist category, we can certainly place "The Hunger Artist," about the declining popularity of self-starvation as an art form; "First Sorrow," about a trapeze artist who keeps himself very isolated but becomes unhinged when his request for a second trapeze is granted; and certainly "Josefine the Mouse Singer," about a mouse who may or may not create music; "Investigations of a Dog," in which the dog encounters singing and dancing dogs; and, arguably, "The Burrow," in which an unspecified mole-like creature constructs an elaborate burrow ultimately for self-preservation from an increasingly intrusive collective of "small" creatures. (Insofar as we can view the land surveyor K. as an artist figure—and this extent may be limited—we can understand *The Castle* as sharing this late preoccupation.) This broader category thus encompasses the three late animal stories, though it is not limited to them.

The animal stories as art-stories turn their attention to both the aesthetic and non-aesthetic qualities of sound, to the way its effects change with the kind and intensity of attention paid by the listener. Often, those in the stories name the sound "music," or use musical terminology to describe it—but this is not always the case, and the distinction is at issue: is it "whistling" or "piping" or "singing"? the mice wonder in "Josefine." For the investigating dog, music is cathartic, almost annihilating—but also difficult for his untrained ear to recognize and distinguish from "sound" when he first encounters it:

> I greeted the morning with an uncertain barking, when—as if I had conjured them up—out of some place of darkness, to the accompaniment of terrible sounds such as I had never heard before, seven dogs stepped into the light. Had I not distinctly seen that they were dogs and that they, themselves brought the sound with them—though I could not recognize how they produced it—I would have run away at once; but as it was I stayed. At that time I still knew hardly anything of the creative gift for music [Musikalität] with which the canine race alone is endowed, it had naturally enough escaped my but slowly

> developing powers of observation; for though music had surrounded me as a perfectly natural and indispensable element of existence ever since I was a suckling, an element which nothing impelled me to distinguish from the rest of existence, my elders had drawn my attention to it only by such hints as were suitable for a childish understanding; all the more astonishing, then, indeed devastating, were these seven great musical artists to me.[18]

As the story continues, we see that the music is only ambiguously connected with the dogs—that if the investigating dog could conceive of humans, he might well find humans producing an accompaniment for trained dogs—but this does not occur. The dogs, though silent themselves, seem to pull the music (which, although "natural" to dogs, is recognizable only to the ear that has been trained to distinguish it) out of the air. A central claim, however, is that music—though unrecognizable and incomprehensible—is at once natural and species-specific, although what makes it music rather than "sound" seems to rest entirely with the listener. Throughout these late stories, then, what distinguishes "sound" from "music" is unclear, but sound, whether musical or not, signifies or even performs a particular collective identity among the dogs, mice, and the "kleine" antagonists of the Burrow-creature. This social, collective experience and signifying function of sound is a particular focus of the late work, although the association of music with animals is not. That is, only as a verminous beetle does Gregor Samsa develop a taste for music, a visceral, bodily taste that causes him to fling himself at his violin-playing sister. Gregor, however, has no collective identity as a vermin—his animal status only serves to exclude him from the human communities of work and family. It is in the later animal stories that we see more concern with larger, species- or kind-wide traits and associations—a trend generalizable throughout most of the late work. As Thomas H. Ford observes in writing on "Josefine," "the correspondence between collectivity and animality has a long if somewhat subterranean history," and crowd theory has long turned to animals to figure "the loss of the boundaries that keep individuals distinct from one another."[19] Kafka seems to draw on this association most in "Josefine."

"The Duty of Czech Music"

The role of music and its function within a social collective could not have been more prominently discussed in the Czech press during this era. The press was filled with debates about the role of music—whether the musicality of Wagner, in particular, justified its production in the Czech National Theater: if such a performance was an offense against the nation, if it was a testament to the newfound strength of the nation that such performances no longer had the power to threaten Czechness, or if it was wrong to withhold from

Czech performers the opportunity to stage such exciting work. These kinds of debates were hardly peculiar to a Prague context, but there, the concern with music and nationality ran even deeper than the problem of staging the national music of the recent German-speaking "tyrants" in the great temple of the Czech nation. A sense of Czech "natural" musicianship was a common self-stereotype: musicality was folkishness, and folkishness was Czech. The major composers of the previous generation—Dvořák, Smetana—composed based on Czech folk songs, and these compositions were seen to have had a crucial nation-building, nation-binding function, particularly when political speech was subject to censorship. *Venkov*, the ultra-nationalist, anti-German and often antisemitic Agrarian Party organ discussed in chapter 2, published the following essay from the feuilleton section, expressing fairly typical sentiments with regard to "The Duty of Czech Music":

> We know well what Czech music was to us during the greatest oppression, how, alone free and untouched by the censor's bullying hand, it spoke to our hearts and strengthened our desires and hopes. We know how much Smetana . . . carried out that work by telling the people everything they needed to know and what otherwise there was no way of saying—how [his music] provided the opportunity to vent without fear those feelings which teemed within and which had otherwise to be kept hidden. Indeed, only during those times did we learn to understand their deep, noble meaning and unfading, pure beauty. We found a source of joy and strength in Smetana . . . and Dvořák . . . and in the creations of other composers in whose work we find that rare element of Czechness in thought and musical expression. Although lost in . . . many works of the contemporary musical generation, nevertheless, the founders of Czech national music, the oldest generation of Czech-feeling and Czech-expressing musical artists pursued one main goal. They were the most sought after, they were most often given the opportunity to speak to the hearts of the people, and they were the most supported in the press and the most appreciated. Under their sign have we experienced the greatest and most recent national celebration.

Music, the *Venkov* editorialists felt, had been a language of nationalism at a time when nationalist language in a political venue would be censored—and often had been, particularly on *Venkov*'s pages. Under the sign, too, of this inspiring true Czechness, the article goes on to insist, must the present and the future of Czech music continue to lead the young nation on its path of ever-increasing and greater Czechness. Music is to speak with a single "word"—or goal, but the Czech term used is literally "slovo," or "word"—to speak directly to hearts, to create not aesthetic enjoyment, but to communicate unmediated nationhood. Music seems to speak without mediation of ear or indeed any perception: it is direct communication.

As if offering a counter-argument to such prevalent understandings of music, Kafka's late animal stories that so emphasize the collective experience of sound or music place an equal emphasis on perception. Like *The Castle*, these stories have a distinctly phenomenological turn: the investigating dog, for example, is meticulous in describing perceptions and the conclusions he (and more broadly, the dog world) have drawn from them. The reader in turn is made aware of the limits of these perceptions and the attendant knowledge they afford as, for example, we begin to notice that the dogs are apparently incapable of seeing the humans that feed them, instead devising elaborate theories to explain the appearance of their food. Whether Josefine the Singer actually sings, furthermore, is a question often pronounced upon, but never actually decided by the story's shifting collective voice. So the question of whether or not these late animal-artist stories are, in fact, artist stories (that is, is this art? are these artists?) is posed by the stories themselves. And to a great extent, the answer to this question seems to lie with the perceiving audience, whether collective (dogs or mice) or individual (paranoid burrow creature).

Czech Sound and Speech

Keeping in mind these late concerns with sound, perception, and their relationship to that intentional arrangement or experience of sound we call music, I would like to return to what was then the most hotly debated, most stringently politicized, and most concretely nation-determining issue both in Czechoslovak cultural life and in Kafka's late writing: language. And again, I would refer to earlier discussions about the peculiarly divided nature of spoken and written Czech, and to the particularly spoken, aural relationship Kafka had with the Czech language, despite his increased attention to Czech as a literary language after 1918. The complex set of relations of "Czech as sound" vs. "Czech as music" vs. "Czech as literature" come together in a striking way in the Jesenská correspondence (discussed below), but manifestations of these dynamics resurface time and again in the late fiction—and are consistently presented as related to shifts in the perceptions of a listening audience. The investigating dog, for example, reflects on the sounds emitted by other creatures:

> Apart from us dogs there are all sorts of creatures in the world, wretched, limited, dumb creatures who have no language but mechanical cries; many of us dogs study them, have given them names, try to help them, educate them, uplift them, and so on. For my part I am quite indifferent to them except when they try to disturb me, I confuse them with one another, I ignore them.[20]

This passage resonates with the attitude of the Burrow creature, and that story in turn recalls from Kafka's correspondence with Felice Bauer the structure of Czech as a minor annoyance. In both stories, the distinction between the narrator and other creatures is represented as the distinction between species—and hence in the case of the dog, between sound and language. Whereas the dog and his kind exhibit curiosity, the Burrow creature exhibits antagonism and, increasingly, fear. The title's ("Der Bau") anagrammatic reprise of Felice Bauer's surname suggests that the connections to themes from *that* correspondence do not stop with the vague sense of spoken Czech as an annoyance: indeed, few themes recur more powerfully and destructively in the course of that relationship than Kafka's desire for a kind of underground isolation. Read in light of Kafka's changing experience of linguistic multiplicity, however, "The Burrow" charts an increasing recognition of the impossibility of such isolation: the sounds of others demand the creature's attention. This fear of loss—the loss of isolation and comparative safety—is accompanied by a change in focus, a change in listening attention, that parallels the kind of change that Kafka's new relationship to the Czech language would increasingly have demanded.

The Burrow creature's characterizations of the sounds made by what he calls the "kleine Volk" or "Kleinzeug" (in the best-known translation, the "small fry") begin, at least, in a similar vein: he, a perceiving consciousness, is surrounded by annoying sounds without structure. The Burrow creature, however, undergoes changes in his perception and attitude towards the sounds that pervade his burrow, and these changes map suggestively onto changes in Kafka's relationship to the Czech language, as I discussed with relation to the representation of Czech in Kafka's letters to Felice Bauer (see chapter 1). The story goes from silence to the small fry's "Zischen" ("whistling" or "hissing"): the sound moves from annoyance, then to "innocence," then to threat. But the Burrow creature later claims that he had heard it all along and had only needed to become more used to it, to gain a sense of stakes.[21] Over the course of the story, the more attention the creature pays, the more the noise "goes on always in the same thin note, with regular pauses, now a sort of whistling, but again like a kind of piping" ("Pfeifen"),[22] distinctions that resurface in "Josefine." The distinctions are not, he believes, the result of any change in the nature of the sound, but in his own perceptions: "I hear it now more and more distinctly, for my ear has grown keener through practice."[23] The "kleine Volk"—his former food source—generate an annoyance that he increasingly perceives as a threat, although not one aimed, as he thinks, at him. "They" are occupied entirely with their own affairs as long as they meet no obstacle. But slowly, as he becomes convinced that the "piping" or rather "whistling" or "hissing" "is not to be interpreted as a gurgling" ("Rauschen"), he begins also to fear that it is made not by a collection of "small fry" but by "a single big one" with a "muzzle" ("Schnauze") of enormous (or monstrous) strength ("ungeheuren Kraft").[24]

If we are to understand the "kleine Volk" as akin to the citizens of a "small nation," or people, then such a people's newly acquired nation-state might seem to speak with a larger voice. That is, the nature of its sound may not have changed, but its power with relation to the former predator-listener might well have. In fact, viewed in this light, "The Burrow" reprises the same "pursuit/assault" dynamic Kafka wrote about in his journal before starting in on *The Castle*—power exhibiting the directional flexibility associated with metaphor, but with literal, political analogues everywhere apparent. In terms of those analogues, and in terms of the question of national sound and national voice, despite what a foreign ear might have heard (Kafka writes of Czech's harsh grating on the German ear) and despite what the *Venkov* nationalists might have claimed for the "language" of music and nationality, it is a prominent feature of Prague life at this time that the Czech language did not "speak" with a singularity of "voice"—by which I refer here not to political or ethnic diversity of opinion, but to an actual difference within the language: the marked division between spoken and written forms.

To return, for a moment, to *Švejk*: the text that would go on to become an unrivaled reference point for the Czech nation derives much of its humor from representing this spoken-written division (and many other linguistic varieties besides). Indeed, this is a literal statement; that is, the humor is literally in representing visually, in print, that which is typically only heard. It is almost akin to a score—written sound. Specific features of spoken Prague Czech characterize Švejk's dialogue—grammatical and morphological features, a "v" added to words beginning with "o," dropped letters and vowel shifts, and simplified endings, in addition to a more colloquial lexicon. Unlike in typical dialect writing, however, the joke is less on Švejk and his companions than on the official language that bars these near-universal and universally comprehensible spoken features. "*We* speak like this," the story seems to suggest, "who the hell are you written people?" Švejk's first line, "So they've killed our Ferdinand," or even "So they've killed Ferdinand on us" ("Tak nám zabili Ferdinanda"), immediately raises the question of "we"—the first iteration of a "we" implying the collective voice of an empire's loyal subjects. Švejk's response then troubles this presumptive we—his mind goes first not to an archduke (how, the implication is, could he be considered "ours"?) but as follows: "Which Ferdinand? . . . I know two Ferdinands. One of them, he works for Průši the druggist, one time he drank a bottle of hair oil by mistake. Besides him, I know Ferdinand Kokošká, who picks up dog turds. Neither one is any big loss" ("Kerýho Ferdinand . . . Já znám dva Ferdinandy. Jednoho, ten je sluhou u drogisty Průši, a vypil mu tam jednou omylem láhev nějakého mazáni na vlasy, a potom znám ještě Ferdinanda Kokošku, co sbírá ty psí hovinka. Vobou není žádná škoda").[25] As it is clarified that the Ferdinand in question is the archduke, "you know, the fat, religious one, from Konopiště," ("toho z Konopiště, toho tlustýho, nábožnýho.") Švejk goes on to consider that whoever did it probably used a fancy gun and probably even got dressed up for the occasion—while in the bar he frequents in the evening, a portrait of the emperor has been removed to the attic because it is so covered with fly dung. "Shit falls everywhere," one theme of *Švejk* might be summarized.

The potentially unifying function of music enters the story much later, when a Catholic hymn printed in many languages and distributed to the troops ends with remarkable ubiquity—clogging latrines in a time of paper shortage, a reminder that the word "shit" and its many rich variants are also dispersed on paper throughout the text. Such colloquialisms aside, though, it is the familiar *sound* of the unfamiliar graphically portrayed spoken language—this disjunction—that makes (particularly in its day) the text so distinctive. It *creates* a "we"—we who speak this way—and, in writing, distinguishes itself from the "written," the "literary Czech" whose protection from German incursion has been the topic of much conversation—not just on the pages of *Naše řeč,* but on the front pages of newspaper dailies. This spoken-written distinction in Czech, however, is a separate distinction from, on the one hand, the *represented* distinction between those in the provinces who could ask "which Ferdinand?" and those close to the center of the empire (a topic Kafka addresses in the earlier story "The Great Wall of China") or, on the other, the German-Czech divide. Throughout *Švejk,* language implies community or distinguishes difference. But it also, on the novel's very first page, certifies a main character's idiocy, and constructs the pedigrees that render the visible "ugly mongrel monsters" into saleable purebred dogs. For Hašek, even the animal, even the species distinctions come down to language, perception, and whatever idiocy will support. Purity is a line sold by thugs to rip off the gullible—a different variety of language skepticism from the kind displayed by Kafka, a different kind of game.

Josefine

If Kafka has come down to us as occupying a different world from the Prague Linguistic Circle, Hašek must seem to be from a different ontological universe—and yet the relationships between individual art and the collective perceiving audience, and between "standard" language and "poetic" or "aesthetic" language, are precisely the main concerns of the Prague School. And, while Kafka can hardly be relied upon to come to the same (or any) conclusions as his theoretical or literary compatriots, "Josefine," like *The Castle*, amply illustrates that he entertained many of the same questions—and even critiqued Prague School premises and conclusions *avant la lettre*. The first sentence—"Our singer is called Josefine" ("Unsere Sängerin heißt Josefine")[26] establishes the tension between collective audience and individual artist. She is not "a" singer but "our" singer: she is claimed by a community and, it might follow, is the particular voice of that community—perhaps even a particular taste. Yet the collective voice presents Josefine's singing as absolute, or at least as granting a singular and absolute knowledge of a particular power: "Anyone who has not heard her does not know the power of song" ("Wer sie nicht gehört hat, kennt nicht die Macht des Gesanges").[27] Here, Josefine's singing does not so much identify or bind community as exclude those who cannot hear it. And furthermore, hearing Josefine does not confer the knowledge of song's power but only the possibility of such knowledge. Those who haven't heard the song won't know song's power, but their ignorance doesn't guarantee, logically speaking, that those who have heard her *will* understand this power—only that they can. Josefine's talent is singular, particular, and yet universal: "there is no one but is carried away by her singing" ("Es gibt niemanden, den ihr Gesang nicht fortreißt"), a truth that seems to hold despite the early assertion that "we are not as a whole a music-loving race" ("als unser Geschlecht im ganzen Musik nicht liebt"). Thus music is in the curious position of defining (by exclusion) a community of hearers and potential power-comprehenders, but it also "carries away." Music is defined as being that which transcends or uplifts; the Mouse folk don't like music because, according to the narrator, "we are no longer able, even on occasions when we have tried to shake off the cares of our daily life, to rise to anything so high and remote from our usual life as music" ("wir können uns, auch wenn wir einmal Tagessorgen abzuschütteln versucht haben, nicht mehr zu solchen, unserem sonstigen Leben so fernen Dingen erheben, wie es die Musik ist"). Josefine stands out; in fact, "Josefine is the sole exception" ("Nur Josefine macht eine Ausnahme").[28]

Much like elements of K.'s efforts and failures in *The Castle*, these initial formulations of aesthetic—here, musical, or unmusical—identity align with future Prague School formulations of the aesthetic versus the "standard" or "quotidian," or even the "everyday" norm. In "Standard Language and Poetic Language" (1932), Jan Mukařovský establishes "poetic language" as "the intentional violation of the norm of the standard"; "the standard language is the background against which is reflected the aesthetically intentional distortion of the linguistic components of the work."[29] *The Castle*'s K. wants the tower before him to clearly distinguish itself from the everyday dwelling-place of which it confoundingly forms a part, and precisely such a clear distinction from the quotidian is what singles out Josefine and her art from her defined race (*Geschlecht*) or community. The norms are spontaneously comprehensible to them, so much so, in fact, that aesthetic experience seems out of reach. Josefine's position is singular because she understands how to reach out of the everyday: she defines the artistic, and this relationship between community norms and aesthetic definitions truly renders her "their" ("our") singer.

Even in this first paragraph, however, where all seems clear enough, the lack of musicality on the part of the musician's audience is problematic; while music certainly "violates the norm of the standard" where the standard of beauty is silence, so would any noise at all: hence the question—how do we know if Josefine sings at all? Following the structuralist paradigm the story often seems to both anticipate and critique, aesthetic function must measure up against *both* the "standard" everyday, communicative norm *and* the elusive "aesthetic norm" that governs the variety of art in which the artist works. How is music to be made and recognized in the absence of a "native musical language" that defines the norms that music may aesthetically violate? Or, as the text puts it, since the mouse folk are unmusical:

> how is it that we understand Josefine's singing or, since Josefine denies that, at least think we can understand it. The simplest answer would be that the beauty of her singing is so great that even the most insensitive cannot be deaf to it, but this answer is not satisfactory.[30]

At this point the story embarks on a series of logical shifts—shifts that *seem* to share the logic of collective, normative understanding and automatization but that go against any consistent system of logic a reader might identify or define. The conclusions shift, but the narrative makes no mention of this, no acknowledgment: norms shift without warning and each time present themselves as "spontaneously comprehensible." The passage continues:

> If it were really so [that the beauty of her singing was absolute and non-contingent], her singing would have to give one an immediate and lasting feeling of being something out of the ordinary . . . But in my opinion that is just what does not happen, I do not feel this and have never observed that others feel anything of the kind. Among intimates we admit freely to one another that Josefine's singing, as singing, is nothing out of the ordinary.
>
> Is it in fact singing at all?[31]

Thus the story's second paragraph contradicts each agreed-upon premise that the first paragraph initiated: that Josefine is the community's singer, that her singing is such that it singularly can lead to a spontaneous understanding of the "power of song," and that it is, as music, distinct from "the everyday" of the mouse community. In other words, each "norm" established by the first paragraph is "violated" by the norms suggested by the second, which nonetheless present themselves not as contradictions or violations of prior codes, but as "spontaneously agreed-upon" community norms. The norms of the second paragraph seem to have no awareness of a relation to the norms that came before them; each paragraph presents a tidy Saussurean synchronic system, a spontaneously comprehensible language to which the language scene of only moments before (in readerly time) bears no relation.

The third paragraph continues this pattern. Here, the recently defined unmusical Mouse folk are identified as having an ancient tradition of song—"this is mentioned in legend and some songs have actually survived, although no one can now sing"—and "thus we know what singing is, and Josefine's art does not really correspond to it."[32] With these revelations, which contradict the community norms established at the outset, the problem of the aesthetic norm is (at least temporarily) solved—the folk do have an established tradition of song, and Josefine's art is in violation of it—hence, potentially meeting the second criterion of aesthetic value as established in a Prague School model. Problematically, however, just as it is suggested that her song indeed violates the (previously impossible) community linguistic norms, we hear that "piping" (as opposed to singing) is first the "real artistic accomplishment of our people" ("die eigentliche Kunstfertigkeit unseres Volkes") and "a characteristic expression of our life" (eine charakteristiche Lebensäußerung).[33] Thus this "piping" is both an aesthetic *and* a standard norm, or, in other words, a categorical impossibility. In the same stylistic vein, the text continues to contradict itself in a matter-of-fact, normative, communicative manner; although two sentences before, "piping" was a "real artistic achievement," now "no one dreams of making out that our piping is an art, we pipe without thinking of it, indeed without noticing it, and there are even many among us who are quite unaware that piping is one of our characteristics"—now, it would seem, piping is the very definition of the automatized norm of the standard for the collective of the Mouse folk.[34] And, although Josefine's song was identified as absolutely singular and transcendent scarcely a page before, it is now speculated that "it hardly rises above the level of our usual piping" ("über die Grenzen des üblichen Pfeifens kaum hinauskommt") or perhaps wasn't as good, and what begins in paragraph three as a line of speculation is, by the first sentence of the fourth paragraph, an acknowledgment of fact: "After all, it is only a kind of piping that she produces" ("Es ist aber eben doch nicht nur Pfeifen, was sie produziert").

From afar, it is stipulated, it is a "quite ordinary piping"—it is only "if you sit down before her" in her actual presence that her art comes through. Specifically, "to comprehend her art it is necessary not only to hear but to see her. Even if hers were only our usual workaday piping, there is first of all this peculiarity to consider, that here is someone making a ceremonial performance out of doing the usual thing."[35] To wit,

> To crack a nut is truly no feat [*Kunst*], so no one would ever dare to collect an audience in order to entertain it with nut-cracking. But if all the same one does do that and succeeds in entertaining the public, then it cannot be a matter of simple nut-cracking. Or it is a matter of nut-cracking, but it turns out that we have overlooked the art of cracking nuts because we were too skilled in it and that this newcomer to it first shows us its real nature, even finding it useful in making his effects to be rather less expert in nut-cracking than most of us.[36]

In this formulation, it seems that a "new nut-cracker"—that is, someone explicitly outside the collective quotidian practice—has in a way a kind of aesthetic advantage, since its "less expert" use "actualizes" or brings out the aesthetic potential of an automatized activity. In structuralist terminology, the "intentionality" of the nut-cracking artist has shifted the functionality of the nut-cracking from practicality to ceremonialized entertainment; in his later essay on architecture and function, Mukařovský will argue that "the aesthetic function emerges and vanishes without being unalterably bound to any object"; that "no art is separated from the rest of the world of phenomena in a hermetically sealed compartment"; that "there are unnoticeable transitions and a constant fluctuation between art and the extra-artistic"; and that "such a violation of functionality as a rule derives from the decision of an individual." Thus whereas the first paragraph of Kafka's "Josefine" seems to recapitulate the core assumptions of formalist and early structuralist definitions of aesthetic value—just at this time making their way into Czech journals—the ensuing paragraphs perform and ultimately restate later, more dynamic formulations of structure, in which relations between individual and collective, standardized norm and aesthetic violation are characterized by an ever-increasing instability—and in which a foreign perspective can "aestheticize" quotidian aspects of another culture where no aesthetic intentionality was present.

As the polemics around the language census (and the language *of* the language census) made clear, the issue of "everyday speech" was extremely charged at this time, having been used by the Austrian government as a proxy question for national affiliation—a linkage the Czechs found extremely unfair, protested, and changed in their own 1920 census. But the entire link between language and ethnic identity raised such problems: no version of the language questions—required by law in the new linguistically based Czechoslovak nation-state—could accurately depict the ethnic makeup of the Czech lands. The questions left no room for "ethnic feeling"; for bilingual or dual identity; for the possibility of a national identity not tied to a common language (of which Prague's Jewish population stubbornly served as a reminder). Both art and state, then, relied for stability and identity on the premise of a common (shared) language commonly spoken. Yet as "Josefine" illustrates—like *Švejk*, although in a very different way—what is commonly shared and commonly spoken is subject to change without warning, consistency, or acknowledgment. One primary distinction between the fictional worlds of Hašek and Kafka emerges in their treatment of this issue of a common language: *Švejk* presumptively *includes* the reader as a "speaker" of the language that philologists insist must conform to an outdated written standard—the jokes are jokes of inclusion. With "Josefine" as with *The Castle*, by contrast, we as readers are on the outside looking in. Yet in "Josefine," the readerly perspective is outside the community altogether, able to see the delusion of continuity nonetheless agreed upon by the mouse folk, whereas in *The Castle*, readers must share "stranger" status with the uncomprehending K. In the case of the novel, we can either assume the Castle world is crazy, or that they do in fact have a "common language"—it is just not a language to which we have access. In "Josefine," however, our second-person-plural access to the collective thoughts of the people does not even allow the illusion of normative consistency. The apparently inclusive voice is, if anything, more alienating.

Early in his correspondence with Jesenská, Kafka claims to hear spoken Czech as an assault, an assault clearly related to the ethnic slurs pronounced in Czech on the streets of Prague against the Jews ("an assault from below"? an "assault from above, directed at [him] from above"?):

> And then Milena still talks about anxiousness, gives me a blow on the chest or asks, which in Czech amounts to the same thing in terms of sound and rhythm: "Jste žid?" [Are you a Jew?] Don't you see how in "jste," the fist is withdrawn to gather muscular strength? And then in the "žid" the joyful, unfailing, forward-flying blow? These are the side-effects that the Czech language often has for the German ear.[37]

> Und dann redet noch Milena von Ängstlichkeit, gibt mir einen Stoß vor die Brust oder fragt, was im Tschechischen an Bewegung und Klang ganz dasselbe ist: jste žid? Sehen Sie nicht, wie im: "jste" die Faust zurückgezogen wird, um . . . Muskelkraft anzusammeln? Und dann im "žid" den freudigen, unfehlbaren, vorwärts fliegenden Stoß? Solche Nebenwirkungen hat für das deutsche Ohr die tschechische Sprache öfters.[38]

This passage shows Kafka's relationship to the Czech language to be quite fraught, written over by Prague's ubiquitous issues of linguistic identification and ethnic identity and by the violent clashes they fueled. With this connection in mind, we should note that despite the markedly aural, syllabic nature of his reception of Jesenská's written Czech and despite his automatic association of it with the Jew-assaulting street rhythms of Prague Czech, Kafka earlier remarks on a quality in Jesenská's writing that he finds *nearly* unique to her:

> But in any case, this was not written by any ordinary writer. After reading it I have almost as much faith in your writing as I do in yourself. The only linguistic music I know in Czech (given my limited knowledge) is that of Božena Němcová, this music is different, but related to Němcová's in its resolution, passion, charm, and above all in a certain clairvoyant [or, literally, clear-sighted] intelligence.[39]

> Aber jedenfalls: das ist keine gewöhnliche Schreiberin, die das geschrieben hat. Ich habe danach zu Ihrem Schreiben fast so viel Vertrauen wie zu Ihnen selbst. Ich kenne (bei meiner geringen Kenntnis)

> im Tschechischen nur eine *Sprachmusik*, die der Božena Němcová, hier ist eine andere Musik, aber jener verwandt an Entschlossenheit, Leidenschaft, Lieblichkeit und vor allem einer hellsichtigen Klugheit.[40]

"Sprachmusik" condenses a number of categories crucial to Kafka's relationship to language as well as to Jesenská—written language (his own), Czech language (as aural language), and Czech language (as spoken language in written form)—and maps them in relation to women's writing. Clearly, this written spoken language that qualifies as "Sprachmusik" differs in tonality and association from the harsh rhythms of assault he hears in spoken Czech, but in condensing language and music in a single sign, Kafka also aligns this rarer, laudable Czech with a category he repeatedly insists he lacks. Kafka's estimation of his own insensitivity towards music is well known; he classed it along with bodily activities as something that must be renounced for writing's sake.[41] Mark Anderson argues that with "Josefine," "Kafka took up a subject which he had explicitly sought to eliminate from his writing," quoting the 1912 journal entry in which Kafka claims that as soon as he realized that "writing was the most productive direction" for him, "everything rushed in that direction and left empty all those abilities which were directed toward the joys of sex, eating, drinking, philosophical reflection, and above all music."[42] Thus musicality is linked both with pleasures of the flesh and of the mind—and opposed to writing. In a July 1920 letter to Milena Jesenská, Kafka defines as a "gewisse Stärke" ("certain strength") his "Unmusikalisch-Sein" ("unmusicality" but literally "unmusical-being," an unmusical quality is essential to his being).[43] In his fiction, however, music is consistently identified as the province of women (Brunelda the opera singer in the *Amerika* novel, Gregor's sister in *The Metamorphosis*, the singing sirens) or animals (Gregor's appreciation of his sister's violin, the floating singing dogs). In "Josefine" these two associations come together. So, on the one hand, we have music aligned with the body and sexuality, and on the other, with the female and the animal—all of which thus appear in a binary relation to Kafka and writing. Music is the unKafka. Corngold and Wagner take issue with Anderson's stark opposition, arguing that Kafka consistently resisted antithesis and further troubling Anderson's conflation of the "organic," "the sensual," and "the ornamental" in music.[44] Certainly these qualities form no part of what Kafka values in Jesenská's "Sprachmusik," and I agree that the more nuanced portrayal of music in these late stories *is* less binary than Kafka's comments on his unmusicality would suggest. I further argue, however, that the mediation of this binary, particularly in "Josefine," represents a change in his thinking. Kafka may have hated antitheses, but it does not necessarily follow that he was not susceptible to their logic in defining his various identities, including that of writer.

Especially as it appears in these late stories, music is an art form explicitly related to the vocal and sonorous part of language that writing—silent letters on a page—necessarily excludes. Czech, as we have seen, accentuates this division between speech and writing, and Kafka's own experience of Czech as a spoken language would only emphasize it further. Czechs were also strongly stereotyped as "natural" musicians, while racial and ethnic chauvinism everywhere casts otherness in terms of animal species. Finally, Kafka only very rarely specifically mentions any Czech writers, but of these, most are women—he expressed an interest, for example, in meeting Gabriela Preissová, who was even more strongly associated with music for Kafka by being Leoš Janáček's librettist and the author of the play on which he based his opera *Její Pastorkyňa* (*Her Foster Daughter*). Max Brod had translated Preissová's libretto into German and changed the Czech title, which articulates a relationship between two women, to *Jenůfa*, thereby singling out the play's sexual victim and effacing the centrality of the older, more powerful and disturbing Kostelnička, whose presence is implicit in the original Czech title. Since Kostelnička commits infanticide in an effort to save "her foster daughter" from disgrace, it is safe to say that neither play nor opera provides a neutral association between music and women, or Czech and women, or sexuality and any of these terms. There is evidence that Kafka had either the play or opera in mind when writing *The Castle*, beyond even the obvious theme of sexual violence that resurfaces throughout the novel. In 1922 after his frenetic relationship with Jesenská had ended in an impasse, Kafka wrote to Max Brod that he was living near "Frau Preissová" and that he had "at one time a great desire to speak with her" but was overcome with fear. Max Brod replied: "Under no circumstances should you meet with Frau Preiss." Kafka also refers to Jesenská's aunt Růžena Jesenská, the Decadent novelist turned chauvinist nationalist, and apparently had read a good deal of Němcová, including her correspondence.

"Sprachmusik"—so resonant with Janáček's speech melodies—is here found *in writing*, that category Kafka had most opposed to music. In Kafka's letter the "musik" of Sprachmusik violates the "norm of the standard" of Czech language, at least insofar as Kafka is aware of it—but this "musik" is also the quality that writing had pushed *out* of Kafka himself, as per the 1912 journal entry. "Sprachmusik" retains the association with women, since the only practitioners of it Kafka mentions are Božena Němcová and Jesenská herself. But clearly this "Sprachmusik" cannot be the same music as ordinary music, which was widely associated with Czechs and would therefore not have come as a surprise to Kafka in a Czech context. The referents, furthermore, are to silent written texts—Kafka's relationship with Jesenská is textual only, and Němcová is long dead. Kafka, however, does not refer to Jesenská's "prose" as writing, here. It is "Sprachmusik," which could translate either as "music of language" or as "music of speech." Thus "music" violates the norm of writing, but not of speech, and "music" would not violate the norm of Czech cultural identity, but would violate the norm of Czech language, elsewhere akin to "the blow of a fist." "Music" would not violate the norm of women, but "writing" almost certainly would. And while Kafka only rarely refers to any woman writer, before this correspondence with Jesenská, the references were always negative; afterwards, they were always Czech.

Meeting the definitional demands of so many identities—aesthetic as well as social—all of which are to be defined by operationally contradictory binaries proves, as it did in *The Castle*, difficult. If, taking a Prague School definition by way of example, aesthetic function is the violation of a collectively recognized norm: which collective? When? Who? Czech women—for a German Jewish city dweller such as Kafka—were strongly associated with the quotidian: they were cooks, servants, shopgirls. They belonged to the life Kafka repudiated in favor of writing. Now they were showing up in writing: in Jesenská's case, translating his own writing: the writing woman's very existence multiply violated "the norm of the standards" around which his own life and identity as a writer had been structured.

Almost as if the category of a Czech woman writer is too much for him to compute, throughout their almost exclusively written relationship, Kafka compulsively locates Jesenská's written prose in her mouth. This association is particularly dramatic in Kafka's extraordinary reading of the Czech for "I don't understand":

> "Nechápu." A strange word in Czech and even in your mouth [speech], it is so severe, callous, cold-eyed, stingy and most of all like a nutcracker, pronouncing it requires three consecutive cracks of the jaw or, more exactly, the first syllable makes an attempt at holding the nut, in vain, the second syllable then tears the mouth wide open, the nut now fits inside, where it is finally cracked by the third syllable, can you hear your teeth? Particularly this final, absolute closing of the lips at the end prohibits the other person from expressing anything to the contrary, which is actually quite good at times, for instance when the other person is babbling as much as I am now.[45]

> "Nechápu." Ein fremdartiges Wort im Tschechischen und gar in Ihre Sprache, est is so streng, teilnahmslos, kaltäugig, sparsam und vor allem nußknackerhaft, dreimal krachen im Wort die Kiefer aufeinander oder richtiger die erste Silbe macht einen Versuch die Nuß zu fassen, es geht nicht, dann reißt die zweite Silbe den Mund ganz groß auf, nun paßt schon die Nuß hinein und die dritte Silbe endlich knackt, hören Sie die Zähne? Besonders dieses endgiltige Schließen der Lippen zum Schluß verbietet dem andern jede andere weitere gegenteilige Erklärung, was ja allerdings manchmal recht gut ist z. B wenn der andere so schwätzt wie jetzt ich.[46]

This all clusters around the Czech for "I don't understand," around the strangeness of understanding "not understanding" in a foreign tongue.

"Tongue" is the apt word, for despite the entirely textual nature of their relationship at this time, Kafka nonetheless grounds his reading of the word in a female mouth's castrating lips and teeth. The same mouth that indicts the lack of communication or understanding also holds out the potential for and, indeed, the actual fact of communication across the languages (since the word is understood)—but also cuts off the possibility of further discourse, with lips and teeth. This slippage into hearing the written additionally accentuates Kafka's experience of Czech as a spoken, rather than a literary, language, as if he needed to distinguish between the two even further even as he merges them in his letter. In an actual footnote to his own letter, Kafka also relates this tri-syllabic phenomenon to the Apostles on the Orloj clock in Prague, illustrating the strong connection between religious-ethnic identity and language as well—Czech is a language spoken, not written, by angry gentiles. The passage sheds light on Kafka's surprise at the "fidelity" he sees in Jesenská's translations and his sense that Czech might not be pleased with the translation of German Jewish writing into its Jew-assaulting spoken rhythms. Kafka's "hearing" of Czech speech also, however, incorporates the eyes (the organs for reading)—the cold eyes, eyes which surely resurface in the silent yet curiously linguistic gaze of Amalia in *The Castle*.

We have only Kafka's reaction to Jesenská's text to refer to, but it seems that Jesenská's *textual* performance of the foreign (to Kafka) yet very quotidian *lack* of understanding—the word "nechápu" is a phrase more colloquial than formal, along the lines of "I don't get it"—has violated in some way Kafka's sense of "the norm of the standard." By appearing in writing, this primarily spoken phrase has violently actualized the act of speech it never was; it produces a bodily nut-cracking performance that it is hard to imagine could ever be "quotidian"—although Czechs might say "nechápu" fifty times a day (especially, one imagines, in the context of a difficult conversation with a non-native speaker). In this case, however, it is less the "new" nut-cracker than the "new" audience—as opposed to the nut-cracker treatment of the image in "Josefine"—that confers the "actualized" and violently violating status on the rematerialized (in speech by writing) word.

The nut-cracker image in "Josefine" recalls the passage in Kafka's letter, although in the later fictional text, the castrating threat is much mitigated. In place of the claustrophobic interpersonal misunderstandings that characterize the Jesenská correspondence, "Josefine" opens up to the broader issues of aesthetic and artistic status: anticipating, again, later Prague School topics like the question of whether artistic intentionality or audience reception and recognition determines the aesthetic status of a work of art. Josefine, who *insists* that "no one understands" her art (a significant shift from the first-person "nechápu" to the lack of understanding on the part of the collective), ultimately chooses silence over song. But the collective itself, presented as unified in the first paragraph, devolves into factions throughout the story—maybe. An art or artist reliant on recognition by the mouse folk for its aesthetic status would have an unstable and frustrating career, since their opinions are subject to change without notice *and without any recognition that any change has taken place*. Since on the most basic criterion of aesthetic status—whether the work in question is ordinary or extraordinary—there can be no more than momentary consensus that nonetheless presents itself as absolute, it seems that any stable source or marker of aesthetic identity is beyond reach.

But what of the potentially aesthetic or aestheticizing work that is the story itself? As earlier suggested, each successive paragraph violates the *logical* norm of the standard set by the previous one. In this sense, initially at least, it is a self-actualizing text, an aesthetic text that, in disrupting communication in this perpetually contradicting way, draws attention to itself as a work of art (in the Prague structuralist sense). In the broader context of Kafka's work, however, it suggests several other evocations and violations of norms established elsewhere. Take, for instance, the eponymous heroine. Names are always of significance in Kafka, and Josefine recalls the earlier *Trial*'s hapless "Josef"—whose efforts to control his definition in the eyes of the collective of the courts proved at least equally frustrating and fatal. This parallel has been one argument in favor of reading Josefine as a figure for Kafka himself. But Josefine also *violates* the norm set not only by Josef K., but by all the rest of Kafka's central characters as well: it is a woman's name, and a woman, at the center. The femininity of both the linguistic item that is the name and the character it represents "violate the norm of the standard" that is Kafka's fiction. Names indicate identity in Kafka, but initials do as well, and the floating initials of "Josefine" and "Maus" that between them name the individual and collective polarities that struggle to define the "singer's" identity also function as the name, in Kafka's personal writings and often in journalistic publication, Milena Jesenská. In the diaries, she is always M.; Kafka remarks in the correspondence how they shed letters with their increasing intimacy until their names disappear entirely. In "Josefine" the initials have acquired new names, the relationship is long over, intimacy is broken and the initials enter (at least potentially) the collective experience of literature as opposed to the communicative sphere of letter-writing (although if there is one opposition the late writings entirely break down, this is definitely it). The letter "J" appears as a capital letter (in which it most resembles an initial) 94 times in the course of "Josefine"; in "Der Bau," which is more than twice the length, it appears 18 times. ("K" appears 101 times as a capital letter in "Josefine," as opposed to 56 times in the longer "Burrow" [that is, in "Der Bau"], although the ubiquity of the letter K. in a story by Kafka rather reaffirms a Kafkan norm rather than violates it.)

What emerges from this tangle of associations is a mapping of the challenging cluster "Czech/ woman/ writer" onto a system that, while written, corresponds to another system of notation and valence (music) inherently different in kind from Kafka's own. Jesenská writes in a system that retains its aural (spoken) resonance, but a system for which Kafka strongly feels he is missing a "native

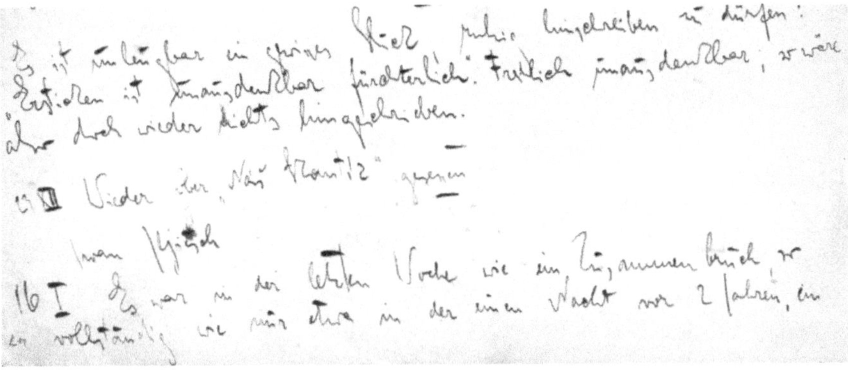

Figure 12. Diary entries of December 23, 1921, and January 16, 1922. Detail of Ms. Kafka 12.2, fol 47r. The Bodleian Library, University of Oxford.

ear." On an ominous closing note for this image, however, with regard to the Jesenská-Kafka harmonics: when Jesenská asked him whether he saw the Haas-Reiner suicide affair at the *Tribuna* offices as a warning to them, Kafka replied no, not exactly—he saw it more as "Musik zum Text."[47]

Nowhere in Kafka's life is the intense and disruptive interrelation of national, ethnic, gender, and sexual norms more apparent than in his textual relations with Milena Jesenská, a living violation of so many norms that various strains within Prague culture strove to police and maintain. Her life and work demonstrate that education can be used for purposes the educators never wished; independence will be wielded not only against vetted, chosen, oppressors, and heritage offers no guarantee against sexual desire. And, in terms of Kafka's own personal store of normative delineations, her textual presence demonstrates that Czech is a literary language that can, after all, speak to and even for him, and that intimate relations with a woman need not be inimical to the writing life, but might rather be integral to it.

But. But she was married, he was dying: these belated discoveries might open up "an infinite amount of hope," but not for them, not as a couple, at any rate. A series of four visits from Jesenská in late 1921 plunge Kafka into a terrible despair. He feels she visits him out of pity; he had previously given her all his diaries, and wonders if they might have been "final proof" against him. He addresses parts of his diary to her; he muses that after all, they might have been happy, it might have been possible—but it didn't happen. In the last entry before the downward spiral is chronicled, Kafka refers to some curious reading material. (See figure 12.)

> 23 December. Again sat over *Náš Skautík*. Ivan Ilyich.
>
> 16 January. This past week I suffered something very like a breakdown;

Figure 13. Front cover of *Náš skautík* by Ladislav Tůma (Zevloun). Prague: Pražská akciová tiskárna, 1922. Moravská zemská knihovna v Brně / The Moravian Library in Brno.

The division—between entries, between years—as we see it in the edited volumes of Kafka's journals belies the actual physical proximity of these odd pagefellows. Very little space separates the Czech boy scout of *Náš skautík* (*Our Little Scout*) from the fevered exploration of Kafka's inner conflict. Kafka's agonized concern about the relationship between world and his writing, world and himself; his famous thoughts on metaphor and pursuit; a literature that assaults boundaries; a new Kabbala—all this appears on the page under the sign of scouting . . . and Ivan Ilyich, an odd enough juxtaposition on its own.

Max Brod's note on this journal entry misidentifies *Náš skautík*—it is not the magazine of the Czech scouting movement, but rather a recently published novella (see figure 13). The novella had been serialized beginning in August

1921 in the feuilleton space of the widely read newspaper *Národní listy* and had been released as an illustrated book earlier in December 1921, advertised as a Christmas gift for young readers. The author, Ladislav Tůma, was a prolific journalist and feuilletonist of several pseudonyms (including Zevloun, the name under which he published *Náš skautík*) with the increasingly nationalist paper—for which Milena Jesenská had also recently begun writing (with the help of her aunt Růžena, also a very regular contributor). This context, in combination with Jesenská's difficult visits and Kafka's sense that she came out of pity for his poor health, would create a very weighted atmosphere for reading this particular book. *Náš skautík* tells of a young boy—Czech, of course—raised in the city. He is weak, spoiled, and urban. But nature, fresh air, exercise—the pleasures and challenges of a bodily life lived in harmony with a community of like-minded people (other boy scouts) and kind adults—restore this sickly child to the pinnacle of mental and physical health. *Náš skautík* is, as much as it is possible to be, the diametric opposite of Ivan Ilyich—and the opposite of Kafka. Clearly, the one represents the worlds of youth, health, community, and the pleasures of bodily life, from which Kafka, tubercular, solitary, unwed, is irrevocably closed off. The world of health and youth is Czech (like the much younger Jesenská); Kafka is old world, old regime. He is tending toward Ilyich. In fact, Milena Jesenská would publish his obituary in this same paper a short two and a half years later.

The breakdown chronicled in the next line of the diary, however, did usher in a new, final period of productivity for Kafka, the period during which all of the fiction I have considered in detail in this book was written. Like *The Castle* and the letters to Jesenská themselves, these animal stories arise from the nexus of a newly energized consideration of language, gender, sexuality, community, writing, and the ways in which these areas might intersect one another, ways that Kafka had theretofore not fully considered. The effects were not solely felt in his fiction—Kafka's last relationship with a woman, the domestic living and language-learning he shared with Dora Diamant, may have been rendered possible by the insights earned at such cost in his relationship with Jesenská and her Czech writing.

CONCLUSION

But by that time, everyone was too involved to leave the city.

—Kafka, "The City Coat of Arms"

Kafka's late work is unflinching in its determination to confront the way language at once establishes the distinctions that divide us and withholds the stable categories these divisions lead us to crave—including the division between his world and his writings. Reading Kafka's late work in tandem with his Prague context requires us to interrogate the tension between language "as such," the purely verbal text it is sometimes seen to constitute (a perspective embraced by earlier generations of Kafka critics), and the world that contestably exists outside it, indicated or represented by its signs. Kafka himself seems convinced that a dividing line exists between them, but where exactly that line may be drawn is less clear. Language *can* have physical effects, and in Kafka's Prague, it often does—and yet, while the question "Are you a Jew?" may feel or sound like the blow of a fist, it isn't one. Kafka agonized over the relation between writing and world. When in his journal, he imagines a literature of assault against boundaries, he is concerned with precisely this relationship, and its closeness troubles him. He "despairs" of writing, particularly its "lack of independence of the world, its dependence on the maid who tends the fire, on the cat warming itself by the stove; it is even dependent on the poor old human being warming himself by the stove. All these are independent activities ruled by their own laws; only writing is helpless, cannot live in itself, is a joke and a despair."[1] He wrote that—and then he started in on *The Castle*, which first began with a maid and greatly depends on maids throughout. This relationship between fiction and world—a line between them to be drawn, a line of great importance, but a line impossible to chart or rely on to remain in one place—troubled Kafka, but worrying this line was productive for him. Worrying, as one worries a tooth.

What troubled him was precisely the insight to be gained from this period in Prague culture: that no question of language leads *very* far away from social fact. This insight is reflected in the origins of the Prague Linguistic Circle that formally convened in Prague in 1927, several years after Kafka's death. Prague School theory is born of an insistence that literary analysis might retain attention to form and language and yet "not deprive literature of its relations to the outside world." This insistence lies at the heart of the difference between Prague School structuralism and its Russian formalist antecedent: the Prague School charged that formalism in its stress on texts and language had "placed literary activity in a vacuum."[2] Prague reminds us that a turn to language and literary form does not lead away from the world—however much Kafka may at times have wanted it to. It leads, however circuitously, back to a world that (like literature) must rely on language for its structure in increasingly literal and concrete ways. And, just as the Prague School would argue for the reintegration of history—what they called "other historical series"—into the analysis of literary form, their theories themselves emerged from a political and literary historical context shared, in part at least, with Franz Kafka.

The particular clarity with which Prague culture can lay bare intercultural and interlinguistic dynamics that are by no means peculiar to it make the city a privileged territory for anyone interested in understanding European modernism as a process of intercultural interaction. If its bilingual, tri-ethnic status is unusual (though not unique), this status also renders Prague exemplary, a model of cultural life that generally transpires over greater physical space. Prague history reminds us that national, ethnic, and even gender identities do not exist as stable unities any more than language does. Like language, such identities rely on a system of similarity and difference, fixed only at a particular moment in a particular context, but seeming to make claims, in that moment, to permanence. Actual biological, species-level difference—as opposed to linguistic (or disciplinary) difference—does not rely on language to keep its distinctions: a dog does not rely on language to know he's not a cat, and cats do not mate with birds; there can be no confusion on that count. By contrast, the historical inhabitants of the Czech lands/Bohemia (even the choice between the English words for this place has a politics to it)—Czechs, Germans, and Jews—had long occupied the same territory. They had intermarried. The languages they spoke changed and shifted over time. The lines within and between the languages were also in flux, even as they presented themselves, at every moment, as permanent and unyielding. As Hillel Kieval quite beautifully puts it,

> The very categories German, Czech, Jew; liberal, Communist, patriot; mystic, rationalist, Orthodox, and assimilationist . . . existed in a state of perpetual movement—seeming to appear only to collapse, regroup, and melt away. Any attempt to establish hard and fast categories of ethnicity and social status is fraught with danger . . . And when the point of reference is Jewish Prague between the wars, one might as well give up.[3]

The instability and even the insufficiency of difference among and between kinds—of language, of writing, of peoples, of sounds in "The Burrow"; of song in "Josefine"; of buildings in *The Castle*—increasingly preoccupied the writer who previously had explored the difference (in kind) between a man and an insect. That earlier Kafka had also decided, repeatedly and at great cost, that his writer kind was not the marrying kind. He too had investments in stable divisions among peoples and kinds—*The Metamorphosis* is not a happy story of liberation. Yet his late work questions the stability of these divisions as he had believed them to be drawn even as it raises the stakes entailed in drawing them. In this, too, he mirrored his home city.

It is a commonplace to see Kafka's work as uncannily prophetic of the historical disasters that soon followed on his death. Viewing this work in terms of languages alongside the sloppy, unchartable history of intermarriage and shifting identities, reading Kafka's responses to new circumstances and interests alongside the conciliatory and hopeful if "minor" overtures of Prague's intellectuals and artists to one another, renders legible an imperfect but less devastating potentional trajectory for the region. On a small scale, shared interests and influences, streets and coffeeshops—even lovers, even families—suggested the possibility of a different future that, simultaneously with the development of the coming disaster, was taking shape in the new Czechoslovakia. Although radical nationalism and the logic of the nation-state insisted on sorting people into sharply delineated linguistic groups, other forces within the government and other radicals sought to bridge differences through translation, cultural engagement, and shared page space—all with their own political and personal agendas. 1920s Prague has much to teach us about the relations of power, ethnicity, majority and minority rule and, above all, how reliant these categories are on language. From his vantage point on the unfolding of this more positive trajectory, Kafka saw intractable problems both political and personal, as the late fiction he wrote reflecting on this world makes manifest. But like Kafka, who found in his relationship with Milena Jesenská the possibility of a shared life of the mind and body that his beliefs had not allowed him to entertain, I have been unable to look at this fraught, contentious, and messy period in Prague's history without a sense of loss, not because of its ideal virtues or the inevitability of its failure, but because one of the many tantalizing proximities it entails is this possibility that things *could* have gone very differently.

NOTES

Introduction

1. Scott Spector, *Prague Territories: National Conflict and Cultural Innovation in Franz Kafka's Fin de Siècle* (Berkeley: California University Press, 2000), 2.

2. Franz Kafka, letter to Oskar Pollak, August 24, 1902, as quoted by Spector, *Prague Territories*, 2.

3. Franz Kafka, October 25, 1921. *The Diaries of Franz Kafka, 1914–1923*, trans. Martin Greenberg (New York: Schocken, 1949), 395. "Daß ich von Prag nie loskam"; "Nur das Sinnlose bekam Zutritt, das Jusstudium, das Bureau . . . ," in Franz Kafka, *Tagebücher 1910–1923* (Frankfurt: Fischer, 1989), 341.

4. Franz Kafka, letter to Milena Jesenská, May 1920. *Letters to Milena*, trans. Philip Boehm (New York: Schocken, 1990), 14.

5. Franz Kafka, *Briefe an Milena* (Frankfurt: Fischer, 1997), 17.

6. Stanley Corngold and Benno Wagner, *Franz Kafka: The Ghosts in the Machine* (Evanston, Ill.: Northwestern University Press, 2011), 134.

7. Franz Kafka, January 3, 1912. *Diaries of Franz Kafka*, 163. ". . . drängte sich alles hin und leiß alle Fähigkeiten leer stehn, die sich auf die Freuden des Geschlechtes, des Essens, des Trinkens, des philosophischen Nachdenkens, der Musik zuallererst, richteten," *Tagebücher*, 144.

8. The 1920 language law adopted simultaneously with the new state's constitution subsumed all previous language laws, including the 1918 statute that established Slovak as the official language of Slovakia. The first article of the language law nonetheless established "Czechoslovak" as the official language in what Tomasz Kamusella sees as "a purely ideological statement to emphasize the national, that is to say Czechoslovak, character of the state" which changed nothing in practice, as Czech continued to be used in the Czech lands, and Slovak in Slovakia. Yet, as Kamusella also explains, matters presented in Czech and dealt with in Slovak and vice versa "were deemed to have been dealt with in the language in which they were presented. This was possible due to the tacit claim construct of the Czechoslovak language as consisting of its two varieties of Czech and Slovak." Tomasz Kamusella, *The Politics of Language and Nationalism in Modern Central Europe* (London: Palgrave, 2009), 743.

9. The reasons for Prague's more Western-assimilated Jewish population are complex, ranging from Prague Jews' almost uninterrupted residency leading to a comparatively more integrated population; language laws; the lack of an Orthodox community; a dearth of migration from Eastern communities as compared to other cities such as Berlin and Vienna, and even the fear of the Czech language barrier. See Kateřina Čapková, *Czechs, Germans, Jews? National Identity and the Jews of Bohemia*, trans. Derek Paton and Marzia Paton (New York: Berghahn, 2012).

10. Chapter 3 explains in greater detail how the presence and formulation of such census questions were a matter of extensive and contentious public debate.

11. Judith Butler, "Who Owns Kafka?" *London Review of Books* 33, no. 5 (March 2011): 3–8; Pascale Casanova, *The World Republic of Letters*, trans. M. B. DeBevoise (Cambridge, Mass.: Harvard University Press, 2004): "his work can be understood as entirely translated from a language that he could not write, Yiddish," 269; David Suchoff, *Kafka's Jewish Languages: The Hidden Openness of Tradition* (Philadelphia: University of Pennsylvania Press, 2011).

12. See Suchoff, *Kafka's Jewish Languages*; Čapková, *Czechs, Germans, Jews?*; Hillel Kieval, *Languages of Community: The Jewish Experience in the Czech Lands* (Berkeley: University of California Press, 2000); and Iris Bruce, *Kafka and Cultural Zionism: Dates in Palestine* (Madison: University of Wisconsin Press, 2007).

13. Kieval, *Languages of Community*, 33.

14. Kafka, January 8, 1914. *Diaries of Franz Kafka*, 252. "Was habe ich mit Juden gemeinsam? Ich habe kaum etwas mit mir gemeinsam," *Tagebücher*, 219.

15. Kafka, October 30, 1921. *Diaries of Franz Kafka*, 396. "Was verbindet sich mit diesen festabgesetzten, sorechendenm augenblitzenden Körpern enger als mit irgendeiner Sache . . . Etwa daß du von ihrer Art bist? Aber du bist nicht von ihrer Art, darum hast du ja diese Frage aufgeworfen," *Tagebücher*, 342.

16. Letter to Max Brod and Felix Weltsch, April 8, 1920. The Kafka-Jesenská correspondence incidentally began that same month. The "Casino" was another name for the Deutsche Haus, the center of German cultural life in Prague. "Dann ein Prager Jude, der bis zum Umsturz (im Vertrauen) Mitglied sowohl des Deutschen Hauses als der Městanská [sic] beseda gewesen ist, jetzt nur mit großer Protektion die Entlassung aus dem Kasino durchgesetzt hat (Streichung bis zur vollständigsten Unlesbarkeit) und seinen Sohn sofort in die tschechische Realschule hat übertreten lassen 'er wird jetzt nicht deutsch, und nicht tschechisch können, wird er bellen.' " Max Brod, Franz Kafka, *Ein Freundschaft: Briefwechsel* (Frankfurt: Fischer, 1989), 272.

17. Franz Kafka, *Die Erzählungen* (Frankfurt: Fischer, 1997), 373 (my translation).

18. Ibid.

19. See Derek Sayer, *Prague, Capital of the Twentieth Century: A Surrealist History* (Princeton: Princeton University Press, 2013), 73.

20. Tara Zahra, *Kidnapped Souls: National Indifference and the Battle for Children in the Bohemian Lands, 1900–1948* (Ithaca: Cornell University Press, 2008), 4.

21. Pavel Eisner, *Kafka and Prague*, trans. Lowry Nelson and René Wellek (New York: Golden Griften Books, 1950), 19–21.

22. Klaus Wagenbach, *Kafka*, trans. Ewald Osers (Cambridge, Mass.: Harvard University Press, 2003), 51.

23. Pavel Eisner, *Milenky (Německý básník a česká žena)* [*Sweethearts: German Poets and Czech Women*] (Prague: Helios, 1930).

24. Michelle Woods, *Kafka Translated: How Translators Have Shaped Our Reading of Kafka* (Bloomsbury, 2013), 13–44.

25. František Langer described the meetings of Hašek's "Party of Moderate Progress within the Bounds of the Law," under whose auspices Hašek ran for

Parliament and received thirty-five votes. Party leadership was limited by the number of people who could fit at two tables pushed together in the dining room of the leadership's favorite pub, but Hašek's antics as a typical "politician" with pitch-perfect lampoons of political and bureaucratic style soon filled the pub nightly. František Langer, *Byli a bylo* [*They Were and It Was*] (Prague, 1963; Akropolis, 2003), 38–40.

26. Shaun Jacob Halper provides a thorough account of J. Langer's highly unusual career, not only publishing in three languages, Hebrew, German, and ultimately Czech, but also "articulating a specifically *Jewish* homosexual identity," in his excellent dissertation "Mordecai Langer (1894–1943) and the Birth of the Modern Jewish Homosexual" (Berkeley, 2013), and in publication in "Coming Out of the Hasidic Closet: Jiří Mordechai Langer (1894–1943) and the Fashioning of Homosexual-Jewish Identity," *Jewish Quarterly Review* 101, no. 2 (spring 2011): 189. As Halper also notes, "Publishers have made our lives easier by citing Jiří Langer using various combinations of his German, Hebrew, and Czech names: Mordechai Dov, Georg/Georgio, Georg M., Jiří M., and M. D. Georg," 189 n.2.

27. František Langer, "My Brother Jiří." Foreword to Jiří Langer, *Nine Gates to the Chasidic Mysteries*, trans. Stephen Jolly (New York: Behrman House, 1976), xv–xvii.

28. Kafka, September 14, 1915. *Diaries of Franz Kafka*, 341. "Mit Max und Langer Samstag beim Wunderrabbi. . . . 'Alle Rabbi sehen wild aus,' sagte Langer. Dieser im Seidenkaftan, darunter schon Unterhosen sichtbar. Haare auf dem Nasenrücken. Mit Fell eingefaßte Kappe, die er immerfort hin und rückt. Schmutzig und rein, Eigentümlichkeit intensive denkender Menschen. Kratzt sich am Bartansatz, schneuzt durch die Hand auf den Fußboden, greift mit den fingern in die Speisen—wenn er aber ein Weilchen die Hand auf dem Tisch liegen läßt, sieht man das Weiß der Haut, wie man ein ähnliches Weiß nur in Vorstellungen der Kindheit gesehn zu haben glaubt. Damals allerdings waren auch die Eltern rein," *Tagebücher*, 297–98.

29. Kafka, September 15, 1917. *Diaries of Franz Kafka*, 383. "Die Weisheit der Kleinen, Vorherrschaft der Tiere. Die Frauen.—Kühe, mit äußerster Selbstverständlichkeit über den Platz ziehend," *Tagebücher*, 330.

30. Marek Nekula, ". . . *v jednom poschodí vnitřní babylonské vese* . . ." / *Jazyky Franze Kafky* [*"On one of the floors of my inner tower of Babel . . ." Franz Kafka's Languages*] (Prague: Nakladatelství Franze Kafky, 2004), 336–37.

31. Spector, *Prague Territories*, 19.

32. Kafka mentions his subscription in a letter to Jesenská dated June 24, 1920. *Letters to Milena*, 58; *Briefe an Milena*, 78.

33. Spector, *Prague Territories*, 20.

34. Ibid., 89.

35. Franz Kafka, "The City Coat of Arms," trans. Willa and Edwin Muir, in *The Complete Stories*, ed. Nahum Glatzer (New York: Schocken, 1971), 433–34. "Jede Landsmannschaft wollte das schönste Quartier haben, dadurch ergaben sich Streitigkeiten, die sich bis zu blutigen Kämpfen steigerten. Diese Kämpfe hörten nicht mehr auf; den Führern waren sie ein neues Argument dafür, daß der Turm auch mangels der nötigen Konzentration sehr langsam oder lieber erst nach allgemeinem Friedensschluß gebaut werden sollte. Doch verbrachte man die

Zeit nicht nur mit Kämpfen, in den Pausen verschönerte man die Stadt, wodurch man allerdings neuen Neid und neue Kämpfe hervorrief," Kafka, *Die Erzählungen*, 375.

36. Marek Nekula, "The Divided City: Prague's Public Space and Franz Kafka's Readings of Prague," in *Franz Kafka im sprachnationalen Kontext seiner Zeit: Sprache und national identität in öffentlichen Institutionen der Böhmischen Länder*, ed. Marek Nekula, Ingrid Fleischmann, and Albrecht Greule (Cologne: Böhlau Verlag, 2007), 93–94.

37. Kafka, *Complete Stories*, 434. "Dazu kam, daß schon die zweite oder dritte Generation die Sinnlosigkeit des Himmelsturmbaues erkannte, doch war man schon viel zu sehr miteinander verbunden, um die Stadt zu verlassen," Kafka, *Die Erzählungen*, 375.

38. Alfred Thomas, *Prague Palimpsest: Writing, Memory, and the City* (Chicago: University of Chicago Press, 2010), 100.

39. Ibid., 101–2.

40. For a detailed account of the toppling of the Marian column, see Cynthia Paces, *Prague Panoramas: National Memory and Sacred Space in the Twentieth Century* (Pittsburgh, Pa.: University of Pittsburgh Press, 2009), 87–96.

41. Walter Benjamin, *Illuminations*, trans. Harry Zohn (New York: Schocken, 1969), 110.

Chapter 1

1. Zhang Xudong, for example, evokes the paradigm to analyze Shanghai literature's position within Chinese and modernist "major" literatures in "Shanghai Image: Critical Iconography, Minor Literature, and the Un-Making of a Modern Chinese Mythology," in *New Literary History: A Journal of Theory and Interpretation* 33, no. 1 (2002): 137–69; Maher Jarrar addresses the Palestinian writer Emile Habibi in terms of the paradigm in "A Narration of 'Deterritorialization': Imil Habibi's *The Pessoptimist*," in *Middle Eastern Literatures* 5, no. 1 (2002): 15–28; Mario Cancel considers Puerto Rican "minority" in the context of the Spanish-American War in "Mitos, nación, y militarismo: La literatura menor y el 1898,"*Atenea* 22, no. 1–2 (2002): 31–55—to name just a few of the many articles indexed.

2. See Stanley Corngold, "Kafka and the Dialect of Minor Literature," in *Debating World Literature*, ed. Christopher Prendergast (New York: Verso, 2004). In addition to illustrating the problems with *Minor Literature*'s claims about Kafka and German, Corngold offers a detailed reading of Kafka's own claims about Yiddish and Czech in the 1911 journal passage. Others in the field—most extensively and successfully Scott Spector in his *Prague Territories*—have engaged to recontextualize the key terms of *Minor Literature*'s arguments in a richer, more historically based understanding of Prague's complex ethnic and linguistic tensions.

3. Lowell Edmunds, "Kafka on Minor Literature," *German Studies Review* 33, no. 2 (2010): 354, http://www.jstor.org/stable/20787912.

4. While *Prague Territories* provides the most nuanced cultural study to date, it is far less extensive and detailed in its presentation of the Czech aspects of culture. Czech scholarship, of course, has tended to find Kafka's relationship to Czech of more interest, as in the work of František Kautman collected in *Franz Kafka*

(Prague: Academia, 1994), but publication, distribution, and institutional support faced political restrictions prior to the 1990s. Famously, the 1963 Kafka conference in Liblice, which argued for the rehabilitation of Kafka as a part of the country's cultural history and relevance to socialism, hosted several papers exploring Kafka's connections to Czech literature and culture and furthermore proved to be a political and cultural watershed, often understood as a harbinger of the Prague Spring. The following period of "normalization," however, saw serious consequences for these outspoken scholars. Outside of Czechoslovakia, before 1989 books such as Ritchie Robertson's *Kafka: Judaism, Politics, and Literature* (Oxford: Clarendon, 1985) set out to remedy this deficit in understanding Kafka's Czech context, but lacked access to Czech materials. Robertson, however, provides a good, brief overview of the traditional terms in which Kafka's cultural affiliation and experience had been viewed (1–3), as well as making great strides towards filling in the gaps as he could. Today, the most detailed and exhaustive study of Kafka's relationship to the Czech language may be found in Marek Nekula's *Jazyky Franze Kafky*, available in German as *Franz Kafkas Sprachen: ". . . in einem Stockwerk des innern babylonischen Turmes . . .* " (Tübingen: Max Niemeyer Verlag, 2003). A collection of Nekula's work drawn largely from this volume is now available in English translation in Marek Nekula, *Franz Kafka and His Prague Contexts* (Prague: Karolinium, 2016). See also *Brücken nach Prag: Deutschsprachige Literatur im kulturellen Kontext der Donaumonarchie und der Tschechoslowakei*, ed. Klaas-Hinrich Ehlers, Steffen Höhne et al. (Frankfurt: Peter Lang, 2000) and *Kafka a Čechy/ Kafka und Böhmen* (Nakladatelství Franze Kafky, 2007).

5. In addition to the many such works discussed or cited previously, the particular concerns raised by Deleuze and Guattari have been recently engaged by work on the topic of monolingualism that draws on Kafka and Prague's linguistic multiplicity and explores the theoretical implications in different directions from "minor literature." See Yasemin Yildiz, *Beyond the Mother Tongue: The Postmonolingual Condition* (New York: Fordham University Press, 2011), who argues (as I do) that Kafka becomes increasingly skeptical of monolingualism and the nation-state insistence on language-as-identity, and David Gramling, who sees Kafka as more invested in multilingualism from the start, in *The Invention of Monolingualism* (New York: Bloomsbury, 2016), especially chapter 2, "Kafka's Well-Tempered Piano."

6. Gilles Deleuze and Felix Guattari, *Kafka: Toward a Minor Literature*, trans. Dana Polan (Minneapolis: University of Minnesota Press, 1986), 16.

7. For an English-language book-length study of the Czech spoken-written dynamic, see Charles Townsend's *Spoken Prague Czech* (Columbus, Ohio: Slavica, 1990).

8. Kafka, December 18, 1911. *Diaries,* 140. "Traurig muß das alles für einen nur etwas herumgekommenen Tschechen sein," *Tagebücher*, 123.

9. Charles Sabatos, "Multilingualism and the Czechoslovak Context of 'Minor Literature,' " in *1616: Anuario de Literatura Comparada* 2 (2012), 281–94, 287.

10. Kafka, *Diaries*, 141.

11. Both Mareš and Janouch would go on to long careers of elaborating in surely fictitious detail their friendships with Kafka, as examined and often debunked by Josef Čermák. *Franz Kafka: Fables et Mystifications*, ed. and trans. Hélène Beletto-Sussel (Villeneuve d'Ascq, France: Presses Universitaires de Septentrion, 2010).

12. Franz Kafka, *Letters to Felice*, trans. James Stern and Elisabeth Duckworth, ed. Erich Heller and Jürgen Born (New York: Schocken, 1973), 176. *Briefe an Felice*, ed. Erich Heller and Jürgen Born (Frankfurt: S. Fischer, 1990), 276.

13. Kafka, *Letters to Felice*, 227. "Und heute sind tatsächlich 2 solcher Einladungen gekommen. Der Verband der tschechischen Müllereigenossenschaften hat Montag in Prag eine Versammlung, die tschechischen Baumeister der Sudetenländer am Dienstag in Brünn. Das Glück ist, daß es tschechische Versammlungen sind und mein Tschechisch höchst traurig ist, [aber] . . . Kongresse aller möglichen Vereinigungen, wo über Unfallversicherung gesprochen wird und Vertreter der Anstalt irgendetwas vortragen. . . . Und heute sind tatsächlich 2 solcher Einladungen gekommen. Der Verband der tschechischen Müllereigenossenschaften hat Montag in Prag eine Versammlung, die tschechischen Baumeister der Sudetenländer am Dienstag in Brünn. Das Glück ist, daß es tschechische Versammlungen sind und mein Tschechisch höchst traurig ist, [aber] . . . es wäre auch nach der Verteilung der Arbeit innerhalb der Anstalt durchaus meine Sache," *Briefe an Felice*, 343–44.

14. Kafka, *Letters to Felice*, 417. "Kleine tschechische Lektion," *Briefe an Felice*, 591.

15. Kafka, letter of April 4, 1913. *Letters to Felice*, 234. "Er ist Lehrer und schreibt erotische Romane . . . und auf dem Titelblatt ist eine Dame abgebildet, die mit brennenden Herzen jongliert. . . . Ich weiß nicht eigentlich, aus welchen Gründen ich mir den Menschen, ohne mich irgendwie um ihn zu bekümmern, als einen kleinen schwarzen Schleicher vorstellte," *Briefe an Felice*, 353–54.

16. Kafka, *Letters to Felice*, 235. "natürlich nur etwas lächerliche erotische Romane herauskommen können, wenn sie ein Lehrer, ohne Welterfahrung, in trockener Manier, aus seinem kleinen Erdloch heraus schreib."; "Weißt Du, die Tschechen streben ja sehr zum französischen Wesen hin," *Briefe an Felice*, 354.

17. Franz Kafka, "The Burrow," trans. Willa Muir and Edwin Muir, in *The Complete Stories*, ed. Nahum N. Glatzer (New York: Schocken, 1971), 343. "Dieses Geräusch ist übrigens ein verhältnismäßig unschuldiges; ich habe es gar nicht gehört, als ich kam . . . es ist gewissermaßen nur mit dem Ohr des Hausbesitzers hörbar," Franz Kafka, "Der Bau," in *Die Erzählungen* (Frankfurt: Fischer, 1997), 488.

18. Kafka, *Complete Stories*, 345.

19. Kafka, *Die Erzählungen*, 489.

20. Kafka, *Complete Stories*, 345. "ich höre es freilich jetzt mit dem durch die Übung geschärften Ohr immer deutlicher," *Die Erzählungen*, 489.

21. Nekula, *Jazyky Franze Kafky*, 14.

22. Ibid., 15.

23. Ibid., 22–23.

24. Marek Nekula, *Franz Kafka and His Prague Contexts* (Prague: Karolinium, 2016), 156–58.

25. *Dalimil* is the first Czech-language treatment; Cosmas's earlier twelfth-century Latin text *Chronica Boemorum* (*The Chronicle of the Czechs*) gives the first written account of the legends.

26. Hans Dieter Zimmerman offers the most complete account of Kafka's reading of Němcová in "Franz Kafka liest Božena Němcová," *Kafka und Bömen*, 51–65.

27. I discuss these brothers more fully in the introduction.

28. Josef Kroutvor, *Praha, město ostrých hran* (Prague: Vovox globator, 1992), 17.

29. Kafka first mentions Bílek in the postscript of a letter postmarked July 1922, suggesting him as a topic for Brod to write about in the *Abendblatt* (*Letters to Friends, Family, and Editors*, 344; Kafka, *Briefe, 1902–1924* [Frankfurt: Fischer, 1966], 397). More detailed discussion follows in the subsequent letter, dated only late July 1922: "It is a wanton and senseless impoverishment of Prague and Bohemia that mediocre stuff like Šaloun's Hus or wretched stuff like Sucharda's Palacký are erected with all honors, while on the other hand sketches of Bílek's for a Žižka or Komenský monument, sketches of incomparable quality, remain unexecuted" (*Letters to Friends, Family, and Editors*, 347; *Ein Freundschaft*, 395). In a letter dated July 31, Kafka delights that Brod has agreed to write on Bílek, comparing his cause to Brod's advocacy for Janáček.

30. Kafka, *Letters to Friends, Family, and Editors*, 347.

Chapter 2

1. Gustav Janouch, *Conversations with Kafka*, ed. Hugh Haughton (London: Encounter, 1985), 128. I discuss the dubious reliability of Janouch's text in more detail in chapter 8.

2. *Conversations with Kafka*, 138. In the same passage, however, Janouch has Kafka claiming not to speak Czech, which is clearly untrue. While in context, Kafka might have been self-deprecating about his own language skills as compared with Max Brod's superior command, these words attributed to him leave a mistaken impression. Kafka mentions subscribing to the journal in a letter to Milena Jesenská of June 24, 1920, citing it as his authority for making claims about the Czechness of her name, as referenced also in chapters 3, 5, and 7. See also my discussion of the journal with regard to Božena Němcová in chapter 4. The text of the passage is quoted in full in chapter 5.

3. Janouch, *Conversations*, 138–39.

4. Kafka, January 1921, letter to Max Brod. *Letters to Friends, Family, and Editors*, 257; Kafka, *Briefe 1902–1924*, 298.

5. Kafka, *Letters to Friends, Family, and Editors*, 257.

6. Ibid., 256.

7. For a more extensive discussion of *Tribuna*'s founding and political fortunes, see Čapková, *Czechs, Germans, Jews?*, 124–26.

8. Thomas Ort, *Art and Life in Modernist Prague, 1911–1938* (New York: Palgrave, 2013), 211, n.10.

9. Čermák, *Franz Kafka: Fables et Mystifications*, 50–51.

10. "Ti, jimž záleží na docílení smíru s Němci, měli by se především zasadit o odstranění nadávky Němec. Nic není, psychologicky hluboce vzato, způsobilo do té míry rozněcovat stále národní odpor Čechů ke Germánům a následkem toho Germánů k Čechům, jako toto hnusné slovo, chromné opovržení a ošklivost vyjadřující. Jen ono to bylo, které ve mně v prvných dětských letech vzbudilo o Germánech představu, že jsou něco medvědovitě, huhňajícího, zvířecky tupého, obludného a nezbavil jsem se jí dodnes zcela otrávilo mi to z velké části germánskou kulturu. Je jisto, že každý Čech zažil zde, třeba v menší míře a neuvědomění, něco podobného. Následky však jsou příšerné, Národ, který pokřtil svého

souseda nadávkou, rozhodl tím někdy o své budoucnosti, napsal snat tím ortel své smrti . . . Psychická impnderabilia jsou tím nejtěžším éterem je těžší, než olovo" (my translation). Ladislav Klíma, "Myšlenky," *Tribuna*, May 14, 1920, 5.

11. The topic of performativity in Kafka has a long critical history, beginning with Stanley Corngold's "The Hermeneutic of the Judgment" in Angel Flores, ed. *The Problem of the Judgment: Eleven Approaches to Kafka's Story* (New York: Gordian Press, 1977). Recent discussions include Graham Fallows, "Power and Performativity: 'Doing Things with Words' in Kafka's *Proceß*," *Oxford German Studies* 44 (2015): 199–225; Michael Huffmaster, "The Success of Failure: Performatives in 'The Judgment,'" *Poetics Today* 37, no. 4 (2016): 605–39. See also the discussion of cadastral surveying in chapter 3 and of gender in *The Castle* in chapter 7.

12. Kafka, letter of July 12, 1920. *Letters to Milena*, 82–83. "So saß ich bei Laurin, hörte öfters Deinen Namen und war ihm dankbar. Allerdings es ist weder leicht noch angenehm mit ihm zu reden"; " . . Güte Teilnahme Hilfsbereitschaft anlangt ein großer und sehr ernsthafter Erwachsener ist," *Briefe an Milena*, 105–6.

13. Reiner Stach, ed., *Kafka: The Years of Insight*, trans. Shelley Frisch (Princeton, N.J.: Princeton University Press, 2013), 335–37.

14. For references in the correspondence to material in progress for, or appearing in, *Kmen*, see Franz Kafka, *Briefe an Milena*: 7—letter dated April 1920, thanking Jesenská for receipt of an issue; 135—asking about her publications in a variety of journals; 228—letter of August 20, 1920, discussing Vladislav Vančura; 245—letter of September 2, 1920, apparently confirming to Jesenská that her translation of Landauer had, in fact, appeared over several issues; and 277—letter dated September 1920, thanking Jesenská for her work in *Kmen* and *Tribuna*, the daily for which she wrote a regular column.

15. Jesenská's translations appear in *Kmen* 4 (March 1920–March 1921). From 1920: Franz Kafka: "Topič" ("Der Heizer/The Stoker"), April 22; "Náhlá procházka" ("Der plötzliche Spaziergang/The Sudden Walk"); "Výlet do hor" ("Der Ausflug ins Gebirge/Excursion to the Mountains"); "Neštěstí mládence" ("Das Unglück des Junggesellen/The Bachelor's Ill Luck"); "Kupec" ("Der Kaufmann/The Tradesman"); "Cesta domů" ("Der Nachhauseweg/The Way Home"); "Ti, kteří běží mimo" ("Die Vorüberlaufenden/The Passersby"), all September 9. Other translations: Gustav Schulz: "Zítra nebo již dnes" ("Tomorrow—or Today"), June 17; Upton Sinclair: excerpts from *Jimmie Higgins*, June 24; "Anonymous Russian Thinker: Individuality," August 5; Gustav Landauer: "Friedrich Hölderlin," August 19 and 26, September 2; Franz Werfel, "Den z chlapectví" ("A Boyhood Day"), September 9. From 1921: "Blasfemie blázna" ("The Blasphemy of a Fool"), March 3; Rosa Luxemburg: "Duše ruské literatury" ("The Soul of Russian Literature"), November 18; Charles Péguy: "Bída" ("Woe"), November 25, December 2.

16. Scott Spector gives the definitive account of the development and complexity of this anachronistically named, loosely associated group of German Jewish writers and intellectuals in his *Prague Territories*. Max Brod coined the name and his book, too, provides a vital if hindsighted insider's account. Max Brod, *Der Prager Kreis* (Stuttgart: Kohlhammer, 1966).

17. Cited by Jaromir Lang in *Neumannův Červen* (Prague: Orbis, 1957), 97.

18. Jindřich Toman, *The Magic of a Common Language: Jakobson, Mathesius, Trubetzkoy, and the Prague Linguistic Circle* (Cambridge, Mass.: MIT Press, 1997), 88.

19. *Kmen* 4: 46 (February 10, 1921) 545–46. An excerpt from his *Noveishaya russkaya poeziya* [New Russian Poetry]: *Velimir Khlebnikov* (Prague: Typography Politika, 1921).

20. Kafka, *Letters to Milena*, 168. "In diesem Kmen-Heft ist auch das erste gute Original-Stück das ich dort gelesen habe, den Verfassernamen habe ich nicht genau in der Erinnerung Vladislav Vančura oder ähnlich," Kafka, *Briefe an Milena*, 228.

21. Kafka, *Briefe an Milena*, 266–67.

22. "Ve skutečnosti ovšem žádným "dekadentem" nebo "novoromantikem" nebyl." Jaromír Lang, *St. K. Neumann* (Prague: Československý spisovatel, 1957), 21. My translation.

23. For a detailed and thorough overview of Neumann's role in the Czech reception of the international avant-garde, see Jiří Stromšík, "Rezeption der europäischen Moderne in der tschechischen Avantgarde nach 1910," in *Moderne in der deutschen und der tschechischen Literatur*, ed. Klaus Schank (Tübingen: Franke Verlag, 2000), 29–68; for Neumann's influence, see esp. 31–49.

24. Adam McKible, *The Space and Place of Modernism: The Russian Revolution, Little Magazines, and New York* (New York: Routledge, 2002), 10.

25. The text of Neumann's note: "Povídka, kterou jsme vyplnili toto číslo, patří k nejlepším moderním povídkám německým. Domníváme se, že jest lépe, když taková věc netrhá se na pokračování, nybrž předloží se čtenářům celá jako neobvyklá, ale šťastná výjimka. Čtenář není tím nikterak poškozen a redakce v dnešní situaci často dosti obtížné—nabude času" (S. K. Neumann, editor's note to Kafka's *Topič*, *Kmen* 4, 72).

26. Ibid.

27. "The Stoker" was originally published in isolation from the novel (like all Kafka's novels, never published during his lifetime), so this was the text Jesenská saw and based her version on. The novel is now published under the title *Der Verschollene*, translated into English as *The Boy Who Dropped Out of Sight*, but remains better known in English as *Amerika*.

28. jeel, "Nacionalismus a "anacionalismus" v umění" in *Kmen* 4, no. 29, July 22, 1920, 227.

29. "Jsem na pohybách, je-li možna vážná polemika s někým, kdo . . . humanitní ideál socialismu utopí v hrubém antisemitickém výpadu i kdo se domnívá, že snížil mezinárodnost socialismu poukazem na specificky tvůrčí schopnosti národního celku, kdo mysl národa jako kulturní jednotky ztotožní s politickým nacionalismem a na podkladě tohoto záměrně útočí proti 'anacionalismu,' " ibid., my translation.

30. "'Anacionalismus' je *politicko*-kulturní program, žádající od umění přihlížení k sociálním proudům doby, řešení kulturních otázek ve smyslu socialismu, že je voláním po nové tendenci, namířené proti staré *politicko-nacionální*. Že útok na 'anacionalismus' je útokem na tendenci v umění vůbec, a že jen na tomto poli měl býti veden," ibid., my translation.

31. Ibid., 151.

32. Ibid., 174.

33. Mark Morrison, *The Public Face of Modernism: Little Magazines, Audiences and Reception, 1905–1920* (Madison: University of Wisconsin Press, 2002).

Chapter 3

1. Benedict Anderson, *Imagined Communities: Reflections on the Origins and Spread of Nationalism*, rev. ed. (New York: Verso, 2006).

2. Peter Bugge, "Czech Nation-Building, National Self-Perception, and Politics 1780–1914" (dissertation, Aarhus University, 1994), 17–18.

3. Ernst Pawel, *The Nightmare of Reason: The Life of Franz Kafka* (New York: Farrar, Straus and Giroux, 1984), 23–24.

4. "Pročež musí, kdo chce být Čechem, přestati být Židem." As quoted in Bugge, "Czech Nation-Building," 59.

5. Jonathan Bolton, "Czech Literature," in *YIVO Encyclopedia of Jews in Eastern Europe*, March 7, 2011, http://www.yivoencyclopedia.org/article.aspx/Czech_Literature.

6. Mark Twain, "Stirring Times in Austria, 1898," *Harper's New Monthly Magazine*, vol. 96 (March 1898): 530–40.

7. František Weyr, "Národnost či mateřská řeč?" (Nationality or Mother Tongue?), *Lidové noviny* 28, no. 320 (Brno: July 1, 1920): 1. My translation.

8. Tara Zahra, *Kidnapped Souls*, 4.

9. Ibid., 121–24.

10. Franz Kafka, *Das Schloß* (Frankfurt: Fischer, 1993), 5. All German citations in the text are to this edition.

11. Franz Kafka, *The Castle*, trans. Mark Harman (New York: Schocken, 1998), 1. All English citations in the text are to this edition unless otherwise indicated.

12. Kafka, *The Castle*, 59. "Die Grenzen unserer kleinen Wirtschaften sind abgesteckt, alles ist ordentlich eingetragen, Besitzwechsel kommt kaum vor und kleine Grenzstreitigkeiten regeln wir selbst. Was soll uns also ein Landvermesser?" Kafka, *Das Schloß*, 74.

13. Francis Fodor, *The Geographic Impossibility of the Czech State* (London: Dawson; New York: Steiger; Budapest: Ferdinand Pfeiffer, 1920), 1.

14. James C. Scott, *Seeing Like a State: How Certain Schemes to Improve the Human Condition Have Failed* (New Haven, Conn.: Yale University Press, 1999), 24.

15. Ibid., 2.

16. Ibid., 3.

Chapter 4

1. Kafka, January 16, 1922. *Tagebücher*, 345.

2. Kafka, *Diaries*, 202.

3. Kafka, *Tagebücher*, 345.

4. Stanley Corngold makes the key distinction that Kafka does not only literalize the metaphor, but transforms it, distorts it such that it is neither tenor nor vehicle, but alternates fluidly between the two, "the process of literalization in various directions and not its end state" (*Franz Kafka: The Necessity of Form* [Ithaca, N.Y.: Cornell University Press, 1990], 56). More recently, Mark Christian Thompson has connected "Mistkäfer" with the derogatory racial

epithet "Kaffer." Thompson, *Kafka's Blues: Figurations of Racial Blackness in the Construction of the Aesthetic* (Evanston, Ill.: Northwestern University Press, 2016), 56–58.

5. Günther Anders suggested that a primary accomplishment of Kafka's work was to literalize metaphor; *Franz Kafka* (London: Bowes and Bowes, 1960), 42. Corngold countered that Gregor Samsa was depicted in the process of becoming literalized, not presented as a fait accompli; *Necessity*, 80. For a thorough consideration and extension of these long-standing debates on metaphor in Kafka, see Schuman, "Metamorphosis and the Limits of Metaphorical Language" in *Kafka and Wittgenstein: The Case for Analytic Modernism* (Evanston, Ill.: Northwestern University Press, 2015), 55–84.

6. Originally published in *Noveishaya russkaya poeziya*: *Velimir Khlebnikov* (Prague: Typography Politika, 1921). A partial translation appears as Roman Jakobson, "Vivisekce jako nejblížší úkol vědy a umění," in *Kmen* 4 (1920–21). English trans. "Modern Russian Poetry: Velimir Khlebnikov," in *Major Soviet Writers: Essays in Criticism*, ed. E. J. Brown (New York: Oxford University Press, 1973), 58–82.

7. Jakobson's position is most famously articulated in "Two Aspects of Language and Two Types of Aphasic Disturbances" in *On Language*, ed. Linda R. Waugh and M . Monville-Burston (Cambridge: Harvard University Press, 1956), 115–33. The basic structures of this paradigm, however, are already present in the early work on Khlebnikov and other figures he was publishing in Prague in the early 1920s.

8. Kafka, *The Castle*, 10. "Die Straße nämlich, diese Hauptstraße des Dorfes führte nicht zum Schloßberg, sie führte nur nahe heran, dann aber wie absichtlich bog sie ab und wenn sie sich auch vom Schloß nicht entfernte, so kam sie ihm doch auch nicht näher. Immer erwartete K., daß nun endlich die Straße zum Schloß einlenken müsse, und nur weil er es erwartete ging er weiter . . ." Kafka, *Das Schloß*, 16.

9. Kafka, *The Castle*, 57. "K. war . . . nicht weit davon entfert, seine Lage zufriedenstellend zu finden, trotzdem er sich immer nach solchen Anfällen des Behagens schnell sagte, daß gerade darin die Gefahr lag. Der direkte Verkehr mit Behörden war ja nicht allzu schwer, denn die Behörden hatten, so gut sie auch organisiert sein mochten, immer nur im Namen entlegener unsichtbarer Herren entlegene unsichtbare Dinge zu verteidigen, während K. für etwas lebendigst Nahes kämpfte, für sich selbst, überdies zumindest in der allerersten Zeit aus eigenem Willen, denn er war der Angreifer, und nicht nur er kämpfte für sich, sondern offenbar noch ander Kräfte, die er nicht kannte, aber an die er nach den Maßnahmen der Behörden glauben konnte," Kafka, *Das Schloß*, 72.

10. Kafka, *The Castle*, 58. "Dadurch nun aber, daß die Behörden K. von vorherein in unwesentlicheren Dingen . . . weit entgegenkamen, nahmen sie ihm die Möglichkeit kleiner leichter Siege und mit dieser Möglichkeit auch die zugehörige Genugtuung und die aus ihr sich ergebende gut begründete Sicherheit für weitere größere Kämpfe. Statt dessen ließen sie K., allerdings nur innerhalb des Dorfes, überall durchgleiten, wo er wollte, verwöhnten und schwächten ihn dadurch, schalteten hier überhaupt jeden Kampf aus und verlegten ihn dafür in das außeramtliche, völlig unübersichtliche, trübe, fremdartige Leben. Auf diese Weise konnte es, wenn er nicht immer auf der Hut war, wohl geschehn, daß er

eines Tages trotz aller Liebenswürdigkeit der Behörden und trotz der vollständigen Erfüllung aller so übertrieben leichten amtlichen Verpflichtungen, getäuscht durch die ihm erwiesene scheinbare Gunst sein sonstiges Leben so unvorsichtig führte, daß er hier zusammenbrach, und die Behörde, noch immer sanft und freundlich, gleichsam gegen ihren Willen aber im Namen irgendeiner ihm unbekannten öffentlichen Ordnung, kommen mußte, um ihn aus dem Weg zu räumen," Kafka, *Das Schloß*, 72–73.

11. Kafka, *The Castle*, 8.

12. Kafka, *Das Schloß*, 13.

13. K., like Kafka's other protagonists, occupies "a world which has not even believed in its own unbelief. Kafka's heroes struggle in vain for spiritual survival. Thus his creations are symbolic, for they are infused with, and not only allegorical of, negative transcendence." Eric Heller, *Franz Kafka* (New York: Viking, 1974), 114.

14. Charles Bernheimer, *Flaubert and Kafka: Studies in Psychopoetic Structure* (New Haven, Conn.: Yale University Press, 1982), 191–98. See also Theodor Adorno, "Notes on Kafka," in *Prisms*, Samuel and Sherry Weber, trans. (Cambridge, Mass.: MIT, 1983), 246. Walter Benjamin's correspondence with Gershom Scholem repeatedly visits this notion of the allegorical in Kafka's work, with Benjamin insisting on the "non-presence" asserted by allegory in Kafka, a phenomenon Scholem understands in relation to what he calls the "incompleteness" of the phenomenal world. Walter Benjamin and Gershom Scholem, *Walter Benjamin-Gershom Scholem Briefwechsel: 1933–1940* (Frankfurt: Suhrkamp 1980), 157.

15. "Man hat die Weisheit gelegentlich als die epische Seite der Warheit definieren wollen. Damit ist die Weisheit als ein Traditionsgut gekennzeichnet; sie ist die Warheit in ihrer hagadischen Konsistenz," Benjamin and Scholem, *Briefswechsel*, 272. My translation.

16. "Er gab die Wahrheit preis, um an der Tradierbarkeit, an dem hagadischen Element festzuhalten" ibid., 272.

17. Corngold, *Necessity*, 89.

18. Ibid.

19. Jakobson, "Modern Russian Poetry: Velimir Khlebnikov," 58–82.

20. Kafka, *The Castle*, 28. "Der Friedhof hatte vor ihnen kein Geheimnis mehr, durch seine kleine Gittertür waren sie schon oft hineingekommen, nur die glatte hohe Mauer wollten sie bezwingen," Kafka, *Das Schloß*, 38.

21. Elizabeth Boa discusses Kafka's treatment of "Heimat" in *The Castle* in relation to other of his writings that touch on it, or are written in a similar mode. She finds that K.'s idealization of this homeland is "signaled . . . by an obtrusively rhetorical tone, suggesting sentimental self-deception on his part." Elizabeth Boa, "The Castle," in *The Cambridge Companion to Kafka*, ed. Julian Pierce (Cambridge: Cambridge University Press, 2002), 63–64.

22. Kafka, *The Castle*, 9; *Das Schloß*, 15.

23. Kafka, *The Castle*, 65; *Das Schloß*, 82.

24. Kafka, *The Castle*, 71; *Das Schloß*, 89.

25. Sergei Karcevskij, "The Asymmetric Dualism of the Linguistic Sign," trans. Wendy Steiner, in *The Prague School: Selected Writings, 1929–1946*, ed. Peter Steiner (Austin: University of Texas Press, 1983), 47–53.

26. Jan Mukařovský, "On the Problem of Function in Architecture," in *Structure, Sign, and Function: Selected Essays*, trans. and ed. J. Burbank and P. Steiner (New Haven: Yale University Press, 1978), 236.

27. Ibid., 236–37.

28. Ibid., 240–41.

29. Ibid., 237.

30. Ibid., 239.

31. Ibid., 241–42.

32. A phrase borrowed from the title of Jindřich Toman's excellent study of the Prague School.

33. For a brief overview, see Richard Burton, *Prague: A Cultural and Literary History* (Northampton, Eng.: Interlink, 2003), 102–5. For a more in-depth treatment, see Stanley Kimball, *Czech Nationalism: A Study of the National Theatre Movement, 1845–83* (Urbana: University of Illinois Press, 1964).

34. This importance endured: the first post-Communist president, Vaclav Havel, was a playwright whose father was the architect of the important Lucerna Theater, and the physical as well as political center of Velvet Revolutionary activities was the Magic Lantern Theater.

35. Spector, *Prague Territories*, 242.

36. Ronald Gray, "To Deny Whatever Is Affirmed," in *Franz Kafka's "The Castle": Modern Critical Interpretations*, ed. Harold Bloom (New York: Chelsea House, 1988), 55. The connection to "V zámku a v podzámčí" was first suggested by František Kautman.

37. See Alois Získal, "O řeči Boženy Němcové v 'Babičce,'" *Naše řeč* 4, no. 10 (1920): 289–99, http://nase-rec.ujc.cas.cz/archiv.php?lang=en&vol=5#h9.

38. Thomas, *Prague Palimpsest*, 94.

39. Božena Němcová, "V zámku a v podzámčí," in *Sebráné Spisy Boženy Němcové* (Prague: Jan Laichter, 1906), 11–12, my translation. "Zámek stál na vršku a pod ním leželo městečko. Řeka tekoucí okolo města u paty vršku dělala hranice mezi majetností panskou a městskou a jedním pramenem jejím bylo město kolkolem obehnáno. Obyvatelé městečka dělili se na tři třídy. Do první třídy počítali se zámožní hospodáři, co měli svůj dům, dvorec a hodně polí a jejichž paní a dcery klobouky nosily a v parádním pokoji kávové společnosti dávaly.

"Z těch boháčů volila se obyčejně městská rada a starosta dle rady starého přísloví 'kde peníze, tu i rozum.' Do druhé třídy počítali se chudší řemeslníci, co měli jen kousek pole a domek; těch ženy nosily se v čepcích a velmi za zlé jim to měla ta první třída, jestli dovolili dcerám klobouky nosit, rovnajíce se jejich dcerám. Třetí třída konečně byla tak zvaná lůza, podruhovina, která živa byla »z ruky do úst«. Tuto by chtěl kdo přirovnat v čemkoli s třídou první, bylo by největší urážkou pro ně bývalo; když podruhyně milostpaní z první třídy ruku políbila, honem si ji utřela, aby se jí od polibku nečistého neposkvrnila, aneb jí nastrčila jen rukáv.

"Dvorce boháčů a baráky chudších řemeslníků byly z většího dílu u vody, na valech. V každém tom dvoru bylo po několika komorách, schválně pro podruhy zřízených, komory ty byly tmavé, v každé bylo malinké okýnko, podlaha žádná ani kamna ani pec. Ohřívat se v zimě a vařit svoji potravu chodili tito podruzi do velké ratajny k nádvorníku. Za takovou komoru musel podruh platit dvanácte zlatých stříbra nájmu do roka; za tu lacinou činži ale byl zase zavázán majiteli dvora, u něhož bydlel. . . .”

40. Germanized Bohemian nobility were frequent targets of nationalist ire from the nineteenth century onward, and this story reflects resentment of what could be construed as land hogging going hand in hand with cosmopolitanism, Germanization (often conflated), and the abandonment of Czech identity. Eagle Glassheim details the considerably more complex reality alongside competing contemporary and historiographic accounts of the nobility's relationship to the changing tides of nationalism in *Noble Nationalists: The Transformation of the Bohemian Aristocracy* (Cambridge, Mass.: Harvard University Press, 2005).

41. Kafka, *Das Schloß*, 5.

42. Kafka, *The Castle*, 1.

43. Kafka, *The Castle*, 3. “Ein junger Mann, städtisch angezogen, mit schauspielerhaftem Gesicht, die Augen schmal, die Augenbrauen stark, stand mit dem Wirt neben ihm. Die Bauern waren auch noch da, einige hatten ihre Sessel herumgedreht um besser zu sehn und zu hören. Der junge Mann entschuldigte sich sehr höflich K. geweckt zu haben, stellte sich als Sohn des Schloßkastellans vor und sagte dann: ‘Dieses Dorf ist Besitz des Schlosses, wer hier wohnt oder übernachtet, wohnt oder übernachtet gewissermaßen im Schloß. Niemand darf das ohne gräfliche Erlaubnis. Sie aber haben eine solche Erlaubnis nicht oder haben sie wenigstens nicht vorgezeigt’,” Kafka, *Das Schloß*, 5.

44. Kafka, *Das Schloß*, 6.

45. Kafka, *The Castle*, 5.

46. Ibid., 6.

47. Kafka, *Das Schloß*, 12.

48. Kafka, *The Castle*, 7.

49. Kafka, *Das Schloß*, 13.

50. Kafka, *The Castle*, 8.

51. Kafka, *Das Schloß*, 13.

52. Kafka, *The Castle*, 8.

53. Kafka, *Das Schloß*, 13.

54. Kafka, *The Castle*, 8.

55. Kafka, *Das Schloß*, 13–14.

56. Mukařovský, “On the Problem of Function in Architecture,” 239.

57. English does not have an analogous term: “castle” translates both *Schloß* and *Burg*. The term “manor” translates the social function of *Schloß* better than “castle,” but provides an incomplete idea of the physical structure and historical development of the building. The French loan word “chateau” is often used in English as a close equivalent of *Schloß*.

Chapter 5

1. Kafka, letter of June 24, 1920. *Letters to Milena*, 58. “Und was Milena betrifft, so hat das mit Deutschtum und Judentum gar nichts zu tun. Am besten verstehen tschechisch (abgesehen von den tschechischen Juden natürlich) die Herren von *Naše Řeč*, am zweitbesten die Leser der Zeitschrift, am drittbesten die Abonnenten und Abonnent bin ich. Als solcher sage ich Dir, daß an Milena tschechisch eigentlich nur das Diminutiv ist: milenka. Ob es Dir gefällt oder nicht, das sagt die Philologie,” *Briefe an Milena*, 78.

2. Bernheimer, *Flaubert and Kafka*, 216.

3. Malte Kleinwort, *Der Späte Kafka: Spätstil als Stilsuspension* (Munich: Fink, 2013), 115–19.

4. Karcevskij, "Asymmetric Dualism," 49.

5. Corngold, *Necessity*, 94.

6. Michelle Woods comments on Kafka's "obvious delight" at receiving Jesenska's translation, and goes on to explain the three notes he gave her, for example: "From the second line of [Jesenska's] translation, Kafka notes that 'arm' in 'armen Eltern,' translated by Jesenská as 'chudymi rodici' ['(by his) poor parents'] . . . here also has the secondary meaning: *pitiable*, but without any special emphasis of feeling, a sympathy without understanding that Karl has with his parents as well." Woods, *Kafka Translated*, 26.

7. Kafka, June 11, 1914. *Diaries*, 282. "'Er ist ein Fremder. Er treibt sich hier ganz unnötigerweise herum. Sieh nur.' Er redete von mir, als sei ich taub oder als verstände ich seine Sprache nicht," *Tagebücher*, 244.

Chapter 6

1. Milena Jesenská, "Plavky," *Tribuna* 8, no. 1 (August 1, 1920). "Jsou dvojí lidé: Ti, kteří se koupají pro pohyb, pro rozkoš chladné vody, kterým je řeka velikou radostí, pro které jsou oblaka na nebi, vlny ve vodě a teplý vzduch světem, samým pro sebe. Ti plavou dlouhými tempy, plavou na znaku, plavou pod vodou, skáčí do vody, mazlí se, laskají s vlnami a jsou v nich šťastni. Nejraději by plavali nazí, voda je jim živlem, tělo je živlem, slunce je živlem, nahota je dobrá a radostná. Nu a proto, že to není dovoleno a že to není možno, nutno se obléci. [. . . .] Ti druzí: To jsou ti, co plavou ve vodě a ani nefuní, ani neprskají, ani nemají bradu ustavičně pod vodou—ne, ti plavou pěkně způsobně, tělo stojí ve vodě, jako tyčka, která má dole závaží, i ramena z vody ven, ani vlásku si nenamočí, celé plavání nemá se sportem a pohybem co dělat, ale prostě jakousi náhodou se člověk udržuje nad vodou a nespadne dolů." My translation.

2. Kafka, letter of August 1, 1920. *Letters to Milena*, 129; Kafka, *Briefe an Milena*, 172.

3. Kafka, *Letters to Milena*, 129. "Ich Weiß nicht wie es geschieht, ich lese es doch nur mit den Augen, wie hat es gleich auch mein Blut erfahren . . . ?" Kafka, *Briefe an Milena*, 172.

4. Kafka, *Letters to Milena*, 129. "Ich gehöre natürlich zu der zweiten Gruppe; dieses Gewicht an den Füßen ist geradezu mein Eigentum und ich bin gar nicht damit einverstanden, daß meine rein persönliche Angelegenheit veröffentlicht wird; jemand hat einmal gesagt, daß ich wie ein Schwan schwimme, aber das war kein Kompliment. Aber auch aufregend ist es. Ich komme mir vor wie ein Riese, der mit ausgestreckten Armen das Publikum von Dir abhält—er hat es schwer, er soll das Publikum abhalten und will doch auch kein Wort und keine Sekunde Deines Anblicks verlieren," Kafka, *Briefe an Milena*, 172–73.

5. Any irony that English speakers may find in the juxtaposition is anachronistic and linguistically unfounded.

6. Kafka, letter of May 30, 1920. *Letters to Milena*, 20–21. "Das ist ja das eigentlich Schöne bei Ihrer Übersetzung, daß sie treu ist (zanken Sie mich nur wegen des 'treu' aus, Sie können alles, aber zanken können Sie vielleicht am besten, ich wollte Ihr Schüler sein und immerfort Fehler machen, um nur immerfort von Ihnen

ausgezankt werden zu dürfen; man sitzt auf der Schulbank, wagt kaum aufzuschauen, Sie sind über einen gebeugt und immerfort flimmert oben Ihr Zeigefinger, mit dem Sie Aussetzungen machen, ist es so?)" Kafka, *Briefe an Milena*, 26–27.

7. See Kees Teszelszky on Jesenský's account of a Hungarian coronation in "The Hungarian Roots of a Bohemian Humanist: Johann Jessenius a Jessen and Early Modern National Identity," which is itself a testament to the incommensurability of nineteenth- and twentieth-century nationalist claims with an early modern central European intellectual and political landscape. In *Whose Love of Which Country? Composite States, National Histories, and Patriotic Discourses in Early Modern East Central Europe* (Brill, 2010), 315–32.

8. Alena Wagnerová, *Milena Jesenská*, trans. Alena Bláhová (Prague: Prostor, 1996), 34.

9. For English-language discussion of some prominent women writers of the period, see Dobrova Moldanová, "Czech Women Writers from the National Revival to the Fin-de-Siècle," trans. Robert Pynsent; and Robert Pynsent, "Czech Women Writers: 1890–1945," both in *A History of Central European Women's Writing*, ed. Celia Hawkesworth (Gordonsville, Va.: Palgrave, 2001).

10. Reiner Stach, *Is That Kafka?: 99 Finds* (New Directions, 2016), 43.

11. The rhyme, "Divky z Minervy, nervi mi nervy," puns visually and homophonically, an effect entirely lost in translation.

12. See my discussion of Eisner in chapter 1.

13. Kafka, June 25, 1920. *Letters to Milena*, 58–59; Kafka, *Briefe an Milena*, 78–79.

14. Kleinwort discusses this connection at length as a source of insight into *The Castle*'s relationship to psychoanalysis, *Der Späte Kafka*, 153–54.

15. Wagnerová discusses this dynamic in *Milena Jesenská*, 77–78.

16. Woods, *Kafka Translated*, 15–16. Woods also goes on to suggest Jílovská and her "particularly difficult relationship" with Kafka as a potential touchstone for the character of the Landlady in *The Castle.*

17. Both Jesenská's translator Kathleen Hayes and Michelle Woods have commented on this text and its clear parallels with *The Castle*. Both these publications postdate my own 2001 dissertation on which the reading here builds, but the parallels are so striking that I have no doubt that discussion of "The Coffeehouse" (also translated as "The Café") alongside *The Castle* and *Letters to Milena* would long have been a truism in Kafka criticism had Jesenská's text been widely known and available—especially as critical attention has turned more to gender as a topic and Jesenská as a figure of interest. See *The Journalism of Milena Jesenská,* ed. and trans. Kathleen Hayes (New York: Berghahn, 2003) and Woods, *Kafka Translated.*

18. "Stýkali se lidé na fóru, stýkali se v klášteřích, stýkali se v salonech. Dnes není ani fóra, ani klášterů s tímto významem, ani salonů s tímto ovzduším. Dnes jsou kavárny. Nemyslím ty způsobné kavárny, kam vodí v neděli odpoledne maminky své dcerušky a kam se chodí vypít čokoládu nebo sníst par koláčků. Nemyslím ani ty, které jsou ve dne unavené, pološedivé, ospalé a které večer obživnou kapelou a několika namalovanými děvčaty a několika "dobrodruhy života" a na štít vývěsní červenou lampičku.

"Myslím ty vysloveně 'literární' kavárny, daleko známé, celým městem známé kavárny, shromaždiště duchovního i bohémského světa, jako je pražská 'Unionka,' vídeňská 'Central,' berlínská 'des Westens,' pařížská 'Montmartre.'

Kavárny s docela zvláštní existencí, kterou nikdo nepochopí, dokud ji neproni-kne až na dno, dokud se vzduchu v ní nenadýchá z plných plic," Milena Jesenská, *Tribuna* 2, no. 187 (August 8, 1920), my translation.

19. "Ti první hosté jsou ti velcí. Ti, kteří mají již svá jména v oficiálním světě, ti, kteří jsou cíl kavárny, a jejich obrazy a karikatury visí po stěnách lokálu, kteří, když přijdou, sedí jako kapitalisté ducha za stolem a jen několika málo je dovoleno zasednouti vedle," ibid.

20. Kafka, letter of June 15, 1920. *Letters to Milena*, 50. "(nun verliere ich auch noch den Namen, immerfort ist er kürzer geworden und jetzt heißt er: Dein)," *Briefe an Milena*, 67.

21. Kafka, letter of August 11, 1920. *Letters to Milena*, 157; *Briefe an Milena*, 212.

22. Corngold and Wagner undertake a sustained discussion on *Verkehr* and its role in "The Judgment," particularly as it relates to what they see as Kafka's "second-order sublimation" of sex to writing. "Kafka and Sex," in *Franz Kafka: The Ghosts in the Machine*, 334–36 and following.

23. Kafka, letter of June 13, 1920. *Letters to Milena*, 45.

24. Kafka, *Briefe an Milena*, 59.

25. Kafka, letter of May 29, 1920. *Letters to Milena*, 17.

26. Kafka, *Briefe an Milena*, 22.

27. Kafka, *The Castle*, 10.

28. Kafka, *Das Schloß*, 16.

Chapter 7

1. Kleinwort, *Der Späte Kafka*, 108–9.

2. Evelyn Tornton Beck, "Kafka's Traffic in Women: Gender, Power, and Sexuality," *The Literary Review* 26, no. 4 (summer 1983).

3. Deleuze and Guattari, *Kafka: Toward a Minor Literature*, 66.

4. Larysa Mykyta, "Woman as the Obstacle and the Way," *MLN* 95, no. 3 (April 1980): 627–40.

5. Kafka, *The Castle*, 28.

6. Kafka, *Das Schloß*, 37.

7. Marthe Robert, *The Old and the New: From Don Quixote to Kafka* (Berkeley: University of California Press, 1977), 194.

8. W. T. H. Jackson, *The Literature of the Middle Ages* (New York: Columbia University Press, 1960), 85.

9. K.'s accomplishments are notoriously small in number—aside from seducing Frieda, he manages to write a letter and to shovel the schoolhouse walk.

10. Kafka, letter of May 29, 1920. *Briefe an Milena*, 22; *Letters to Milena*, 17. This passage is discussed at greater length in the next chapter.

11. Kafka, *Das Schloß*, 13–14; Kafka, *The Castle*, 8. I cite and discuss this description of the Castle in chapter 4 and return to it later in this chapter with relation to Amalia.

12. Kafka, *The Castle*, 30.

13. Kafka, *Das Schloß*, 40.

14. The surprising importance of clothes in Kafka's fiction has been identified and discussed at length by Mark Anderson in *Kafka's Clothes: Ornament and Aestheticism in the Habsburg Fin de Siècle* (Oxford: Clarendon, 1992), 223.

15. As cited by Reiner Stach, "Kafka's Egoless Woman: Otto Weininger's Sex and Character," in *Reading Kafka: Prague, Politics, and the Fin de Siècle*, ed. Mark Anderson (New York: Schocken, 1989), 151.

16. Ibid., 155.

17. Kafka, *The Castle*, 1-2; Kafka, *Das Schloß*, 5.

18. Kafka, *The Castle*, 3.

19. Kafka, *Das Schloß*, 7.

20. Kafka, *The Castle*, 3–4.

21. Kafka, *Das Schloß*, 7–8.

22. Kafka, *The Castle*, 11.

23. Kafka, *Das Schloß*, 17.

24. Jan Hus is flanked by a number of figures in this enormous statue.

25. Paces, *Prague Panoramas*, 47.

26. Kafka, *Das Schloß*, 13. My translation for this and the following short passages.

27. See, for example, my discussion of Klamm's name (chapter 5) and of the passage describing K.'s initial encounter with Frieda (chapter 7).

28. Kafka, *Das Schloß*, 11.

29. Ibid., 18.

30. Arthur Schopenhauer, "Über die Weiber," in *Parerga und Paralipomena*, vol. 2 (Leipzig: Broduaus, 1877), 654.

31. Anderson, *Kafka's Clothes*, 22–23.

32. Kafka, *Das Schloß*, 21.

33. Eric Miller, "Without a Key: The Narrative Structure of Das Schloß," *The Germanic Review* 66, no. 3 (1991).

34. Franz Kafka, *The Castle*, trans. Willa and Edwin Muir (London, Everyman, 1992), 43. For this passage, I defer to the Muirs' translation based on Max Brod's version of the text because it captures more of the sense of rhythm I'm discussing here.

35. Kafka, *Das Schloß*, 53–54.

36. Corngold and Wagner, *Franz Kafka: The Ghosts in the Machine*, 127.

37. I cite and discuss this early description of the Castle (Kafka, *The Castle*, 1–2; Kafka, *Das Schloß*, 5) and the contrast between K.'s experience of the Castle world and his expectations based on his homeland at greater length in Chapter 4.

38. Kafka, *Das Schloß*, 54.

39. Kafka, *The Castle*, 41.

40. Kafka, letter of June 12, 1920, *Briefe an Milena*, 56. *Letters to Milena*, 42.

41. Kafka, *The Castle*, 167.

42. Kafka, *Das Schloß*, 209.

43. Kafka, *Das Schloß*, 216; Kafka, *The Castle*,173.

44. Kafka, *Das Schloß*, 210; Kafka, *The Castle*,168.

45. Elizabeth Boa, *Gender, Class, and Race in the Letters and Fiction* (Oxford: Clarendon, 1996), 267–69.

Chapter 8

1. Kafka, letter to Felix Weltsch, Zürau, November 15, 1917, *Letters to Friends, Family and Editors*, 168; "der erste große Fehler von Zürau: eine Mäusenacht, ein schreckliches Erlebnis. [. . .] Schon früher hatte ich es hie und da . . . in der

Nacht zart knabbern gehört . . .—diesmal aber war es ein Aufruhr. Was für ein schreckliches stummes lärmendes Volk das ist. Um zwei Uhr wurde ich durch ein Rascheln bei meinem Bett geweckt und von da an hörte es nicht auf bis zum Morgen. Auf die Kohlenkiste hinauf, von der Kohlenkiste hinunter, die Diagonale des Zimmers abgelaufen, Kreise gezogen, am Holz genagt, im Ruhen leise gepfiffen und dabei immer das Gefühl der Stille, der heimlichen Arbeit eines gedrückten proletarischen Volkes, dem die Nacht gehört. Um mich gedanklich zu retten, lokalisierte ich den Hauptlärm beim Ofen, den die Länge des Zimmers von mir trennt, aber es war überall, am schlimmsten, wenn einmal ein ganzer Haufen irgendwo gemeinsam hinuntersprang. Ich war gänzlich hilflos, nirgends in meinem ganzen Wesen ein Halt . . ." *Briefe 1914–1917*, 365.

2. Robert Klopstock's note on a conversation slip from Kafka's last days in *Letters to Friends, Family and Editors*, 495 n.20.

3. Kafka, letter to Max Brod, "postmarked on arrival, October 5, 1923," in *Letters to Friends*, 387.

4. Kafka, letter to Felix Waltsch, September 22, 1917; ibid., 145.

5. Ibid.

6. Kafka, letter to Felix Waltsch, October 1917; ibid., 153.

7. Janouch, *Conversations with Kafka*, 22.

8. Kafka, letter to Max Brod, Zurau, September 1917, *Letters to Friends, Family, and Editors*, 140.

9. Goldstücker provides the most thorough, factual dismantling of Janouch's truth claims, largely on the basis of error involving dates and the geographical locations of the two interlocutors. Eduard Goldstücker, "Gustav Janouch—Kafkas Eckermann?" in *Franz Kafka: Themen und Probleme*, ed. Claude David (Göttingen: Vanderhoek and Ruprecht, 1980), 238–55.

10. In his critical introduction to Gustav Janouch, *Conversations with Kafka*, ed. Hugh Haughton (London: Encounter, 1985), xix–xx. Haughton also summarizes the range of critical reception, from Max Brod and Kafka's last companion Dora Diamant's raptures to the skepticism that became more prevalent after Janouch published a second, much expanded version of the conversations in 1968.

11. Janáček did not always take Brod's advice on the opera, and Brod did not undertake the translation despite several requests. Nonetheless, they corresponded about the opera at its various stages since at least 1917. See Jiří Zahrádka, "Matěj Brouček a Max Brod," *Sborník Prací Filozofické Fakulty Brněnské Univerzity* (Brno, 2003), https://digilib.phil.muni.cz/bitstream/handle/11222.digilib/112038/H_Musicologica_38-2003-1_36.pdf?sequence=1.

12. Max Brod discusses Janáček's practice of surreptitiously listening to passersby in conversation and notating "every rise and fall of the speech melody." As cited by Leon Botstein, "The Cultural Politics of Language and Music: Max Brod and Leoš Janáček." In *Janáček and His World*, ed. Michael Beckerman (Princeton, N.J.: Princeton University Press, 2011) 39.

13. Ripellino, *Magic Prague*, 223.

14. Ibid., 223–24.

15. Ibid., 224; Alfred Brehm, *Tierleben*, ten-volume encyclopedia.

16. "rozplácnutá mrtvola blešího samce, prvotřídního umělce, který byl duší cirkusu. Mestek říkal mu něžně 'Františku.' Mrtvola umělce byla ztotožněna

pod zvětšovacím sklem a poznána dle toho, že mu scházela jedna noha" Hašek, "Reelní podnik," *Tribuna* 3, no. 108 (May 8, 1921).

17. As quoted in Hugh LeCaine Agnew, *The Czechs and the Lands of the Bohemian Crown* (Stanford, Calif.: Hoover Institution, 2004), 149.

18. Kafka, *Complete Stories*, 280. "ich begrüßte den Morgen mit wirren Lauten, da—als hätte ich sie heraufbeschworen—traten aus irgendwelcher Finsternis unter Hervorbringung eines entsetzlichen Lärms, wie ich ihn noch nie gehört hatte, sieben Hunde ans Licht.

Hätte ich nicht deutlich gesehn, daß es Hunde waren und daß sie selbst diesen Lärm mitbrachten, trotzdem ich nicht erkennen konnte wie sie ihn erzeugten—ich wäre sofort weggelaufen, so aber blieb ich. Damals wußte ich noch fast nichts von der nur dem Hundegeschlecht verliehenen schöpferischen Musikalität, sie war meiner sich erst langsam entwickelnden Beobachtungskraft bisher entgangen, natürlicher Weise, hatte mich doch die Musik schon seit meiner Säuglingszeit umgeben, als ein mir selbstverständliches, unentbehrliches Lebenselement, welches von meinem sonstigen Leben zu sondern nichts mich zwang; nur in Andeutungen, dem kindlichen Verstand entsprechend, hatte man mich darauf hinzuweisen versucht, umso überraschender, geradezu niederwerfend waren jene sieben großen Musikkünstler für mich," "Forschungen eines Hundes," in Franz Kafka, *Kritische Ausgabe: Nachgelassene Schriften und Fragmente II*, ed. Jost Schillemeit (Frankfurt: Fischer, 1992), 489–90. Like many of Kafka's texts that were published posthumously (and against his explicit directive), the manuscript for this story is fragmented, and published versions are thus more subject to editorial intervention than in the case of those, like "Der Bau" and "Josefine," which appeared during his lifetime. For that reason, I have cited from the critical edition, which reproduces as closely as possible the text that appears in Kafka's journal.

19. Thomas A. Ford, "Crowds, Animality, and Aesthetic Language in 'Josefine' in *Kafka's Creatures: Animals, Hybrids, and Other Fantastic Beings*, ed. Mark Lucht and Donna Yarri (Blue Ridge Summit: Lexington Books, 2010), 114. See also Marianne Schuller, "Gesang vom Tierleben: Kafkas Erzählung "Josefine, di Sängerin oder Das Volk der Mäuse" in *Singularitäten* (Frieburg: Literatur Wissenschaft Verrantwortung, 2001), 209–18.

20. Kafka, *Complete Stories*, 279. "Es gibt außer uns Hunden vielerlei Arten von Geschöpfen ringsumher, arme, geringe, stumme, nur auf gewisse Schreie eingeschränkte Wesen, viele unter uns Hunden studieren sie, haben ihnen Namen gegeben, suchen ihnen zu helfen, sie zu erziehen, zu veredeln udgl.; mir sind sie gleichgültig, wenn sie mich nicht etwa zu stören versuchen oder ein guter Bissen von ihnen zu erhoffen ist (in unserer Gegend ist dies sehr selten), ich verwechsle sie, ich sehe über sie hinweg. . . ." The translation is based on a version of the text that omits the following after "versuchen": "oder ein guter Bissen von ihnen zu erhoffen ist (in unserer Gegend ist dies sehr selten)" ("or I can expect a good morsel from them [in our area this is rare]") "Forschungen," *Kritische Ausgabe*, 486–87.

21. See my earlier discussion of Czech as background noise in chapter 1.

22. Kafka, *Complete Stories*, 344. "immer klingt es unveränderet dünn in regelmäßigen Pausen, einmal wie Zischen, einmal eher wie Pfeifen," Kafka, *Die Erzählungen*, 488.

23. Kafka, *Complete Stories*, 345. "ich höre es freilich jetzt mit dem durch die Übung geschärften Ohr immer deutlicher," *Die Erzählungen,* 489.

24. Kafka, *Complete Stories*, 354; *Die Erzählungen*, 501.

25. Jaroslav Hašek, *Osudy dobrého vojáka Švejka za světové války* (Prague: KLHU, 1960), 9–10.

26. Kafka, *Complete Stories*, 360; *Die Erzählungen*, 518

27. Kafka, *Complete Stories*, 360; *Die Erzählungen*, 518.

28. Kafka, *Complete Stories*, 360; *Die Erzählungen*, 518.

29. Mukařovský, "Standard Language and Poetic Language" in Paul Garvin, ed., *A Prague School Reader in Esthetics, Literary Structure, and Style* (Georgetown: Georgetown University Press, 1964), 18.

30. Kafka, *Complete Stories*, 360. "wie kommt es, daß wir Josefinens Gesang verstehn oder, da Josefine unser Verständnis leugnet, wenigstens zu verstehen glauben. Die enfachste Antwort wäre, daß die Schönheit dieses Gesanges so groß ist, daß auch der stumpfste Sinn ihr nicht widerstehen kann, aber diese Antwort ist nicht befriedigend," *Die Erzählungen*, 518.

31. Kafka, *Complete Stories*, 360–61. "Wenn es wirklich so wäre, müßte man vor diesem Gesang zunächst und immer das Gefühl des Außerordentlichen haben, das Gefühl, aus dieser Kehle erklinge etwas, was wir nie vorher gehört haben und das zu hören wir auch gar nicht die Fähigkeit haben, etwas, was zu hören uns nur diese eine Josefine und niemand sonst befahigt. Gerade das trifft aber meiner Meinung nach nicht zu, ich fühle es nicht und habe auch bei andern nichts dergleichen bemerkt. Im vertrauten Kreise gestehen wir einander offen, daß Josefinens Gesang als Gesang nichts Außerordentliches darstellt. Ist es denn überhaupt Gesang?" *Die Erzählungen*, 518–19.

32. Kafka, *Complete Stories*, 360. "Sagen erzählen davon und sogar Lieder sind erhalten, die freilich niemand mehr singen kann {. . . .} Eine Ahnung dessen, was Gesang ist, haben wir also und dieser Ahnung nun entspricht Josefinens Kunst eigentlich nicht," Kafka, *Die Erzählungen*, 518–19.

33. *Complete Stories*, 361; *Tagebücher*, 519.

34. *Complete Stories*, 361. "aber freilich denkt niemand daran, das als Kunst auszugeben, wir pfeifen, ohne darauf zu achten, ja, ohne zu merken und es gibt sogar viele unter uns, die gar nicht wissen, daß das Pfeifen zu unsern Eigentümlichkeiten gehört," *Die Erzählungen*, 519.

35. Kafka, *Complete Stories*, 361. "es ist zum Verständnis ihrer Kunst notwendig, sie nicht nur zu hören sondern auch zu sehn. Selbst wenn es nur unser tagtägliches Pfeifen wäre, so besteht hier doch schon zunächst die Sonderbarkeit, daß jemand sich feierlich hinstellt, um nichts anderes also das Übliche zu tun," *Die Erzählungen*, 520.

36. Kafka, *Complete Stories*, 361–62. "Eine Nuß aufknacken ist wahrhaftig keine Kunst, deshalb wird es auch niemand wagen, ein Publikum zusammenzurufen und vor ihm, um es zu unterhalten, Nüsse knacken. Tut er es dennoch und gelingt seine Absicht, dann kann es sich eben doch nicht nur um bloßes Nüsseknacken handeln. Oder es handelt sich um Nüsseknacken, aber es stellt sich heraus, daß wir über diese Kunst hinweggesehen haben, weil wir sie glatt beherrschten und daß uns dieser neue Nußknacker erst ihr eigentliches Wesen zeigt, wobei es dann für die Wirkung sogar nützlich sein könnte, wenn er etwas weniger tüchtig im Nüsseknacken ist als die Mehrzahl von uns," *Die Erzählungen*, 520.

37. Kafka, *Letters to Milena*, 21.
38. Kafka, *Briefe an Milena*, 28 (ellipsis in original).
39. Kafka, *Letters to Milena*, 17.
40. Kafka, *Briefe an Milena*, 22.
41. Corngold analyzes this "turn from the natural certainty of the body and senses" in a reading that integrates material from the short fiction and confessional writings (*Necessity*, 105–9).
42. Anderson, *Kafka's Clothes*, 194.
43. *Briefe an Milena*, 122.
44. Corngold and Wagner, *Franz Kafka: The Ghosts in the Machine*, 96.
45. Kafka, *Letters to Milena*, 22.
46. Kafka, *Briefe an Milena*, 28.
47. Kafka, letter of July 5, 1920, *Briefe an Milena*, 90.

Conclusion

1. Kafka, December 6, 1921. *Diaries*, 398. "Die Unselbständigkeit des Schreibens, die Abhängigkeit von dem Dienstmädchen, das einheizt, von der Katze, die sich am Ofen wärmt, selbst vom armen alten Menschen, der sich wärmt. Alles dies sind selbständige, eigengesetzliche Verrichtungen, nur das Schreiben ist hilflos, wohnt nicht in sich selbst, ist Spaß und Verzweiflung," *Tagebücher* 303.
2. Mukařovský, "A Note on the Czech Translation of Sklovskij's *Theory of Prose*" (1934), in *The Word and Verbal Art: Selected Essays by Jan Mukařovský*, ed. and trans. John Burbank and Peter Steiner (New Haven, Conn.: Yale University Press, 1977), 140.
3. Kieval, *Languages of Community*, 224.

INDEX

Page numbers in italics refer to illustrations.

Adorno, Theodor, 81, 83
aesthetic function, 84–85; "Josefine the Singer or the Mouse Folk" on, 177, 178–80, 185–86; of music and sound, 170–71, 177; Prague School on, 102, 177, 179, 184, 185; structuralist theory on, 103, 178, 180
Aleš, Mikuláš, 35
allegory, 83, 84, 206n14
"anationalism," 57–58
Anders, Günther, 205n5
Anderson, Benedict, 61
Anderson, Mark, 145–46, 182
animal stories, 7, 162–71, 189; "The Burrow," 7, 33, 161, 163, 169, 170, 173–75, 186, 214n18; "Investigations of a Dog," 7, 161, 164, 170; Janouch on, 162–64; "Josefine the Singer or the Mouse Folk," 7, 159–61, 162, 169, 170–71, 174, 176–81, 185–86, 214n18
antisemitism, 45–46, 49, 50, 57, 62, 64, 127, 181
Apollinaire, Guillaume, 39–40
architecture: *The Castle* on, 87, 93–94, 96–98, 100–101, 102, 137; "The City Coat of Arms" on, 19–20; functionality of, 87, 88–90, 95, 137; and language, 24, 87–91; Mukařovský on, 87–90, 95, 101–2; in Prague, 22, 35, 40, 90–91; and social space, 87, 95, 122–23
Association of Progressive Czech Jews, 46

Babička (Němcová), 91–92
Battle of White Mountain (1620), 22, 61, 117–18
Bauer, Felice, 32, 41, 115, 119, 122, 174
Beck, Evelyn Tornton, 133
Benjamin, Walter, 22–23, 83, 157, 206n14
Berlin, 160–61
Bernheimer, Charles, 83, 106, 107
Beseda Měšťanská, 8, 9
Bílek, František, 37, 41, 201n29
bilingualism, 66–67, 110, 127
Blei, Franz, 52
Boa, Elizabeth, 155–56, 206n21
Born, Jürgen, 34
boundaries: assault on, 19, 77, 78, 84, 188, 191; in *The Castle*, 64, 69–71, 77–78, 84–86, 98–99, 135, 149; class, 90, 93; and Czechoslovakia, 4, 5, 46, 73, 76, 79, 80, 105; for Jews, 62, 64; and language, 15–16, 18–19, 24, 62, 79, 136, 191; in Prague, 10, 12
Brahe, Tycho, 117
Březina, Otokar, 37
Brod, Max, 7, 49–50, 160–61, 163, 165, 188; on *The Castle*, 83, 92, 126, 150–51; and Czech art scene, 9, 38, 111; engagement with Czech culture, 12, 43, 63; and *The Good Soldier Švejk*, 13; on Hasids in Prague, 15; Janáček work with, 164, 166, 183, 213n12; Kafka letters to, 8, 22, 37, 45, 77, 183; literary estate of, 6; on Prague as polemical city, 10, 52; "Prague Circle" name coined by, 52, 202n16; works: *A Czech Maidservant*, 32
Bugge, Peter, 62
"The Burrow" (Kafka), 7, 161, 169, 186, 214n18; mole-creature in, 33, 163, 170; sound and speech in, 33, 173–75
Butler, Judith, 6

Café Arco, 16, 120, 122
Čapek, Josef, 38, 39–40, 45, 165
Čapek, Karel, 14, 38, 39, 44–45; *The Insect Play*, 164–66, 167
Casanova, Pascale, 6
Castle, The (Kafka): allegorical readings of, 83, 206n13; Amalia in, 134, 135, 141, 153–56; architectural structures and categories in, 87, 96–98, 100–101, 102; Barnabas the messenger in, 85, 138, 144–45, 147; boundaries in, 64, 69–71, 77–78, 84–86, 98–99, 135, 149; Castle depiction in, 80–83, 96–97, 100–101, 102, 131, 139, 143; Castle-Village relationship in, 148, 155–56; "The City Coat of Arms" and, 20, 21; delusional nature of system in, 110, 157–58; double asymmetry in, 87, 110–11; drafts of, 106, 109, 111, 132, 158; Elisabeth character in draft of, 131–32, 133; female characters' depiction in, 25, 131–33, 139–43, 148–58, 191; Frieda in, 108–9, 141, 146–47, 149–50, 152–53; gender and power relations in, 25, 92, 139–41, 146–47, 153; gender attributes and qualities in, 138–45, 148–49; grammatical gender in, 149–52; "Heimat" (home) in, 85, 151, 206n21; and hero quest narratives, 135–36; identity question in, 7,

Castle, The (Kafka), *continued*
105–8, 184; Jesenská as Czech translator of, 111, 128, 209n6; Jesenská influence on, 25, 126, 131, 132, 133–34, 152–53, 154–55, 157; Klamm, character and name in, 105–11, 124, 128, 138, 144, 146, 152; Landlady character in, 134, 140–41, 142, 144, 210n16; Land Surveyor function in, 23–24, 69–72, 74–75; linguistic duality in, 105–8, 108–10; Němcová as influence on, 92, 96, 136–37, 157; nostalgia-for-clarity theme in, 20, 102, 134–35, 137; notebook of, 131–32; planned ending of, 150–51; rhetorical and poetic devices in, 83, 143–44, 150; sexual relations in, 106, 108–9, 138, 146–47, 148, 150–51, 153, 155, 156; social system in, 86–87, 95, 136, 157; spatial relations in, 80–83, 97–98, 99–100; stranger/foreigner status in, 68–69, 90, 96, 111, 132, 151, 156, 180–81; structuralist model of composition in, 85–86; structure of, 19, 24, 96–97, 150, 156–57; teacher in, 86, 102, 144; and territory, 69–72, 74, 151, 152, 155; tower in, 100–102, 137, 139, 141, 154; *Verkehr* concept in, 126, 145–47, 148, 149; weariness characteristic in, 128–29; "Wohnhaus" as category in, 102, 102, 134, 135, 139, 141
Čech, Svatopluk, 164
Červen, 38, 39–40, 45–46, 54, 58
Chesterton, G. K., 46
Chronicle of Dalimil, The, 21, 36
"The City Coat of Arms" (Kafka), 19–22, 20
"The Coffeehouse"/"Kavárna" (Jesenská), 25, 122–24, 125–26, 210n17
Comenius, John, 83, 92
Communism, 11, 53, 60
community, 94, 170, 177, 178–79; and identity, 7, 161; and language, 8, 176, 179; of speakers, 18, 90, 95, 110, 156
"Community" (Kafka), 7, 8, 9
Conversations with Kafka (Janouch), 28, 43, 162–64, 201n2, 213n10
Corngold, Stanley, 4–5, 151, 182; on Deleuze/Guattari conclusions, 27, 198n2; on homonymies, 110–11; on Kafka rhetorical modes, 83; on metaphor and allegory, 84, 204n4
Cubism, 38–39, 40–41
Czech Agrarian Party, 45, 50, 118, 172
Czech culture, 35–42, 43, 63
Czech Decadence, 55
Czech history: Battle of White Mountain, 22, 61, 117–18; and Habsburg Empire, 7, 9–10, 61–62, 63–64; nationalist movement, 118; national mythology around, 22, 35–36; riots of 1897, 63–64. *See also* Czechoslovakia
Czech Jewish movement, 63
Czech language: and Castle world, 157–58; discrepancy between written and spoken, 33, 92, 94, 96, 102, 175–76, 183; in Habsburg Empire, 61–62; and Jews, 6, 12, 62–63; and Kafka-Jesenská correspondence, 115–16, 173–74; Kafka relationship to, 6, 28–29, 30–34, 54, 173, 174, 181, 185, 198n4; Kafka's knowledge and command of, 4, 7–8, 29, 30–31, 33–34, 35, 95–96, 137; Kafka's reading of, 34, 42; *Kmen* on, 58–60; literature in, 29, 36–37, 59, 94–95, 136, 161, 173, 187; publication of Kafka in, 3, 31, 46, 47; and Sprachmusik, 182; translation of Kafka into, 3, 111, 116, 128, 209n6. *See also* language
Czech Maidservant, A (Brod), 32
Czech National Revival, 10, 22; goals of, 20, 61; Němcová and, 94–95, 96
Czech National Theater, 8, 9, 10, 35, 171; and language politics, 90–91
Czechoslovakia: and animal stories, 164, 168–69; bilingualism in, 66–67; borders and boundaries in, 4, 5, 46, 73, 76, 79, 80, 105; census in, 64–65, 66, 67–68, 180; class divisions in, 148; Communism in, 11, 53, 60; forced migration of Germans from, 11; formation of, 5, 11, 30; Jews in, 5–6, 15, 67–68, 80, 195n9; Land Control Act in, 74; language and identity in, 7, 9, 15–16; language areas in, 9, 72–73; language law in, 5, 195n8; minority status in, 68–69; Prague Spring in, 11, 60, 199n5; in World War II, 11. *See also* Prague
Czechoslovak Legion, 16
Czech press, 23, 43–60; censorship of, 46; feuilletons in, 44–45; *Kmen*, 17, 23, 38, 50–60; *Prager Presse*, 42, 43–44, 50; *Tribuna*, 13, 14, 41, 42, 46–50, 49, 113–14, 121–22, 167–68; *Venkov*, 45–46, 49, 50, 172–73

Deleuze, Gilles, 27, 28–29, 42, 52, 60, 133, 199n5
Derrida, Jacques, 107
Der Verschollene (Kafka), 133, 203n27
Deutsche Haus, 8, 9, 196n16
Devětsil, 38, 51
Diamant, Dora, 160, 163, 189, 213n10
Dickens, Charles, 84
double asymmetry, 87, 110–11
Dvořák, Antonín, 172
Dyk, Viktor, 164

Edict of Toleration, 62
Edmunds, Lowell, 28
Ehrenstein, Albert, 53
Einstein, Albert, 44
Eisner, Pavel, 10, 12, 44, 120
Emrich, Wilhelm, 75
Expressionism, 36, 38, 39, 40

"First Sorrow" (Kafka), 170
Flaubert, Gustave, 84
Florian, Josef, 121–22

Fodor, Francis (Ferenc), 73
Ford, Thomas H., 171
formalism, 89, 180, 191–92
Franta, Berta, 118
Franz Kafka: Representative Man (Karl), 13
Freud, Sigmund, 64, 107
Fuchs, Rudolf, 12
functionality: aesthetic, 84–85, 103, 178, 180, 184; of architecture, 87, 88–90, 95, 137

Garnett, David, 162
Gauguin, Paul, 39
Gazette des Ardennes, 43
Gellner, František, 164
gender, 131–58; and Castle attributes, 131–32, 138–45, 148–49; grammatical, 148–52; and national identity, 32, 119–20; and power relations, 25, 92, 139–41, 146–47, 153. *See also* sex and sexuality; women
Geographical Impossibility of the Czech State, The, 73–74
German language: Czechs and, 48–49, 61–62, 73; grammatical gender in, 148–49; Jews and, 10, 52–53, 62, 64, 111; Kafka and, 4, 5, 31
Ghetto, Jewish, 62, 91
"Goat Song, The" (Werfel), 166–67
Goldstücker, Eduard, 12, 163
Good Soldier Švejk, The (Hašek), 13, 25, 167–68, 175–76
Gramling, David, 199n5
Gray, Ronald, 92
Grillparzer, Franz, 35
Gross, Otto, 121
Grüne Bandchen, 75
Guattari, Felix, 27, 28–29, 42, 52, 60, 133, 199n5

Haas, Willy, 50
Habsburg Empire, 62, 72; language in, 7, 9–10, 61–62, 63–64
Hašek, Jaroslav, 47; and Kafka, 13, 180; and Langer, 13, 14; parliamentary campaign of, 14, 196n25; works: *The Good Soldier Švejk*, 13, 25, 167–68, 175–76; *Svět zvířat*, 167
Hasids, 14–15
Haughton, Hugh, 163
Havel, Vaclav, 207n34
Havlíček, Karel, 62–63
Hebrew, 6
Heller, Erich, 83, 206n13
Hesse, Herman, 44
Hippodamie (Vrchlický), 29
Hofman, Vlastislav, 57–58, 110
Hölderlin, Friedrich, 51
homonymy, 110–11, 149
Hora, Josef, 51, 57
House of the Black Madonna, 40
"Hunger Artist, A" (Kafka), 164, 168
Hus monument (Prague), 35, 36, 41, 142, *143*, 201

identity: aesthetic, 61, 170, 184, 186; and architecture, 9, 22; in *The Castle*, 7, 105–8, 184; and community, 7, 161; and Czech-German duality, 105–10; in Czechoslovakia, 7, 9, 15–16, 65–66; ethnic, 3, 6, 106, 170, 180, 181, 185; gender, 30, 32, 119–20, 139, 161, 192; of Jews, 10, 14–15, 67–68; and language, 3–4, 7, 9–10, 15–16, 22, 65–66, 180, 185, 192; and music, 171–73, 183; and names, 9, 186; national, 17, 22, 32, 34, 65–66, 94, 117, 119–20, 149, 180; and nationalism, 58–59; in Prague, 16, 27, 28–29, 59, 79; of small nations, 168–69, 170; of species, 7, 8, 9, 15–16. *See also* Kafka, Franz: identity and influences
Imagined Communities (Anderson), 61
Insect Play, The (Čapek), 164–66, 167
interlinguistic relations, 12, 24, 105–11, 106, 122, 126–27, 192
interlinguistic word play, 6, 24, 108–9, 111, 157–58
"In the Castle and in the Village" (Němcová), 91, 93–94, 145, 157
"In the Penal Colony" (Kafka), 53
"Investigations of a Dog" (Kafka), 7, 161, 164, 170
Israel, 6

Jakobson, Roman, 17, 51, 53, 84, 105; on metamorphosis, 78–79, 80–81, 205n7
Janáček, Leoš, 52, 161, 213n12; *The Cunning Little Vixen*/Liška Bystrouška/Vixen Sharp-ears, 164, 166; *The Excursions of Mr Brouček to the Moon and to the Fifteenth Century*, 164; *Her Foster Daughter/Její Pastokyňa/Jenůfa*, 183
Janouch, Gustav, 28, 31, 43, 201n2; on Kafka and animals, 162–64
Jarrar, Maher, 198n1
Její Pastokyňa (Preissová), 161
Jesenius (Jan Jesenský), 117–18
Jesenská, Milena: on bathing suits, 113–14; "The Coffeehouse" by, 25, 122–24, 125–26, 210n17; Czech name of, 127; family history of, 117–18; influence on Kafka of, 24–25, 108, 127–28, 131, 132, 133–34, 137–38; as journalist, 49, 113–14, 121, 137, 189; Kafka on writing by, 114–15, 137, 181–82, 184–85, 186–87; Kafka relationship with, 3, 49, 122, 127–28, 131, 134, 183, 187, 193; and Pollak, 12, 52, 105, 120–21, 134; schooling of, 118, 120; as translator, 34, 51, 121–22; as translator of Kafka, 3, 111, 116, 128, 209n6; and *Tribuna*, 49, 113–14, *115*, 121–22; visits to Kafka by, 187. *See also* Kafka-Jesenská correspondence
Jesenská, Růžena, 37, 45, 118, 119, 183, 189
Jews, 5–6, 8, 80, 180, 181, 195n9; and antisemitism, 45–46, 49, 50, 57, 62, 64, 127, 181; Czech Jewish movement, 63;

Jews, *continued*
Czech-speaking, 6, 12, 62–63; and German, 10, 52–53, 62, 64, 111; identity of, 10, 14–15, 67–68; and Kafka identity, 4, 6, 7, 8, 64, 119; legal rights of, 5–6, 91; Masaryk and, 169; Prague Ghetto for, 62, 91
Jílovská, Staša, 121–22, 210n16
Josef II, 62
"Josefine the Singer or the Mouse Folk" (Kafka), 7, 169, 174, 214n18; aesthetic status in, 185–86; mouse folk in, 159–61, 178–79, 180; and musicality, 162, 170–71, 176–81
"Judgment, The" (Kafka), 4, 76, 126

Kafka, Franz:
BIOGRAPHICAL: in Berlin, 160; command of Czech language, 4, 7–8, 29, 30–31, 33–34, 35, 95–96, 137; father, 4, 64, 119–20; German speaker, 4, 5, 7; health, 22, 159; interests, 17, 31, 36–37, 38–39, 42, 43–44, 76, 84–85, 122, 126–27; literary legacy, 6; "Paris Street" apartment, 91, 164; relationship with Dora Diamant, 160, 163, 189, 213n10; relationship with Felice Bauer, 32, 115, 119, 122; relationship with Jesenská, 3, 49, 122, 127–28, 131, 134, 183, 187, 193; upbringing, 4; at Workmen's Accident Insurance Institute, 163
GENERAL: identity and influences: contested identity, 6–7; as "František Kafka," 7–8, 30–31, 34; identity as writer, 17, 152, 153; Jesenská influence, 24–25, 108, 127–28, 131, 132, 133–34, 137–38; as Jew, 4, 6, 7, 8, 64, 119; Němcová influence, 84, 92, 137, 157, 161, 183; Prague politics as influence, 17
WORKS: "The Burrow"/"Der Bau," 7, 33, 161, 163, 169, 170, 173–75, 186, 214n18; *The Castle/Das Schloß*, 23–24, 77–87, 96–103, 105–11, 131–58; "The City Coat of Arms"/"Das Stadtwappen," 19–22, 20; "Community"/"Fellowship"/"Gemeinsch aft," 7, 8, 9; *Der Verschollene* (Amerika), 133, 203n27; diary, 15, 29, 134, 187, 189; "First Sorrow," 170; "A Hunger Artist," 164, 168; "In the Penal Colony," 53; "Investigations of a Dog"/"Forschungen eines Hundes," 7, 161, 164, 170; "Josefine the Singer or the Mouse Folk"/"Josefine, die Sängerin oder das Volk der Mäuse," 7, 159–61, 162, 169, 170–71, 174, 176–81, 185–86, 214n18; "The Judgment," 4, 76, 126; letters to Felice Bauer, 32, 41, 115, 119, 122, 174; letters to Max Brod, 8, 22, 37, 45, 77, 183; "A Little Woman," 161; *The Metamorphosis*, 16, 76, 78–79, 83–84, 162, 182, 193; "Report to an Academy," 47, 167; "The Stoker"/"Topič"/"Der Heizer," 16, 56–57, 60, 203n27; *The Trial*, 41, 60, 76, 84, 133
Kafka-Jesenská correspondence, 113–30; beginning of, 122, 196n16; and Czech language, 115–16, 173–74; each writing in own language, 4, 31, 116, 124; first publication of, 134; interlinguistic character of, 124–25, 126, 127; intimacy of, 116, 125–26; as major work, 7; as only half extant, 117, 131; public-private tension in, 114–15. *See also* Jesenská, Milena
Kafka: Judaism, Politics, and Literature (Robertson), 199n4
Kafka's Travels (Zilcosky), 75
Kafka: Toward a Minor Literature (Deleuze and Guattari), 27, 28–29, 42, 52, 60, 133, 199n5
Kafka Translated (Woods), 12–13, 121–22, 210n16
Kamusella, Tomasz, 195n8
Kapper, Siegfried, 62–63
Karcevskij, Sergei, 14, 18, 87, 110. *See also* double asymmetry
Karl, Frederick, 13
Kautman, František, 12, 83, 198n4
"Kavárna." *See* "The Coffeehouse"
Khlebnikov, Velimir, 53, 99, 105, 113
Kieval, Hillel, 192
Kisch, Egon Erwin, 49, 52
Kleinwort, Malte, 108–9, 121, 132
Klíma, Ladislav, 47–49
Klopstock, Robert, 160
Kmen, 17, 23, 51; editorial policy of, 52–53; and Kafka, 38, 51, 52, 56–57, 60; significance of, 50–60
Krásnohorská, Eliška, 118–19
Krejcar, Jaromír, 38
Krolop, Kurt, 12
Kroutvor, Josef, 4, 12, 40–41

Labyrinth of the World, The (Comenius), 83, 92
Lady into Fox (Garnett), 162
Landauer, Gustav, 51
land surveying, 64–65, 75–76; in *The Castle*, 23–24, 69–72, 74–75
Langer, František, 15, 16, 38, 196n25; and Hašek, 13, 14
Langer, Jiří/Georg/Mordechai, 13, 14, 15, 16, 197n26
language: architecture as, 24, 87–91; and bilingualism, 66–67, 110, 127; and boundaries, 15–16, 18–19, 24, 62, 79, 136, 191; common, 19, 24, 83, 86, 90, 91, 95, 124, 180–81; and communication, 18, 90, 116, 158, 185; and community, 8, 176, 179; as contested in Prague, 16, 27, 28–29, 59, 79, 127; in Habsburg Empire, 7, 9–10, 61–62, 63–64; and identity, 3–4, 7, 9–10, 15–16, 22, 65–66, 180, 185, 192; and linguistic duality, 24, 105–10; and monolingualism, 20, 199n5; poetic, 19, 84, 85–86, 177; Prague School on, 18, 19, 84, 85–86, 90, 91, 95, 110, 149, 156, 176,

191; and property relations, 61, 95, 155; significance of in Czechoslovakia, 15–16, 72–73; and society, 149, 191, 193; and territory, 8, 15–16, 18, 52, 65, 79; and Tower of Babel, 21; and women, 157. *See also* Czech language; German language
Lasker-Schüler, Else, 119
Laurin, Arne, 46, 49, 50
Lidové noviny, 14, 65–68, 87, 164, 166
"Little Woman, A" (Kafka), 161
Luxemburg, Rosa, 51

Mácha, Karel Hynek, 62–63
Magic Prague (Ripellino), 13
Mahler, Gustav, 64
"major literature," 27, 30–31, 52, 198n1
Mann, Thomas, 83
Mareš, Michal, 31, 47–48, 50
Marian column, 21, 22, 35
Masaryk, Tomáš, 14, 21, 36, 118; on small nations and cultural identity, 168–69, 170
masculinity, 138
McKible, Adam, 55
Metamorphosis, The (Kafka), 16, 76, 162, 182, 193; metaphor in, 78–79, 83–84
metaphor, 78–80, 83–84, 205n5
metonymy, 3, 9, 80
Meyrink, Gustav, 45, 47
Milenky (Eisner), 120
Miller, Eric, 147
"minor literature": Deleuze and Guattari paradigm of, 27–29, 33, 42, 60; and "major literature," 30–31, 52
Moderní revue, 37
modernism, 34, 60, 192; *Kmen* and, 51, 52, 53, 54, 55–56, 57, 59
Mommsen, Theodor, 169
monolingualism, 20, 199n5
monuments: to Hus, 35, 36, 41, 142, *143*, 201n29; Kafka on, 41, 201n29; and national mythology, 22, 35–36
Moravia, 63, 73, 91
Morrison, Mark, 60
mouse phobia, 159–60
Mukařovský, Jan, 24, 95, 101–2; "On the Problem of Functions in Architecture," 87–90, 95; "Standard Language and Poetic Language," 177
Musaion, 58
music, 30; and Czech identity, 171–73, 183; "Josefine the Singer or the Mouse Folk" and, 170–71, 176–81, 182; and Kafka animal stories, 173, 182–83; and spoken language, 182, 183–84; and women, 182, 183–84
Musil, Robert, 46–47, 64
Mykyta, Larysa, 133
Myslbek, Josef Václav, 35, 36

names, 105–6, 124–27, 148, 162, 186
Národní listy, 189
Naše řeč, 106, 136–37; and Kafka, 17, 18, 31, 43; and Němcová, 91–92
Náš skautík, 188–89
nationalism, 57–59, 193
Nečasová, Jarmila, 50
Nekula, Marek, 20, 35, 66, 199n4; on Kafka and Czech literature, 12, 34, 24, 37; cultural importance of, 94–95, 136; and Czech National Revival, 94–95, 96; Kafka influenced by, 84, 92, 137, 157, 161, 183; as woman writer, 118–19, 121; works: *Babička/The Grandmother*, 91–92; "In the Castle and in the Village," 91, 93–94, 145, 157
Neumann, Stanislav Kostka: on Kafka, 56; and *Kmen*, 51, 59, 60; literary career of, 55; on nationalism, 58–59; politics of, 52–53, 55
New York Times, 169
Nietzsche, Friedrich, 48
Novak, Arne, 45

Old Town Square, 21, 35, 40, 41, 91
Order of Worker Education, 53

Paces, Cynthia, 142
Peroutka, Ferdinand, 46
Pick, Otto, 12, 16, 43, 44
Pilgrim's Progress (Bonyan), 83
Podlipská, Sofie, 31
Pollak, Ernst, 12, 52, 105, 120–21, 134
Pollak, Oskar, 3
Prager Presse, 42, 43–44, 50
Prague: architecture and buildings of, 22, 35, 40, 90–91; Castle district in, *71*; cosmopolitan image of, 16, 23, 44, 91; cultural scene in, 8, 28; Czech/German division in, 9–11; history of, 11–12, 192; Hus monument in, 35, 36, 41, 142, *143*, 201n29; intercultural and interlinguistic dynamics of, 54, 127, 192; Jews in, 4, 5–6, 8, 10, 12, 62, 64, 80, 91, 127, 180, 181, 195n9; Kafka and, 3, 91, 160, 164; language and identity in, 16, 27, 28–29, 59, 79; Marian column in, 21, 22, 35; monuments in, 22, 35–36, 41, 142; Old Town Square in, 21, 35, 40, 41, 91; as polemical city, 10, 52; streets of, 35, 91, 164, 169–70; Wenceslas Square in, 8, 35, 36
Prague Circle, 16, 17, 44, 85; Brod coining of name for, 52, 202n16; Kafka and, 37–42
Prague German, 27
Prague Palimpsests (Thomas), 21
Prague School: on the aesthetic, 102, 177, 179, 184, 185; on community of speakers, 18, 90, 95, 110, 156; expulsion from, 17, 96; historicism of, 192; on language, 18, 19, 84, 85–86, 90, 91, 95, 110, 149, 156, 176, 191; poetic theory of, 84, 85–86; structuralism of, 17, 18, 19, 191–92
Prague Spring, 11, 60, 199n5

Prague Territories (Spector), 3, 12, 198n2, 198n4
Preissová, Gabriela, 119, 161, 183
Procházka, František Serafínský, 164
Pynsent, Robert, 93, 210n9

realism, 36, 83–84, 169
Reiner, Josef, 49–50
"Report to an Academy" (Kafka), 47, 167
Rilke, René (Rainer) Marie, 64
Ripellino, Angelo, 13
Robert, Marthe, 135
Robertson, Ritchie, 199n4

Sabatos, Charles, 29
Šalda, F. X., 45–46
Šaloun, Ladislav, 35, 201n29
Saussure, Ferdinand de, 18, 87, 110, 178
Schopenhauer, Arthur, 48, 144
Schultz, Georg, 51
Scott, James C., 75
Seifert, Jaroslav, 44–45, 51
sex and sexuality: *The Castle* depiction of, 106, 108–9, 138, 146–47, 148, 150–51, 153, 155, 156; and Jesenská, 115, 121, 131–32; Kafka's attitude toward, 5, 152, 182; 211n22; in Vienna, 121; and writing, 4–5, 115, 152. *See also* gender
Shepherd, William, 73
Sheppard, Richard, 155
Sinclair, Upton, 51
Slánský show trials, 11, 60
Služba, 57
small nations, 169
Smetana, Bedřich, 30, 35, 172
Sonnenschein, Hugo, 53
sound: aesthetic and non-aesthetic qualities of, 170–71; in "The Burrow," 33, 173–75; Czech, 173–76. *See also* music
Spector, Scott, 3, 198n2, 198n4; on German Jewish writers, 18, 111; on language and territory, 23; on Prague Circle, 12, 17, 202n16
"Sprachmusik," 182, 183–84
Stach, Reiner, 50, 119, 139, 155
"Stoker, The" (Kafka), 16, 60, 203n27; plot of, 56–57
structuralism, 85–86, 87–88, 95; on aesthetic function, 103, 178, 180; of Prague School, 17, 18, 19, 191–92
Suchoff, David, 6
surveying. *See* land surveying
Svetlá, Karolina, 118–19
Svět zvířat (Hašek), 167

Teige, Karel, 51
territory, 61–76; *The Castle* depiction of, 69–72, 74, 151, 152, 155; contested, 4, 9, 79; for Czech art, 58–59; Deleuze and Guattari on, 23, 27; and language, 8, 15–16, 18, 23–24, 52, 65, 79; shared and mingled, 17, 105, 192
Těsnohlídek, Rudolf, 166
Thomas, Alfred, 21, 92, 93
Thompson, Mark Christian, 204n4
Toman, Jindřich, 53
Trial, The (Kafka), 41, 60, 76, 84, 133
Tribuna, 14, 41, 167–68; cultural significance of, 46–50; Jesenská work for, 49, 113–14, *115*, 121–22; Kafka and, 13, 42, 49–50
Tůma, Ladislav, 189
Twain, Mark, 63–64

Umělecký měsíčník, 16, 54

Váchal, Josef, 39
Vančura, Vladislav, 38, 51, 54
Venkov, 47, 49, 50; editorial character of, 45–46; "The Duty of Czech Music" in, 172–73
Verkehr, 126, 127, 145–47, 148, 149
Vienna, 120, 121, 124
Vienna Neue Freie Presse, 169
Vixen Sharp-Ears (Těsnohlídek), 166
Vrchlický, Jaroslav, 29, 37

Wagenbach, Klaus, 10–11
Wagner, Benno, 4–5, 151, 182
Wagnerová, Alena, 120, 121
Weininger, Otto, 138–39
Weltsch, Felix, 159, 161
Wenceslas Square, 8, 35, 36
Werfel, Franz, 12, 37, 44–45, 53, 64, 164; "The Goat Song" by, 166–67; Jesenská and, 51, 52, 125; Kafka on, 30, 125, 161
Wolker, Jiří, 51
women: in Czech national movement, 118; and domesticity, 119, 122; Kafka's depiction of, 25, 124, 131–33, 139–43, 148–58, 191; and language, 157; as literary figures, 118–19, 137; and music, 182, 183–84. *See also* gender
Woods, Michelle, 111, 117, 209n6; on Jesenská, 12–13, 121–22, 210n16
Workmen's Accident Insurance Institute, 163
World War I, 38, 64
World War II, 11
writing (activity): aesthetic function of, 84–85; and music, 183–84; and sexuality, 4–5, 115, 152; and women, 5, 118–19, 137; and the world, 17, 191–92

Yiddish, 6, 29–30
Yildiz, Yasemin, 199n5

Zahra, Tara, 9
Zhang Xudong, 198n1
Zilcosky, John, 75
Zola, Émile, 52
Zone (Apollinaire), 39–40